The Parting of Ways

Shiela Grant Duff

The Parting of Ways

A Personal Account of the Thirties

PETER OWEN · LONDON

ISBN 0 7206 0586 5

DA
585
.G72
.A3

PETER OWEN LIMITED
73 Kenway Road London SW5 0RE

First published 1982
© Shiela Grant Duff 1982

Printed in Great Britain by
Daedalus Press Somers Road Wisbech Cambs.

Contents

Illustrations

Preface

The Parting of Ways is the story of my youth, a time entirely encompassed by two world wars. My generation were born on the eve of the First World War and our lives were transfigured by its devastation. We spent our youth in the shadow of an impending second world war, and it affected almost everything we thought and did. The 'parting of ways' took place not only in private but in public life, when our world was torn apart for a second time.

The story I tell here first appeared, in a somewhat different form, in Germany. Entitled 'Five Years to War', it was an account of the period, 1934-1939, I spent as a foreign correspondent in Europe, witnessing at first hand the rapid destruction of the continent by the Nazis and Czechoslovakia's tragic struggle for survival. I wrote from personal memory evoked by my returning to a long-stored collection of papers from that period : letters, photographs, newspaper cuttings, press passes, visiting cards, random notes and diaries never completed. A young German friend, Ekkehard Klausa, translated my manuscript and found a publisher, C. H. Beck of Munich, who published *Fünf Jahre bis zum Krieg* in 1978.

It was Beatrice Musgrave and Dan Franklin of Peter Owen Ltd who saw the potential appeal of the book for an English audience. Their youthful sympathy and intelligence emboldened me to tell the whole story, private as well as public, to coax ghosts from the shadows and throw light on some forgotten corners of this significant period of my life.

I am especially grateful to Dan, my editor, for his unfailing kindness and tact. By questioning every detail of my passionate indictment of the fatal errors of British foreign policy between the wars, both in its means and its ends, he has helped me to make this book – based on Foreign Office documents as well as memory – an even more damning account of the mistakes and betrayals of those years.

As I was writing, I was often conscious of the words of Walter Pater, so dear to my grandfather :

> Not to discriminate every moment some passionate attitude in those about us and in the brilliance of their gifts some tragic dividing of forces on their ways is, on this short day of frost and sun, to sleep before evening.

To the many friends who have influenced my life by their 'passionate attitudes' and the 'brilliance of their gifts', and who wrote to me at the time the letters from which much of this story has been reconstructed, I must here record my thanks. I am especially grateful to Douglas Jay, Goronwy Rees, Christopher Cox and Isaiah Berlin, who so enriched my Oxford days; to Diana Hopkinson, my childhood and life-long friend; and to Clarita von Trott, the widow of Adam von Trott, who generously returned to me, after the war, all the letters I had written to him. This correspondence was in many ways my most important source; it documents the most 'tragic dividing of forces' in this book. To Adam himself, above all, I express my deep recognition of all he stood for and of his heroic martyrdom.

I should also like to record my debt to four major public figures who appear in these pages and who made an indelible impression on my life : Edgar Ansel Mowrer, who opened my eyes to the evil of Nazi Germany; Jawaharlal Nehru, who moved me both personally and politically; Hubert Ripka, the Czechoslovak patriot who taught me that the struggle of the First World War had not been in vain but had brought the prospect of freedom and hope to the subject nations of Eastern Europe; and Winston Churchill, who saw that that cause was still essential to the freedom of Europe as a whole.

Finally I should like to thank Conor Fallon, a friend from the present rather than the past, who read this book in manuscript and gave me the courage to think it worth writing; and, most of all, my husband Micheal, who has been so generous and patient with its author and so constructive in its writing.

Grateful acknowledgements are due to Messrs The Bodley Head Ltd for permission to reproduce a passage from *Master of Spies* by Frantisek Moravec.

September 1981   SHIELA GRANT DUFF

The Parting of Ways

1

I was born on Whit Sunday 1913. I should thus have been specially blessed, and indeed in many ways I was. But my birth came on the eve of great desolation : it was the end of an epoch – for my family, for England, and indeed for the whole world.

I was the fourth and last child of Adrian and Ursula Grant Duff. My sisters Jean and Ursula ('Lulu') had been born in 1907 and 1908, and my brother Neill in 1911. In these first years of our lives we lost three of our grandparents, our own father and my mother's two brothers. Those who had formed the strong family background of the Victorian and Edwardian eras had vanished.

My parents were both children of distinguished and well-established families. Although they are seldom remembered today except by historians examining the particular fields in which they were active, both my grandfathers had been eminent Victorians – if by eminent one means the position they occupied in their own lifetimes and the part they played in public affairs. My paternal grandfather, Sir Mountstuart Grant Duff, was a leading Liberal MP and Governor of Madras; he died in 1906, the year my parents were married. My maternal grandfather, Sir John Lubbock, the first Lord Avebury, died in May 1913, the month in which I was born. Although I never knew him, my mother's father undoubtedly had the stronger influence on me, perhaps because less than two years after I was born my father was killed at the Battle of the Aisne.

Despite his enormously active and varied life, Sir John Lubbock is most often remembered as a scientist, the friend of Huxley and Darwin. The latter confided to him that he relied on the opinion of three men only, Hooker, Huxley and Lubbock, and of these he put Lubbock first, 'because of the course of your studies and the clarity of your mind'.

Lubbock mapped out the course of these studies for himself when he was a child. His father, the second Sir John Lubbock, removed him from Eton when he was only fourteen years old because he needed him urgently in the family business, the banking house of Lubbock, Forster & Co; not long after, he made him his partner. Sir John had no compunction in taking this rather drastic step, since he was contemptuous of the education Eton was providing and confident that his son could educate himself. Being a noted mathematician and astronomer, Sir John himself took over the teaching of mathematics. This was not an unqualified success. 'My father's mathematical genius', his pupil recorded some years later, 'was in some respects a disadvantage. He could not see difficulties where I did, and though very patient would often at last say in despair, "Well, if Newton does not make it clear to you, I am afraid I cannot. We must go on." In other respects I made good progress, reading seven or eight hours a day and devouring all sorts of books, but especially those on Biology and Geology.'

Some years earlier, when John was seven, his father announced that he had 'a great piece of news' for him. Asked to guess what it might be, the boy suggested that he was to be given a pony. 'Oh,' said Sir John, 'it is much better than that. Mr. Darwin is coming to live at Down House.' The garden of Down House immediately adjoined High Elms, the Lubbock estate near Farnborough in Kent, and Sir John, being Treasurer of the Royal Society, was already acquainted with Charles Darwin.

John's disappointment was soon forgotten for Darwin took a keen interest in his studies and persuaded his father to give him a microscope. John carefully began to draw what he saw there, taking the sketches to Darwin with whom he often walked and talked. Since Darwin was no draughtsman himself, he was soon using the boy to help him with illustrations to his own work. Over the years, a close relationship developed between the scientist and the rather lonely young man; indeed one of his brothers later remarked that Lubbock 'owed to the great Charles Darwin even a larger debt in the respect of character formation than in the encouragement and direction of his mental gifts'.

It was through Darwin, as well as through Sir John, that Lubbock met all the leading scientists of the day and soon began to make original contributions in the fields of archaeology, biology and entomology, and to write popular books on each of these subjects. He was not content simply with study, though even in this he was active and practical. He devised a sort of moated stand where he could keep ants' nests under observation through glass. By intoxicating a few ants from several nests and then redistributing them, he discovered the ants' tribal loyalties and powers of recognition other than by direct communication. He watched the sober ants carefully examining the bodies, carrying their unfortunate comrades back into the nest and dumping the foreigners firmly in the moat. He also trained bees to come to feed on honey which he placed on glass above papers of different colours and brightness. By this means he was the first to discover the colour vision of bees and the fact that they preferred blue. For twelve years he kept a tame wasp which became so famous that its death was reported in the national newspapers. These stories delighted us as children.

It was this practical and kindly side of Lubbock's nature that made it not enough for him simply to be a researcher. He wanted actively to help the world about him. In 1870, when he was thirty-six years old, he stood for Parliament as a Liberal and was elected MP for Maidstone. He became a very active private member, initiating reforms in a wide range of fields from education to banking. His most famous piece of legislation was the Bank Holidays Act of 1871, which gave to every working man the first public holiday he ever enjoyed. (The holidays, held in August, were popularly known as 'St Lubbock's Days'.) He also initiated the 1882 Act for the Preservation of Ancient Monuments, having already had to intervene personally to save Avebury from speculative builders (by buying the whole site and giving it to the nation) and Stonehenge from the London and South Western Railway who wanted to build a track right through the middle of it.

It would need a whole book (which I hope to write one day) to describe his myriad activities : in the famous X Club; in his presidency of the Metaphysical Society, founded to bridge the gap between science and religion; in the Working Men's College; in the London County Council, of which he was the first Chairman – and in countless other fields. 'Of him as much as of any man,' wrote Professor Pumfrey in the *Notes and Records of the Royal Society of London* (June 1958), 'it can be said : "If you require a monument look about you." The results of his life are unmistakably there, in science, in education, in the preservation of the countryside, in the less seamy aspects of the Welfare State; and if others now get the credit he would not have minded.'

It was also a Grant Duff motto – I forget now whether of my father or grandfather – that you can do anything in this world as long as you do not mind who gets the credit.

I grew up knowing much less about my other grandfather, Sir Mountstuart Elphinstone Grant Duff. He died before my parents married and his wife, my grandmother, died when I was only three years old. The splendid circles in which they had moved and entertained in grand houses like Hampden, Knebworth and York House were all far in the past. I knew that like Lubbock, who was a very close friend of his, he was a Victorian polymath who touched life at many points and believed that the highest duty of a member of the ruling class was to serve not only his country but the world. He served in Parliament for twenty-four years, representing the Elgin Burghs in the Liberal interest, and in India, as Governor of Madras, for five. He travelled widely in Europe, Russia, Turkey, Egypt and North Africa and in all these countries had friends who gave him information which he hoped to put to good use in the conduct of British foreign policy. But in his first Government in 1868, Gladstone put him firmly into the India Office as Under-secretary and in his second Government sent him to India. Lubbock was his companion on many of his journeys and at one stage the two men shared rooms during Parliamentary sessions. They even bought a house together in Algiers, though this was sold after the Grant Duffs went to India in 1881.

Grant Duff trained each of his four sons to serve likewise. The two eldest, Arthur and Evelyn, were placed in the Diplomatic Service, my father, Adrian, in the Army and the youngest, Hampden, in the Navy. But none of them inherited their father's genius for friendship, his broad view of life, or, in fact, sufficient of his private means to make this possible. He left behind him a large number of books, including fourteen volumes of diaries. Originally written to keep in touch with friends to whom they were circulated in manuscript, they present a piquant view of the Victorian age today.

All these, as well as the many scientific works of Sir John Lubbock, were to be found on the many bookshelves in our house, but they did not attract me as much as Lubbock's general books with the intriguing titles *The Pleasures of Life*, *The Use of Life* and *On Peace and Happiness*. These I devoured avidly, and I often think I am the last of the Victorians so deeply did I imbibe their perhaps over-simple ideas of right and wrong – revealed simply by listening to one's own conscience which tells one to work hard, to help other people, to be truthful, courageous, unselfish and strong. Lubbock's message was comforting and inspiring, and indeed quite simple till one began to grow up and was faced by all the choices and the problems in the world.

'We all wish for peace and happiness,' he wrote. 'We cannot hope for more and need not wish for less. Our own happiness ought not, of course, to be our main object nor will it even be secured if selfishly sought. It is wise to seek for interests rather than pleasure.' It amused my grandfather and did not discourage him when Owen Seaman, the parodist, wrote in imitation of his style : 'We cannot all be geniuses but a firm grasp of the obvious may be acquired by the humblest amongst us.'

My mother also enjoyed this parody and used to quote it to us as children on the many occasions on which she felt the 'firm grasp' eluded us. She too tried to live by these Victorian platitudes and to bring us up on these strict but loving injunctions. She was an agnostic, though she taught us to say our prayers. 'Help us to find out what work we have to do in the world' was one of them. Her own work was to bring up four fatherless children and to devote herself to what her father had called 'the two supreme objects of existence – the promotion of the happiness of others and the improvement of one's own soul.'

Ursula, my mother, was the eldest daughter of Lubbock's second marriage. His first wife, Nelly, who bore him six children, had died in 1879. For some years she had been in a decline, as the Victorians put it, and had taken little part in the great friendship with the Grant Duffs. He had come to depend on them more and more and was shattered when Grant Duff's appointment to Madras separated the two families for five years. In this double bereavement, Lubbock fell in love.

The girl he chose was anything but suitable as the wife of a distinguished fifty-year-old scientist, banker, and Member of Parliament. Admittedly she was the daughter of General Lane Fox Pitt Rivers, the archaeologist and anthropologist, but unfortunately Alice Fox Pitt had no interest whatsoever in anthropology or any other branch of science, or even any love for her father. In her veins ran the 'bad blood' of the Stanleys, an eccentric, obstreperous and autocratic brew. Her mother was one of the 'Ladies of Alderley' of whom Nancy Mitford wrote, remarking – much to my grandmother's fury – that she had married 'a Colonel Fox Pitt or Pitt Rivers'. The others had married Russells and Howards and Ogilvies, whom Nancy considered much more distinguished. Certainly they were richer, till the 'Colonel' suddenly inherited the Pitt Rivers estate of Cranborne Chase which comprised nearly 25,000 acres in Dorset and 2,762 in Wiltshire. This was in 1880, when my grandmother was all but grown-up and remembered with bitterness a hard and unhappy childhood. She disliked her father and could not wait to get away from him.

She met Lubbock the next year at Castle Howard, where her formidable aunt Rosalind Carlisle, a fierce radical and teetotaller (who was reputed to have poured the wines from the Castle Howard cellar into the moat), was entertaining a distinguished company of scientists. They were attending the Jubilee Meeting of the British Association which was being held that year in York under Lubbock's presidency.

Alice Fox Pitt, far from interested in the company, came down late for breakfast. Whereupon her imperious aunt Rosalind, scolding her roundly, angrily gathered her guests together and swept from the room. Lubbock, kind as ever, stayed behind to comfort the trembling girl, but when he found that she was trembling with anger, not contrition, and loudly denounced her 'beastly aunt', he was amused and captivated. A year later they were married. A promised visit to the Grant Duffs in India never came off; instead he took his bride on a honeymoon to Switzerland.

The homecoming to High Elms was stormy. Lubbock's two grown-up daughters by his first marriage were not only older than their stepmother but were accustomed to presiding over their father's house. The occasions for mutual rancour and jealousy were many, and the Victorian precepts about love and unselfishness were painfully tested and frequently found wanting. My own mother, Alice's first child, was born six weeks prematurely as a result of one of the many terrible scenes that were to cloud her childhood and embitter her mother. Alice was not a Stanley for nothing, however, and fought back with spirit. She insisted on refashioning the house and destroying all evidence of the first Lady Lubbock. On the ceiling of the great hall she had her own family coat of arms entwined with that of the Lubbocks, in spite of several sons, potential heirs, by his first marriage. She proceeded to bear three more sons of her own and two daughters. Her family was her prime concern, and once she had successfully driven her stepdaughters out of the house, she settled down to a devoted marriage. Her husband's public life meant little to her and his friends still less.

Lubbock (now Lord Avebury) remained faithful to his friends, however, and early in 1906 he had to perform the painful duty of visiting Sir Mountstuart Grant Duff on his death-bed. 'A sad day,' he recorded in his diary on 11 January. 'I went to take leave of poor Grant Duff, who is dying. He was quite himself but very weak. He took my hand and asked me to do what I could for Lady Grant Duff and the children, and then dozed off, but woke up now and then. When I was going he asked me to kiss him, and said how much I had done for him. I was so distressed that I could not say as much as I should have liked. He has been a true friend and I shall cherish his memory. How much we have seen and done together.'

The Grant Duff 'children' were all grown up and older than Lubbock's second family. Adrian, fifteen years older than my mother, was a major in the Black Watch, working in the War Office in London. Invited to High Elms, he fell in love with my mother and they were married before the year was out.

Lubbock, now seventy-two, was delighted with his son-in-law; he looked on him as an elder brother to his own young sons whom he feared he might not live to see properly launched in life. In the later years of his life he became increasingly troubled by developments in the world around him, especially the growing expenditure in all countries on armaments. His anxiety had led him to become chairman of the Anglo-German Friendship Society, formed in 1905 for the purpose of promoting a more friendly feeling between the two countries, but by 1909 he was writing, 'The present state of Europe is a danger and even a disgrace to us all.'

The Government shared his unease. Military talks had been started with the French and, in the Intelligence Section of the Department of Military Operations at the War Office, my father was concerned with the organization of the Expeditionary Force destined for France in the event of German aggression. In 1910 he was appointed Military Assistant Secretary to the Committee of Imperial Defence and went to work at once on the mobilization of the civilian departments in case of war. This was the famous 'War Book' – a detailed plan, never before envisaged in peace-time, by which all Government departments knew the exact procedure they were to follow on the outbreak of war.

17

In August 1913 my father returned to Aldershot, and in May 1914 he took command of the first battalion of the Black Watch. Maurice Hankey, who as Naval Assistant Secretary had been his junior while this work was going on, had by then been appointed Secretary to the Committee.

Whit Sunday 1913 saw my mother rushing across Hyde Park to her parents' house in Grosvenor Street, which she reached just in time for my birth. My grandfather was now seventy-nine and failing rapidly. The final entry in his diary records my birth under his roof.

In a desperate attempt to revive him and prolong his life, my grandmother took him to Kingsgate Castle, which he had built up from a ruin on the North Foreland coast. A week later, on 28 May, he died. My grief-stricken grandmother sent at once for my mother, who struggled down first to Kingsgate and then to High Elms from where the long funeral cortège walked on foot, following the simple oak coffin borne on the shoulders of his friends to its resting place near Farnborough churchyard in the woods he loved so much. This piece of hallowed ground was to be the scene of mounting grief throughout the next few years.

The epoch of peace and security was all but over, not only for my family but far beyond. For most people the outbreak of war on 4 August, 1914 struck out of a blue sky, but my father had seen it coming and had done the only thing he could do as a soldier – *Si vis pacem*. ... He left at once for France with his regiment and described to his colleagues at home how he was carrying out his own secret instructions to the BEF, drawn up several years before at the War Office. At home too it was his instructions in the War Book which went into operation and Hankey wrote to him : 'I shall not forget to let it be known that you designed the War Book. ... Every item went off without a hitch and with a smoothness that really astonished me.'

On 14 September, 1914, at the Battle of the Aisne, the Germans broke through on the Chemin des Dames. My father led a counter-attack and was fatally wounded. He was carried into a cave by two of his men who later told my mother that an unknown figure had come in as they left. When they returned, my father was dead and no one was to be seen. My mother, an agnostic all her life, wondered if it could have been Christ. She also told me – years later, for I was then only sixteen months old – that during her great sorrow she had had a dream that my father had come to her and told her not to grieve. But she did grieve, very deeply. Her entire world was shattered. After eight brief years of marriage to a man she deeply loved and trusted, she was left to struggle alone with the care and upbringing of four small children. It was barely more than a year since she had lost her own father with all that that meant, not least the grief of her own widowed mother and the passing away of the secure and honoured background which had sheltered them both.

Materially this background still existed. My grandfather's successor as baronet, Johnny, his eldest son by his first marriage, was not only unmarried but devoted to my grandmother; he came to live with her at High Elms. Her sorrowing for my grandfather was now filled with agonizing anxiety for her sons. My mother had three brothers : Harold, who was closest to her in age and understanding, Eric, who was passionately loved by his mother, and Maurice, still a schoolboy. Harold and Eric joined up and for three years she waited in dreadful apprehension. Eric, who had enlisted in the Flying Corps, was shot down over Ypres in 1917. Harold, who survived Gallipoli in the West Kent Yeomanry, joined the Grenadier Guards and was killed almost immediately in France in 1918. The heir was now Harold's little son, aged three, on whom my grandmother inflicted the most grief-stricken, disastrous and all-consuming love.

After my father's death, my mother had bought a house in Mulberry Walk in Chelsea, a new development on the Cadogan Estate which had never been lived in before. In those days it was comparatively modest, as was the establishment my mother kept there : cook, house-parlourmaid, lady's maid, nanny and nursery-maid. As we grew older she dispensed with the nursery staff and her maid, Nunn, became a nanny to us all, beloved and cherished till her death. With no breadwinner or means of earning any money – my mother had never even been to school, having been educated by governesses at home – she felt herself to be poor and tried to bring us up as frugally as possible.

Compared to this modest establishment, High Elms, where we went for every holiday throughout our childhood, became a sort of fairy land to us children. For the grown-ups it was a refuge. Gone was its great expansive Victorian life. No one ever came there but my grandmother's relations, her brothers and sisters and her thirteen grandchildren – Lubbocks, Pelhams and Grant Duffs – with their retinue of nannies, nursery maids and ladies' maids.

High Elms was a handsome house built by Philip Hardwick in 1844 for the second Sir John Lubbock, but endlessly altered and added to. It easily absorbed this crowd of dependants every holiday as well as its own vast army of servants – a butler, three footmen and a boot-boy, a cook with many minions under her, a housekeeper with even more. All these lived behind the proverbial baize doors in wings of their own, but since we children used the back stairs and went out of the house by the back door and through the back passage, they were all our friends. So were the numerous outdoor servants in stable, farm, garden and woods, and, of course, their children.

Children and servants alike were isolated from the life which went on downstairs and in the front part of the house. We visited it only at recognized times, carefully washed and dressed. Before breakfast we all trooped down to say good morning to our grandmother and Uncle Johnny, each in their separate wings, as they lay in bed reading their letters and drinking their early-morning tea. If we were late, my grandmother might be in her dressing-room having her beautiful long white hair brushed by her maid. Since her marriage she had never dressed herself or her hair, but since nannies did this for us too, it did not strike us as odd. After tea we went down again, the girls dressed in thin frocks, the boys in velvet shorts or, in the case of my brother Neill, in tartan trews or kilt. We played with wooden bricks and animals on the floor, or with dolls and tea sets, or looked at picture books or very occasionally a magic lantern. I remember the first wireless set. One could only listen to it through ear-phones and there was much squabbling for the only pair.

All this could be rather a strain – there were undoubtedly tensions among the adults, 'stealths' they were called – and I remember enjoying grown-up life only at Christmas-time when we all had tea downstairs and everyone, servants and all, received presents from a huge Christmas tree lit by a hundred candles. But the best of Christmas, as indeed the best of everyday, was up on our own floor where we all played and slept and had our own life.

The nursery floor extended the whole length of the house, with a nursery at each end and a long passage where we could chase up and down, playing wild games of hide-and-seek in and out of all the bedrooms with their interconnecting doors. Our meals were carried up two flights of stone back-stairs on huge trays. I remember the breakfasts where we quarrelled over what coloured cup we were given from the harlequin tea-set and the hilarious suppers in our dressing-gowns when our uncle Maurice came up to joke with us before his own dinner downstairs. On summer evenings we would watch the grown-ups walking on the lawns in their long evening gowns. On wet days we would play roaring games of racing demon which sometimes lasted all day. On fine days we were always out of doors, dressed in old jerseys and boots and allowed to run wild.

High Elms had everything a child could want – swings, dogs, stables, a farm, woods, ponds, a walled kitchen garden, rabbits. There were flat-bottomed boats we could row out to islands in the ponds, a red cart we could drag round the woods. We could climb on to the farm carts bringing logs daily to the house. We learnt to ride on rusty bicycles without tyres. We hunted for Easter eggs in the bushes, for kittens in the haystacks, for plovers' nests in the fields. We played hockey with walking sticks on the lawns ('good for the weeds') and Tom Tiddler's Ground by the back door.

For us it was all joy, but we were aware of the sorrow. My brother and sisters remembered my father, but I was too young. I did remember the Christmas of 1916 when my uncles Harold and Eric came home on leave. The ponds were frozen and they dragged our red cart across the ice with us all shouting and sliding and laughing. And later I remember their life-size portraits in uniform being hung in the dining-room and the monuments to their memory – a stone aeroplane for Eric – being erected in the clearing of the wood where my grandfather lay and my father was commemorated. My grandmother used to cut the grass there and put flowers by the stones, and I remember her asking how one could believe in the goodness, or even the existence, of a God who sacrificed his only son.

We were aware that our grandmother hated the Germans with all her heart. My mother was wiser and more compassionate. She taught us to hate war. The armistice was signed when I was five years old. I had never known a time of peace and did not understand the change. The war still pressed heavily on us. My grandmother's gardeners and farm servants returned still wearing the clothes they had fought in. In London, ex-servicemen in tattered uniforms played barrel-organs in the streets. I passed at least one every day on my way to and from school, and often went to sleep at night with an organ playing under my window. Every Armistice Day we were taken to Whitehall and saw the marching soldiers and ex-servicemen, listened to the guns booming and the still more fearful silence that followed. The Last Post makes me weep to this day. My mother took us to the great war cemetery near Ypres where my uncle Eric lay, and also to the little French churchyard near Soissons from which my mother would not let the body of my father be moved. We saw some of the devastation of France and Belgium with our own childish eyes, and in the sand-dunes near La Panne we picked up empty shell-cases.

But somehow, as children, we never spoke of all this, neither to our friends nor even to each other. At school, I was frightened of being asked what my father did. His death was a dark secret in my heart which I shared with no one but my mother, to whom I was very close. Perhaps because I was the youngest of her four children and her baby when my father was killed, she always clung close to me. My sisters thought I was spoilt and envied me my emerald green hair ribbons when theirs were black. Her life was devoted to all of us; she loved no one else after my father's death. This was a waste for she had remarkable intelligence, energy and independence, a great sense of humour, real beauty and a generous and compassionate heart. She was born in an age when the daughters of the upper classes neither went to school nor had jobs. It was a man's world and now it had been swept away. She was determined that her daughters should have the same education and the same opportunities as her son. In fact we had more – life itself – as Neill, like my father, was killed in another German war and lies also in a French churchyard.

2

At the age of twelve, when my sisters were grown-up, I was sent to St Paul's Girls' School, one of the leading independent schools in London. There I entered a totally different world. My grandmother regarded it as middle-class and deplorable; my mother as progressive and sound. My Pelham cousins, whose father was Permanent Head of the Board of Education, went there too. None of our friends was invited to High Elms.

My two closest friends at school were Diana Hubback and Peggy Garnett. Diana has suggested in her autobiography, *The Incense-Tree*, that the education St Paul's provided was not nearly as good as it was thought to be. But for me, the teaching I was given there, above all the historical teaching, profoundly moulded my moral and political outlook and, perhaps more than anything else, led me to take on the challenge this book is about. I was especially influenced by the portrayal of three periods of history in terms that concerned us directly : the Renaissance with its discovery of the 'full, whole nature of man'; the Reformation with its proclamation of man's right to seek his own path to God; and the French Revolution with its battle-cry of 'Liberty, Equality, Fraternity'.

I learnt much, too, from the backgrounds of my two friends. Diana's mother, Eva Hubback, Principal of Morley College, devoted her life to education and social reform. She was a very impressive figure and a great feminist and I felt in some awe of her. Peggy's father, Maxwell Garnett, Secretary to the League of Nations Union, was also a little alarming; he too devoted his life to education and world peace. Diana, like me, had lost her father in the war and Peggy's mother, like mine, had lost brothers. We never discussed war and peace in these terms nor spoke of our sorrows to each other or regarded it as in any way a bond. Quite different things filled our heads and drew us together.

It was to their holiday homes in North Cornwall and the Isle of Wight that I first ventured beyond the close family circle of High Elms or the Scottish houses bordering on the bleak North Sea to which my mother took us in the summer. The charm of the Solent and the wild beauty of the Atlantic Ocean as it beat on the rocky coast of North Cornwall were as much revelations to me as the family atmosphere so different from my own. Here, the heads of the family, Diana's mother and Peggy's father, were wage-earners – which nobody seemed to be in my own family – were active in public life and discussed the affairs of the world in the presence of their children. At High Elms, even when we joined the grown-up part of the house in our teens, I never remember hearing politics seriously discussed.

Mrs Hubback put the newly published *Intelligent Woman's Guide to Socialism and Capitalism* in our hands and I read Bernard Shaw's views with amazement. As children, my sisters and I had been encouraged to adopt families in the slums of Chelsea, taking their children to play in Battersea Park and giving them toys and clothes. We took it for granted that poverty could only be helped by charity. Shaw's book and the outlook of Diana's mother and her friends were the first indication I had that poverty could be eradicated by changes in the political, social and economic organization of the country. I was also rather pleased with Shaw's idea that women, then a surplus in the population, would have more husbands to choose from once class barriers were removed. I had not yet reached the 'emancipated' phase of my life when I considered marriage a restrictive and unglamorous option which should be delayed as long as possible.

This phase was to open and these lessons were to be amplified when Peggy introduced Douglas Jay into our lives. After his First in Greats, Douglas had studied economics for a year and won an All Souls' Fellowship. His studies had convinced him that socialism was the only just and efficient way of organizing the economy. This and other startling ideas percolated down to me through Peggy. I had been hearing about Douglas for some time even while we were still at school. He was the clever boy next door who was called in to coach Peggy for exams : after a while she was referring to him as 'the platonic' (platonic friendship with boys was much advocated by our parents in those days and warmly espoused by ourselves). By the time we met, a definite relationship of passionate priority was established between them. Douglas wanted to meet me because he believed that

Peggy felt for me with the same exhilaration and intensity that he felt for his immediate friends. This related, of course, to the passionate friendships made in the unreal atmosphere of single-sex schools. Growing up rather slowly and tentatively, we carried these passionate friendships into the heterosexual society of Oxford, painfully attempting to form with young men the same ardent but platonic relationships we had enjoyed in our last years at school. Many of our friends were postgraduates who had completed their student days in the still monastic system of Oxford college life. Like Douglas himself, they were only now awaking to the charms of female companionship. I remember Stephen Spender saying to me in my first term at Oxford : 'How odd that so many of your friends are homosexuals'! But he was wrong. Delayed heterosexuals, perhaps, but the delay did not last very long.

Even before we went up to Oxford, Peggy and I, barely eighteen years old, came under the rigorous barrage of Douglas's trained and first-class mind. It seemed at times as if all its fire was directed to disintegrating every value with which we had grown up and alienating us from the ideas held by our families, alienating us indeed from those families themselves. Douglas was then working on *The Times* and living in Hampstead. He kept up a running battle with Peggy's family who were only just beginning to understand how greatly his ideas differed from theirs. It was mostly on a teasing note. 'Teasing is the only reaction to the public school system which has got permanently ingrained in me,' he said. I can no longer remember which of their remarks and injunctions were held up for scorn but I do remember the day when Douglas announced he could stand no more and was never going to speak to Peggy's mother again. Anxiously, I asked what had happened. 'She says,' Douglas spat out in genuine anger, 'that the Edgware Road runs east and west.'

My family also came in for jokes and scorn. On the occasion of my eighteenth birthday, I managed to open a little crack in the doors of High Elms, always so firmly shut to anyone but family. It was a weekend party of all ages – younger cousins of my mother's generation like Billy Fox Pitt, a dashing major in the Welsh Guards; my sister Jean; Desmond Boyle, one of the glamorous family of colonial governors and merchant princes into which my sister Lulu was marrying. I was rather nervous of how Douglas would react in such circles and the matter seems to have been widely and hilariously discussed among us, for I find a joke letter from Christopher Cox,

Douglas's former tutor at New College : 'Our thoughts will be with you in your anxious hours next week-end. Keep the conversation on motor cars and natural history and ride on horseback and you will find Douglas will behave very well.' There were other pitfalls apart from conversational ones. I knew Douglas had a dinner-jacket because this was also the form at All Souls, but about the rest of his wardrobe he boasted that all he had had to buy since he first went up to Oxford was a pair of white tennis shoes. He was wearing these when he arrived, and they were no longer white. The rest of his change of clothes was wrapped up in his macintosh and I shivered at the jokes that would be cracked below stairs after the footmen had laid out his dinner-jacket for the evening.

I had tried to warn Peggy and Douglas of the conventions at High Elms and the importance of behaving as one was expected to behave if one wanted to escape my grandmother's acid tongue. Douglas solved the problem by removing Peggy and me from sight for any part of the day that was not spent at either tennis or meals. We lay in the beech woods with their carpet of bluebells and read George Moore's *Héloise and Abelard* while the rest of the party enjoyed themselves in more sociable ways and painfully raised their eyebrows. My grand-mother lay in her revolving summer house and read Dornford Yates.

'What a lovely week-end it was,' Douglas wrote afterwards, 'and we thought it would be a joke. . . . I shan't ever lose the impression of the blue sky and warm wind and cows on the green and you with your blue eyes and butterfly coat. It was vivid and perfect, a complete dream in itself, brilliant and shining, and brought me nearer to for-getting the real world than anything for years.' And to make sure the joke aspect was not forgotten, he added : 'I've written to your villainous grandmother, rather punctiliously but with a touch of quiet dignity. Her maiden names, I see, were Alice Augusta Laurentia Lane-Fox-Pitt-Rivers. I've put some of these in the address to show my intimate knowledge of upper-class life.' But he couldn't leave out a warning : 'Don't let me think of you as only flowering when the real world's shut out, will you?'

And so the struggle between my two worlds was engaged. The world I was moving towards won hands down through most of that summer for life with Douglas and his Oxford friends was, I hoped, the 'real world' outside the confines, artificialities and conventions of 'the season' which, as much against the grain for my mother as for me, I was supposed to be having that year. The contrast was exposed, sharply and rather comically, on the evening I was presented at Court. My grandmother had lent us her Rolls-Royce and her men servants and my mother and I were sitting in that long cortège which assembles for such occasions in the Mall, dressed in our ostrich feathers and trains. Suddenly Douglas appeared in his macintosh and tennis shoes and jumped in to sit on the little seat between us and the glass panel which divided us from the chauffeur and footman. Perfectly trained, they never even turned their heads, and on that occasion Douglas had only cheered up a long and boring wait and not destroyed the glitter and glamour of Court. The beauty and ceremony of the state rooms at Buckingham Palace did not fail to move me nor the glorious uniforms of the courtiers and dignitaries to impress. Nevertheless, when later as a journalist I attended royal ceremonies in Belgrade and Bucharest with considerable detachment, I was glad that I had joined the 'real world'.

'Are you prepared to live for a set of unintelligible rules told you with no explanation by a few people who got them from other people who at the beginning had nothing to go on except the power that you have also?' I remember Douglas saying to us. 'Will you do that or will you agree with Plato, who thought that even justice is not right unless you understand the reason why.'

This was a tall order and I doubted whether I was capable of fulfilling it. 'Of course you feel lost and worried,' Douglas said. 'Thinking things out is a long and chaotic process that comes right not gradually but in sudden flashes after seemingly worse and worse confusion.'

Peggy and I wanted these 'sudden flashes' to add up to the real meaning of life. Day after day Douglas read us A. E. Housman :

But men at whiles are sober
And think by fits and starts,
And if they think, they fasten
Their hands upon their hearts.

and the meaning of life, which we both felt gushing so gloriously around us, was presented as something so painful and sad. We knew that Douglas was sorrowing deeply for his sister Helen who had recently died most tragically of polio, but was this a warning of all we could expect life to be? 'I don't think there is any meaning in things,' Douglas said, 'because if there were, the things couldn't happen which do. Do you realize that thousands of people are now

27

lying in hospital just bearing pain until they die, and that the lives of most of the human race are just an incessant struggle with hunger?'

'What are we to do then?' we kept asking. 'What is the point of living at all?' I confided some of these agonies of mind to Diana, who was having a gloriously happy holiday in Munich. 'Alas! so melancholy,' she replied. 'Oh you mustn't. Everything is so lovely. Strange! We seem to play different parts these last few months. Formerly you were the comforter and I the depressed one. Now I attempt to comfort and you seem depressed, but of course it may be a passing stage. "How can one live if one doesn't know what one is living for?" Oh! Shiela! has anyone in this world ever known what they are living for? Are you going to be the first? So much the better, but I think you will find it an impossible riddle to solve.'

'I do think there is a point of living,' Douglas reassured us. 'Because some things, chiefly friendship and knowledge, are better than other things. These things I know to be good when I experience them : about any other sort of good I know nothing and see no reason to believe anybody else does.' He told us we must be prepared to live for them and for them only and 'for other people who were willing to live for them and for those people only'.

There were actually a number of other things Peggy and I felt to be good, but we were frightened of being called fools and determined to live up to Douglas's standards. Fortunately he had many good friends of whom he was convinced this was true, and he was most generous and willing to share them with us.

The summer before we ourselves went up as undergraduates, Peggy and I lapped the cream off the Oxford milk. Weekend after weekend we spent there, staying with Peggy's grandparents in North Oxford, in a little timbered cottage in the Chilterns belonging to her aunt, or in the welcoming, comfortable house the Pilkingtons had built on Boar's Hill for themselves and their children Arnold and Mary.

It was at a dinner party in All Souls that it all began. Peggy and I were in Oxford for the college interviews which were to decide our fate, but far more hung on this evening when both of us were to be presented to Douglas's closest Oxford friends. We were chiefly concerned about our appearance, how we looked and what dresses we should wear; neither of us wore make-up – in those days face powder was the only aid which nature was allowed and we visited hair-dressers only to have our hair cut. I had certainly never been to a grown-up dinner party before and had no idea what to expect. We knew the men would be in dinner-jackets and that we must wear long evening dresses. I remember mine distinctly; it was a stiff powder-pink velvet dress, re-made for me from the court dress of one of my grandest aunts. It was very simple and I liked it.

We came late, of course, delayed by our anxiety to please. The two other girls at the party we already knew from school, and we had long acknowledged the superior beauty of Maire Lynd (now a Home Student living with the Fishers in the Warden's Lodgings of New College) and the superior mind of Nicolette Binyon, a scholar at Lady Margaret Hall. We liked them well and so were not afraid of them.

Then the young men were presented. Douglas had talked about them all, warmly and often. Arnold Pilkington ('Pilks') was tall and blond and handsome, with laughing blue eyes. He had been an outstanding athlete and an intrepid mountaineer but had been struck down by a dire infection from which he was only just recovering. 'Compared with your other friends,' Peggy had said to me, 'he is a seagull to sparrows.' Goronwy Rees was short and dark with green eyes and black curls, as Byronic and beguiling as Douglas had described. Christopher Cox, tutor to all three, immediately inspired confidence, trust and affection. He was old, of course, all of twenty-seven or twenty-eight.

We dined downstairs and were waited on by college servants. Douglas was very insistent that Peggy and I should drink wine, which we had never done before and did not now, at first taste, much like. We belonged to the generation who could still drink tap water with pleasure and did so at every meal. I found parties and people whom I liked quite intoxicating enough and long preferred the taste of water. Douglas profoundly believed in the good effect of wine – he never touched spirits – in heightening the power of intelligence and the awareness of pleasure.

We were too young and unsophisticated to have any qualms about dining in All Souls with these clever young men, but I was nevertheless surprised by the conversation. At dinner it was almost entirely concerned with the news of the day. I have forgotten now what the news was and did not very much care then, but fortunately we had been instructed for our interviews to read *The Times* from cover to cover. It now stood us in good stead. After dinner, with the wine stimulating pleasure rather more than intelligence, the conversation became less general. At one point, when Douglas was beating Goronwy's head on the floor, I fell back on the set-book in my exam – Gibbon's *Decline and Fall* – and tried to engage Christopher, a classical tutor, in talk about the Roman Empire. It was not a great success but it was a magic evening all the same and the door whereby I entered this magic world.

That summer Peggy and I tasted the extraneous joys of university life – lying in boats on the river or walking along its banks, swimming in the Cherwell or in the Pilkingtons' pool on Boar's Hill. In Douglas's open car, whose sole protection from wind and rain was a canvas roof which was only pulled up once the rain had started, we explored the beautiful countryside which still lay open and unspoilt up to the very edges of Oxford. We had picnics in bluebell woods, on the Downs, by the Windrush or, on wet days, in Christopher's large room at the top of a staircase in New College. We went to *Twelfth Night* in the magnificent new theatre which opened that summer of 1931 at Stratford on Avon, to Salisbury and to Winchester, where Douglas and many of his friends had been to school.

Finally, to crown it all, there was a huge party for the Balliol Commem. Ball, at which my two worlds came together once more. My sister Jean was there, with the handsome Desmond Boyle and Conyers Surtees, a staunchly conservative lawyer, my brother Neill from Balliol, and then these new-found friends. I remember Douglas saying what a good investment it would be for my grandmother to pay for Goronwy's ticket because of his great future as a writer. This was the last time these two worlds ever really came together; though Neill and my mother spanned them both, I was aware that neither liked very much what they saw in the other.

But the ball and the breakfast party afterwards at the Trout Inn were superb. Goronwy came, though I doubt if my grandmother paid for his ticket. Douglas had talked endlessly to us about this brilliant, charming and wicked young Welshman at New College, poet, scholar and seducer. 'A scapegrace', some wit had described him. Peggy and I solemnly promised each other we would not allow him to kiss us at the ball. He made no attempt to do so. Right at the end, in the last gallop, I could not resist telling him how foolish we had been, whereupon he flung his arms round me as the music stopped. I accepted it as innocence not seduction and I was right. We promised at our next meeting never to deceive each other and never to do or say anything we did not mean.

3

When, in the autumn of 1931, Peggy and I finally went up to our separate colleges – Peggy to Somerville and I to Lady Margaret Hall – we encountered for the first time the more prosaic reality of undergraduate life : the rules about never entering a man's college unaccompanied, about being safely behind a locked door in our own college by 9 pm unless we had signed for a 'late' leave till 11 pm. We were supervised by moral tutors as well as the subject tutors who demanded two essays a week for which several books had to be read. We were told what lectures to go to, though this was optional, and it was indicated that six hours' work a day was the norm. Being an early riser, I could get through three of these in the empty but heated College library before anyone else was up : and those three hours often had to suffice. I also found that the stern rules dividing the sexes did not apply in New College where Christopher Cox was a senior Fellow and wonderfully open to all one's joys and woes, nor in All Souls where the hall porter, unlike my own college porter who stuck sternly to my surname, greeted me like my grandmother's butler as 'Miss Shiela'. To Douglas, and to that marvellous summer he gave Peggy and me before we went up to Oxford, I owe this privilege – now won for all – of transcending the barriers of age and sex in the choice of friends and companions.

For friendship is, I believe, one of the greatest blessings conferred by a university education. In the whole of the rest of one's life, unless one is very rich or very lucky, one's choice of friends is limited by where one lives and how one earns one's living. At a university, one is thrown together for three long years with large numbers of contemporaries from many quarters of the globe and – even then, and more so now – from all walks of life. Above all, one has time to find oneself and to develop friendships; time to sit and talk, time to go

31

for long walks, time to write letters and time, six months of it (for three terms, of only eight weeks each, leave longer vacations than one ever again has in life), for travel abroad and for reading parties at home. In those days no one took holiday jobs or entered even briefly the daily life of work which was most people's lot. To be at the University, even for the minority with scholarships and no family to support them, meant a certain standard of living whereby the privileges of friendship and study could be carried on into the vacations. I remember those vacations with even greater clarity and gratitude than the terms.

The first, the winter vacation of 1931-2, was spent at the Garnetts' Isle of Wight cottage. Peggy had invited not only Douglas but Arnold Pilkington, Goronwy and me. Christopher Cox was supposed to be coming too, but being a don, he really did have pressure of work. In the end his absence cost him much time healing the wounds we all inflicted on each other.

Douglas lived by a theory he tried to practise too literally and too openly : that 'Love is like understanding, that grows bright gazing on many truths'. At moments we all agreed enthusiastically, and I was delighted to have three of my 'many truths' with us. For me the theory had a sound platonic base. But there were also moments, in an imperfect world, when misunderstandings occurred. These were laid at the feet of poor Christopher Cox many times in the coming two years. And though, philosophically, I remained stubbornly faithful to the Shelleyan principle (till ten years later when I joined the 'great sect' and got married myself), I found out immediately that it was most inimical to my relations with Goronwy. He, for the next three years, and hauntingly and hoveringly for two more years after that, was the centre of my life ; not 'husband material', as my mother firmly and regretfully told me (for she, too, was very fond of him), but as 'a spring of crystal water' which the name Goronwy means.

The great excitement of our first term was when Goronwy, who had only taken finals that summer, sat for and won an All Souls' Fellowship. This was an outstanding achievement by any standard. Quintin Hogg, now Lord Hailsham, who was elected the same year, was heir to a great Conservative tradition, an Eton and Christ Church scholar with four years of Mods and Greats and one of Law behind him. Goronwy was the son of a Welsh Methodist minister, educated at Cardiff Grammar School and with only three years of a New College scholarship and a First in PPE behind him. In addition, he had suffered an overwhelming grief that summer with the death of his mother, for whom he was the youngest and most precious son.

'You must be so happy tonight,' Douglas wrote to me, 'and you deserve to be because you saw Goronwy's worth yourself with your own mind from the letter I sent you from Italy and you accepted and admired him from that moment whatever anyone might have said about him.

'I am happy too. I never thought a year ago I should have that exaltation over again. And yet I have, because Goronwy was elected for the same reasons as me (for though he has lots of supreme talents which I have not got, he was actually elected for the moderate ones he shares with me and the interest in the truth we both care about) and he was elected in the same circumstances [the death of Douglas's sister had occurred just before the All Souls' exam] and for that reason I can hardly conceive of the violence of the struggle he must have gone through.

'I am as happy as last year because this fellowship, for all the intrigues, is given as a prize for the intellectual qualities we value most – a desire for truth about the most important things and a determination not to be weak or lazy or dishonest in finding it. It's a triumph for that, whether it's him or me. That's what you must love him for if you love him for anything.'

It was always Douglas's mistake to think one loved people for reasons. Goronwy, I remember, at that time at any rate, thought love was an act of imagination. I must admit that being loved was one of the most compelling reasons I ever found for caring deeply and feeling responsible for other people and even for entering into a commitment which, in Goronwy's case certainly, I was glad to honour years after our close ties had ended. But this is probably hindsight. Love in youth is full of turmoil and change and uncertainty and pain.

Throughout my three years at Oxford I spent more time with Goronwy than with anyone else, not only in the intermittent weeks he spent there as a newly-elected Fellow but in the vacations when we travelled all over Europe together. I learnt more of books, listened to more music, looked at more pictures with him than with anyone else and also received greater gentleness, affection and consideration. But he was very sensitive and complex. Coming from a religious Welsh home (at the age of sixteen, his father, like Paul on the road to Damascus, received a call from God, so direct, personal and compelling as to leave no doubt of its authenticity), he had to take on

33

protective colouring at New College among the clever, worldly and self-confident Wykehamists. 'I know all the harm it has done me,' he wrote to me in 1934, 'and that it was very bad for me.' Perhaps he would always have had deep internal conflicts, but certainly they were fomented at Oxford. 'By now you will have discovered,' he said in another letter not long after our first meeting, 'that I do not accept happiness and goodness easily, that I am apt to sneer at them and denigrate them, that, as you say, I make vices of my virtues and virtues of my vices. I do not think it is conceit or egomania which makes me believe that I do it because happiness and goodness are so incredibly difficult to achieve, not to be had without immense effort, and so all appearances of them should be mercilessly scrutinised before they are accepted.'

The slump had hit Wales especially hard. I remember him describing his visit to Merthyr Tydfil, where all the miners were out of work. It was just after the Government had cut the dole. 'It's the complete negation of life,' he said angrily. 'What one can do I do not know but at least one needn't live as if it did not exist.'

This was how Oxford had lived in the 'twenties, but in the 'thirties it was changing fast. In the 'twenties the privileged young men who had then made up almost the whole of the undergraduate population, had not had to think about politics or even to bother much what kind of degree they gained. Now both mattered intensely. Furthermore, the forward march of feminism and the growing need for girls from 'establishment' families to think in terms of jobs which required university degrees, was transforming the University. It was no longer the place Goronwy describes so brilliantly in *A Chapter of Accidents*. Women had lately been admitted as full members of the University and were taking an increasing share in its life at all levels. The division was no longer between the 'Aesthetes' and the 'Hearties' but between the 'Politicals' and the rest, almost between those who had friends in the women's colleges and those who did not. It seemed to us, as Douglas wrote in his autobiography, *Change and Fortune*, 'as if our little group had almost instigated the revolution'.

I came up to Oxford not only with Peggy and Diana, but with another much respected and revered school-friend, Jane Rendel. Both she and her brother Sandy were very helpful to me in the next few years, and at Oxford she was the one girl-friend with whom I could talk about non-personal matters. We went together to philosophy tutorials with R. G. Collingwood, and I remember him

34

describing her as 'a great mind'. She also possessed a deeply con-scientious and questioning moral nature and too much responsibility was heaped on her both at St Paul's, where she was head girl, and subsequently. Neither her physical nor her mental health could stand it. Diana and I were both very fond of her and I admired above all her stern political views and her upright character.

It was perhaps also the move to the Left which edged women to the fore in the Oxford of the 'thirties. We all enthusiastically joined the Labour Club and Jane and I (out of a misunderstanding about the class war) even joined the communist October Club when it was formed at the end of 1933 by an American Rhodes Scholar, Frank Meyer.

I often think of the Oxford I knew as a very significant road junction, not only intellectually, because of the avenues of thought and knowledge it opened, but in the unfolding of contemporary history. So many people who were up at that time have made their mark in the world, in the professions, in literature and in politics (I am thinking of the Front Bench of the Labour Party; especially of Michael Foot, who dominated the Oxford Labour Club in those days), that one feels one has somehow looked down the avenues of their lives from this focal point and been part of a contemporary world often quite different from one's own.

It was at the Labour Club that Diana first met Adam von Trott. He was not only to play a poignant part in her life but a prominent and tragic role in the most serious of all the German attempts to rid themselves of Hitler: the 20 July plot of 1944. He also came to occupy a prominent position in my own life, not only personally but, in an even deeper sense, in the cataclysmic struggle with Nazi Germany. But back in 1931 he was a young and romantic Balliol Rhodes Scholar, one of the first Germans to come to Oxford after the Scholarships had been suspended during the First World War.

Adam was an outstanding figure in every sense, not only taller than almost anyone else but with striking features, a ringing laugh and great personal charm. Rhodes Scholars always possessed a certain charisma, being postgraduates from overseas rather than ex-school-boys from round about as were the undergraduates; but to this Adam added an imposing, aristocratic background. His father had been one of the Kaiser's ministers, his mother was a descendant of the great John Jay, the first Chief Justice of the United States; his home, Imshausen, was in the Trottenwald in Hesse, where Trotts had lived

35

since the thirteenth century. None of *us* had forests to which we gave our names!

Born in 1909, Adam had studied at the Universities of Munich, Göttingen and Berlin, and had already written most of his treatise on Hegel. As A. L. Rowse, an early friend of Adam's at Oxford, has said: 'He gave himself up to Hegelianism; it profoundly affected his mind, though his mind must have been inherently disposed to it: for all external appearances, Adam was deeply German. With him black was never black, and white white; black was always in the process of becoming white, white of becoming black.'*

He was the first German I had ever met and for me he personified all the tragic implications of a 'fratricidal war', which was how more and more people were describing the war of 1914-18. How could that terrible slaughter have ever taken place if the slaughterers and the slaughtered were people like Adam, like my uncles, like my father and Diana's father?

This fervent horror of war, this profound conviction that the participants on both sides were not so much armed combatants as fellow sufferers from some terrible wickedness committed against them all, was fed by the films and books that had been flowing onto the market as we were growing up. *The Four Horsemen of the Apocalypse* and *All Quiet on the Western Front* were almost the first films I ever saw, *Journey's End* one of the first plays. We were all reading the war poems of Wilfred Owen, Rupert Brooke and Laurence Binyon, and books like Robert Graves's *Goodbye to All That* and Siegfried Sassoon's *Memoirs of an Infantry Officer*. I had read my uncle Eric's letters to his mother from the front, and they were wholly without martial hatred or bitterness.

It was in this mood that the famous motion at the Oxford Union, never again to fight for King and Country, was proposed and carried. Much more has been made of this than the event warranted: indeed its importance was distorted even at the time. The original vote would probably never have been heard of had it not been taken up by the Beaverbrook press and by two prominent Oxford men of the twenties, who found the new political tone of the 'thirties undergraduates distasteful.

These two young men, Randolph Churchill and Edward Stanley,

* Quoted in Christopher Sykes's biography of Adam von Trott, *Troubled Loyalty*, Collins, London, 1968, p. 56.

both famous rowdies in their student days, took it upon themselves to come back and organize a reversal of the light-hearted undergraduate vote by mobilizing all the senior members of the University. The challenge was taken up not only by undergraduates but by many senior members who disliked the ballyhoo of the whole affair. It stank of outdated shibboleths, of false slogans slanted to excite jingoism, of a cover-up of armaments manufacturers (who in those less cynical days we particularly disliked), and not least of a certain amount of cheap publicity for Randolph and Edward. Both were cousins of mine, but I had no use for either of them, nor had a great number of other people who came to vote them down. Not that I did that. Women were still unable to become members of the Union, though thanks to Brian Davidson, a Tory President of the Union and a good friend of Peggy's and mine, the actual premises were no longer sacrosanct.

The motion was carried for a second time, and of course great indignation was whipped up against the 'lily-livered' young men of Oxford. It was even put about, years later, that it was they and not the Chamberlain Government who were responsible for Hitler's and Ribbentrop's conviction that England would never fight. This, however, is utterly false. The appeasers were the survivors of the tragic generation of 1914-18, not our own contemporaries who fought in the Spanish Civil War even before World War II, and who hated fascism.

4

The summer vacation of 1932, the last before Hitler came to power, was the first of my three long vacations from Oxford. It started with a week in Diana's Cornish cottage of which we all had such happy memories from previous visits. This was the happiest of them all, and for a long time I thought of it as the happiest week of my life. Diana had asked her beloved Adam von Trott as well as Jane and me and our good friends Christopher Cox and Arnold Pilkington. Christopher I felt to be of the same moral calibre as Jane, and Pilks was all that a companion should be by that foaming sea. It was a cloudless week for us all.

Goronwy had just come back from Freiburg and Vienna and was then with his family in Wales, but he wanted to take me back with him to Germany. At that period, Oxford was enjoying the pleasure of discovering Germany and Austria. Their films, their plays, their music, their art galleries, the quality of life in places like Berlin, Hamburg, Munich and Vienna, with their great stretches of water and their free and emancipated youth, seemed to suggest the dawn of a golden age for us all. Diana had written ecstatic letters from Germany the previous summer, begging me to come and share the joys with her. Every new person I met seemed to have just returned from Germany. Stephen Spender, W. H. Auden and Christopher Isherwood were the heroes of the Oxford literary scene, and all were surrounded by a German aura of something new and exciting. Dick Crossman, then a young don at New College and vocal in his appreciation of Germany, actually brought back a German wife and set up house with her in New College Barn, which greatly heightened the drama of life in Oxford. We had all been to see *Mädchen in Uniform* and every film starring Marlene Dietrich. Pilks had taught me to sing *'Ich bin von Kopf bis Fuss auf Liebe eingestellt'* ('I'm Head over Heels in Love'), and one felt this was a German condition which it would be nice to share. I longed to go there with Goronwy.

Young people did not go away alone together in those days as they do now, however, and my mother was anxious, especially for my reputation. 'You do not know how cruel the world is,' she often said to me. Goronwy tried to reassure her that the 'world' she feared was passing away. 'Already their day is over and their spite is meaningless,' he wrote to her. 'These beastly gossipings all come from people who feel "they have a position to maintain" in society : the irony is, of course, that they really have none and deserve to have none. . . . It really does not matter about the mental instability and uneasiness of the educated classes : anyone who like Shiela possesses a considerable amount of spontaneity and passion and a greater amount of courage than most people, will escape these dangers. Her difficulty is likely to be that she will not find a society in which such virtues are valued and respected and common to others.'

I do not know how my mother answered this – I found the letter among her papers after her death – but she let me go. She showed me what courage was.

It was Dick Crossman who suggested Wickersdorf, a progressive school in the hills of Thüringen, as suitable for a reading holiday about which my mother could feel reassured. Gornowy went on ahead.

'I have arrived here safely,' he reported, 'and here is an account of what I found. Fr Cordes lives in a small house in the village. It has a verandah with a most wonderful view, with two rooms opening on to it, one of which is mine and one is to be yours. The village is very small and primitive, about twenty houses in all and the one bad road running through it is crowded with dirty brown children. We can have all our meals at the school, including breakfast, though if we want to, we can have it by ourselves on the verandah. There are about eight people staying at the school, as well as Mr and Mrs Gerhardi who run it. There is one small English boy and a varied assortment of Germans of various ages, including one very handsome young man, and two not very handsome girls who are pupils. Your mother will be pleased to know about the young man. They speak only German so you will be able to learn. There is also a teacher at the school who will give us lessons. The Germans are full of sport but apart from meals we needn't ever see them unless we want to. There is a tennis court we can use and a swimming pool : and also pools in the forest. . . .

'The country is lovely, of hills and valleys covered with woods and huge fields of corn, some new and green and some golden ready to be cut. And one is really in the country. From the verandah one can see nothing but miles of hills and corn and trees. There is a garden where we can lie in the grass and the walks are lovely. They needn't last more than a hundred yards because it is all so lovely. We should be able to do a great deal of work. . . . Come soon.'

So to Wickersdorf I went.

I had never been to Germany. My mother had taken us abroad as children to places like La Panne in Belgium, where I saw those relics of the First World War. She also took us to St Valéry on the coast of Normandy where, in the Second World War, my brother was to be killed. But mercifully the future is hidden from us. No thought of war with Germany, past or future, was in my mind as I arrived at Cologne at six o'clock in the morning and travelled on to Saalfeld, which I reached in the afternoon.

Wickersdorf was as beautiful as Goronwy had described. Perhaps we worked less, but we went for longer walks. The countryside had a peculiar fairy story look, quite unreal, with striped fields of green oats and yellow wheat, dark green pine forests with running streams, villages built of slate that looked as if they had been created by Hans Andersen. Our walks through the forests, especially when night had fallen and we were a little afraid, were the stuff that dreams are made of. Occasionally we dined in the inns of neighbouring villages, watching the young men playing chess or listening to their singing. The local people were very good-looking. Goronwy said it was because the nobility in this area had exercised the *droit de seigneur* to build a peasantry with the rustic strength of their mothers and the fine features of their fathers. The girls would sing as they washed their clothes in the streams which, flowing through the valleys, were dammed by the villagers to form pools. The wooded hills rose steeply from the valleys so that the distance from one hill to another was small and a voice would carry across and roll round the hollows below.

We had long quiet days when Goronwy wrote, and in the evening would read me his new novel. *The Summer Flood*, his first, was published that summer while we were at Wickersdorf.

'My new book promises well,' he wrote to Douglas, 'but I can't get on with it, no satisfactory style, the old will not do and there is an embarrassment of a vague, unformed mass of material. I read it to Shiela and send her to sleep, read on enraptured by my own work and find she has been asleep for hours. . . .

'She is happy and lovely, many complexes, if they existed, gone, she is gay and serious by turns, always beautiful. I could never have thought it possible to live quite alone for six weeks with one person. She will be very different, I think even lovelier, in three years. Her life, I think, is a natural growth in what is good. Now she reads *War and Peace* with fascination.'

Most of the time we were very happy, but we also had terrible quarrels. Once I came in to find Goronwy tearing up his novel. He had been reading my diary and was angry and hurt by its ridiculous childish confessions. I don't think he ever went back to that book. I seized up the bits and have them still.

Goronwy was a very complex character; although he came to know himself well, he baffled many others. In another letter to Douglas he wrote :

'It was a year to-day my mother died : last night I wept, wished to die, and having lived a year without her, found it impossible to face the thought of more years : and indeed as you say, her death seems more like a contraction of the good than a mere personal loss. Shiela and I have been extraordinarily happy : but we quarrel sometimes because she finds my moodiness intolerable. As indeed do I : my mind becomes like a superimposed and detached observer, continually mocking me and hurting me until I could beseech it to cease all activity whatever, to be free of its ceaseless sneers : so they make me moody and we quarrel. Also at times I feel the want of a purely free and masculine life : do you ever feel this? I would like very much if sometimes you could come abroad with me and we could know and see each other alone again for a month or so. Will this ever be possible and would you like it?'

Into the pastoral peace of Wickersdorf broke an agonized letter from my mother. There were machine-guns, she told us, on every street corner in Berlin. Terrible reports of the imminent German elections were in every British newspaper. Were we safe? Of course we were, but of course we also left by the next train for Berlin. Goronwy said it was an opportunity not to be missed to see a European capital under martial law. He had been there before and he took me to a pension in the Kurfürstendamm. Then, as now, it was a brightly lit and noisy thoroughfare. The many cafés and the broad pavements were thronged with every kind of sinister human being one could possibly imagine : slinking men in black capes and huge black sombreros; women with cropped hair and wearing shirts and ties; others, both men and women, with ghastly painted faces; cripples, beggars and, behind them all, the dreadful uniformed and booted strike forces of the political parties swaggering up and down. We were both appalled and I was frightened. I bitterly regretted having left our peaceful countryside. This was a very different Germany and I cursed the march of history.

It was 31 July, 1932, and the first elections to the German Reichstag since 1930 were being held. In these two years, the National Socialists had almost doubled their membership : they had more than 400,000 armed storm troopers who, banned by Brüning in the spring, had now been legalized by the new German Chancellor, von Papen, and once again commanded the streets. Not only were there pitched battles between them and the shock troops of other political parties, but they also indulged in their own form of brutality, beating up Jews and socialists. Nor did they stop at outright murder. Men and women had been shot down in the streets or kicked to death in public every Sunday that month. Now, though armed gangs still roamed the streets, order seemed to have been restored and the fighting to have died down. On this Sunday, Germans flocked to the polls and nearly fourteen million of them voted for Hitler. The Nazis became the strongest party in this or any other Reichstag which the German people had ever elected.

We were utterly repelled by all we had seen and heard : the political atmosphere was highly charged and menacing. We retreated to Wickersdorf, but here too things seemed to be changed. Perhaps it was only the hot summer and harvest time which had changed the face of the countryside : gone were the striped fields, all looked alike now with their stacked sheaves of corn and hay. The laurels had been cut in the woods. '*Nous n'irons plus au bois*,' said Goronwy sadly as we waited for my brother Neill to join us on his way back from a long trip to South Africa. It was seven months since I had seen him and even he seemed changed. We all felt a great urge to leave Germany.

Many Oxford friends were in Vienna, and it was to Vienna we went. As a capital city of a once great empire, it was still infinitely beautiful compared with Berlin, and we spent our days there looking at pictures and going to the Opera, visiting palaces and resting in charmingly ornate and worldly baroque churches. We drank coffee with inches of cream at the top of the glass and ate the world-famous water ices. The smiling, familiar faces of our Oxford friends and acquaintances were infinitely reassuring. William Hayter was there at the Embassy and Duff Dunbar. Martin Cooper was studying music there. Stephen Spender was around and had made a wonderful American friend, Muriel Gardiner, who befriended us all. She was studying psychoanalysis under Freud and living with her little daughter in a flat near the Opera. We used to drop in on her for a late supper and a glass of wine. One night, sitting there under a reproduction of Manet's 'The Absinthe Drinker', I fell asleep, only to awake to a most startling proposition – that Neill, Goronwy and I accompany Muriel on a visit to the Soviet Union, entirely at her expense. Neill, the 'last English gentleman' as he had been described as a child, immediately demurred at so generous an offer. Goronwy and I accepted eagerly, and we managed to persuade Neill to change his mind. A dutiful daughter, I wrote home to my mother for permission, but afterwards she always maintained that I gave her our Moscow address to which to answer.

Muriel had urgent business in London, so she suggested we all meet in Warsaw. On the train we travelled third-class, sleeping on the wooden benches, on the floor, the rack, wherever we could lay our heads. I had no stockings or hat or much of a coat, the boys no ties or overcoats. Feeling like vagabonds when we reached Warsaw, we greeted our sophisticated and immaculate benefactress as she stepped out of her first-class wagon-lit from Paris. Shyly we all boarded the train for Moscow, changing onto the wide-gauge railway at the Soviet frontier. A low white building sufficed for a station, and here all the baggage had to be minutely examined, a very slow and tedious procedure. Any sign of impatience, we noticed, slowed it down still further. People who carried anything new in their luggage – this did not affect us – had it removed and carefully weighed, which rather surprised me. I was surprised too to see a soldier armed with what looked to me like a machine-gun at the ready, watching the train and the officials who descended from it. As we moved off, he stood to attention. The Russian train rapidly asserted the equality of man by subjecting us to a plague of bedbugs which found the clean and sparkling Muriel far tastier than our tired and dirty selves. We arrived in Moscow a united band of bug-bitten travellers.

1932 was the year when it first became fashionable for the idealistic

British Left to look with favour at Russia, a country which claimed to have solved the problems of slumps and unemployment. It was the year when David Low, the cartoonist, and Kingsley Martin, the Editor of the *New Statesman*, produced their *Russian Notebook*, when a delegation from the Fabian Society helped to inspire the Webbs' massive tome *Soviet Communism: A New Civilisation*. Jane Rendel, the most serious of my friends at Oxford, had arranged early in the summer to visit the Soviet Union and had prepared herself accordingly. Our wholly unpremeditated visit, on the other hand, was as near frivolous as we were permitted to be.

It wasn't very near. We visited the Museum of the Revolution, the Kremlin and Lenin's tomb in Red Square; we had seats at the Grand Opera for *Boris Godunov*; but we were also taken to see workers' dwellings, a collective farm, a marriage bureau, a children's nursery and a factory kitchen. We were shown the People's Court and a terrifying prison where the guards, sitting in the centre, could see into every cell throughout the building. Our fifth day in Moscow was spent trudging round a vast textile factory and a frightening clinic where pain and disease were exposed in all their horror.

I had never visited such places in my own country and had not the faintest idea what to look for or what to compare them with. I was sure that these institutions were splendid in their way, but working in a factory or on a collective farm, being ill in a hospital or shut up in prison, seemed to me an unpleasant fate wherever one suffered it, and here in Russia people looked drabber and shabbier and showed more signs of suffering on their faces than anywhere else I had been.

We tried to make some sort of human contact, but the result was absurd. Neill, finding a prisoner who could speak French, asked him why he was in prison. '*Parce que je ne suis bon,*' he answered.

Travelling in a Moscow tram was an experience for which the London rush hour had not prepared us. It was packed solid and one had to get in at one end and out at the other. On one occasion when Goronwy, with his curly hair and bow tie, was battling through the crowd, a Red Army man suddenly shouted: 'Give way! He's got culture.' The mass parted like the waters of the Red Sea.

Respect for culture was indeed what one felt everywhere. The absence of vulgarity, of crude advertisements, of kissing and petting in public, was very striking. Although the Park of Rest and Culture was incredibly staid, the audiences at opera or ballet were warm and enthusiastic. Yet somehow we seemed to be excluded by a great barrier – not simply that of language and tourism – from everything that was happening around us.

After five fiercely serious days in Moscow, we left in some trepidation on the night train for Leningrad; but there were no bedbugs this time and the accommodation was comfortable, even luxurious. (Perhaps I should add here that when I reported the bugs to our London daily help, she laughed and said that we need not have gone to Moscow for those, there were plenty in Battersea.)

Life in Leningrad was somehow gentler and more urbane. We could recognize the city we had read about in Russian novels and it was with relief that we left the twentieth century for the nineteenth. We were taken to Tsarskoe Selo, whose luxury had been preserved as an object lesson for scorn but must, we felt, have made others besides ourselves long for such comfort and elegance. The Winter Palace and the Hermitage, with its magnificent collection of paintings, were a joy and a relief; the Tchaikovsky ballet a soothing contrast to a film by a proletarian poet. Even the propaganda showplaces were more cheerful. The House of Culture was bright, the night sanatorium for tuberculosis sufferers was not frightening, and the hot water in our hotel bedrooms not only ran but actually was hot.

I left the Soviet Union little wiser than when I arrived, and still as prepared as before to defend its 'new civilization'. Russia was our hope of peace and our protection from poverty, for were not wars and unemployment the consequence of an economic system whose motive was private gain rather than public good?

I count myself fortunate to have had in my youth an ideal to believe in which still seemed realizable.

5

I had now completed my first year at Oxford and started on the studies in which I was to take my Finals in the summer of 1934. It was probably the influence of Douglas and Goronwy which made me decide on Philosophy, Politics and Economics. The Honours School of PPE was then relatively new and much criticized as a mixture of disciplines which did not, it was said, seriously train the mind nor give it that depth or concentration which the older Schools provided. Jane Rendel and I (Diana had now gone down and Peggy had decided to take the Economics Diploma in order to shorten her course at Oxford) were among the first of the women undergraduates to take this course, and since Lady Margaret Hall had not yet appointed their own tutors in several of its subjects, the field was open to us. We had powerful friends to advise us on the relative merits of the Oxford tutors and were largely able to make our own choices. We boldly picked Balliol and went together to John Fulton for our philosophy. He was not really a very good philosopher, having the same sort of pragmatic outlook as myself. I thought that moral philosophy would teach me how to live and political philosophy would teach me how States should be governed, but this, I found, was not the case and it was from R. G. Collingwood, recommended by Isaiah Berlin, that I learnt my mistake and Jane received her accolade. But Fulton was a very nice man, and the special interest I had in watching his immensely successful post-war career in the great expansion of university education in England was one of those many assets provided by the 'road junction' of Oxford.

PPE itself gave me exactly the training and, I suspect, the impetus, for the career which I eventually adopted. It was almost like a preliminary course in political journalism, providing the intellectual background to current events as well as the experience and discipline of writing two essays a week for the critical eyes of my tutors. Furthermore my two Special Papers, International Relations and Labour Movements, excited my sympathies as well as informed my mind. After reading about the ideas of the early English socialists, the struggles and sufferings of the early trade unionists, one could not but sympathize with and support all generous movements of the Left. The influence of my friends, of Douglas with his deep Labour Party loyalties, of Goronwy with his home near the Cardiff docks and his feelings for the Welsh miners, and of Jane with her good radical mind, had a similar effect.

The All Souls exams of 1932 and 1933 provided two more excellent friends, Isaiah Berlin and Ian Bowen, as well as two more avenues to look down over the years, watching the brilliant careers of Patrick Reilly in the Foreign Office and Richard Wilberforce at the Bar. Ian Bowen, elected a Fellow in 1932, was of great practical help with my Economics paper in Schools, which I suspect I only passed by learning his essays by heart. He also housed my cat in All Souls at one stage, when Lady Margaret Hall had thrown it out. Isaiah, no canine lover, had to put up with my dogs. At first it was an Old English sheepdog who accompanied us on our sauntering walks through Magdalen deer park or along the Cherwell, or lunched with me in his rooms, first in All Souls and then in New College; later it was a stray mongrel I had adopted.

I cannot boast that Isaiah taught me any philosophy, though no doubt I plagued him with some of the numerous incomprehensibilities I found in the subject. What we both really enjoyed was the intimate panorama of human relations going on around us. We shared several friends and many more acquaintances: peculiar and eccentric, witty and dull, charming and disagreeable. Isaiah, with his literary imagination, extreme sensibility and irrepressible talk, made them all seem far more interesting, I suspect, than they really were. They became characters in the Russian novels we were finding in translation on the bookshelves of Blackwells' but which he, of course, had long possessed and read in Russian. It was fascinating when the characters he portrayed were more distant figures like Maurice Bowra or Kenneth Clarke or Mrs Cameron, with whom we occasionally met for lunch. But when it concerned my closer friends, whom I looked on with innocent eyes, his marvellous portraits gave them dimensions which disturbed me a little, though never for long and perhaps not enough. We went to concerts together and he had a wind-up gramophone with a huge horn which filled his entire room, leaving a narrow passage up which he strolled conducting the music. The walls were lined with books. It was said that no one had ever found Isaiah actually reading. He sat in the middle of the room and imbibed them. (Obviously, as it has turned out, a far more effective means of acquiring knowledge and insight.)

Into this ivory tower, this make-believe world, there broke the horrible reality of Hitler's appointment as Chancellor of Germany on 30 January, 1933. It was a particularly beautiful weekend in Oxford. The rivers were frozen and we all went skating. Goronwy had come from Manchester where he was working on the *Manchester Guardian* and Douglas from London and *The Times*. We skated at Blenheim and thought only, I fear, of private life and how beautiful it could be.

'I am sad that all that skating is over,' Douglas wrote to me when he got back to London. 'If only it would freeze a little longer, one might perhaps become quite good. But it was lovely having Stephen [Spender], Shaiah and [A. L.] Rowse and Herbert [Hart] and Richard [Wilberforce] and everybody there for the weekend all at once. Being with intelligent people after this office [*The Times*] is like the freeze after the fog and rain.

'Hitler seems to have come at last and heaven knows what will happen next. German politics are strange, frenzied and fascinating. Von Trott told me on Saturday that Hitler was definitely finished. I don't see how he can go on coalescing with these men. Anything he does economically different from the last Government will only make things worse and finish him and the other men, I hope.

'I have a vision of all the reactionary Governments falling at just about the time that prices begin to rise and socialist Governments coming in everywhere and getting the credit for the recovery and the opportunity to expand wages and social services enormously out of the enormous wealth that will come as soon as the depression is over. I think there is a good chance that that is how it will end if there are a few sane men.'

There were no sane men, it seemed, in power, anywhere. Adam von Trott was of course utterly dismayed at the gratuitous appointment of Hitler by the venerable and hitherto respected German President, Field-Marshal von Hindenburg. Adam had always voted Social Democrat since he became of voting age, much to the disapproval of his conservative parents. He had spoken out against

National Socialism in the German Club at Oxford and been rebuked for it by his mother. 'I do not think you have done right,' she had written to him. 'You know that as far as I understand the movement, I reject it. Nevertheless this is a national movement which you should not denigrate or belittle outside your own country.'

The roots of Adam's patriotism were deep in his family's traditions. He was very disturbed by events in Germany and waited anxiously for the end of term when he could return and find out what was going on.

That Easter vacation, Peggy and I went down to Diana's cottage in Cornwall with her sister Rachel. Christopher was with a New College reading party in the neighbouring bay and Douglas joined us there for Easter. Fed up with *The Times* and its failure to pass on to its readers the warnings they were receiving from Germany, he was shortly to join *The Economist*. Some of the messages he had read at *The Times* before he joined us had been about the Reichstag Fire, which he was convinced had been started by the Nazis themselves. Now in Cornwall he read out daily reports of how Hitler was riveting his hold on Germany and of the terrible fate being meted out to his political opponents. I had never known Douglas so incensed. It was as if at that moment he saw the whole horror of the next twelve years.

I wrote anxiously and – in view of the censorship that had been introduced in Germany – 'conspiratorially', to Adam, fearing for what might become of him. He was already on the defensive.

'Will I encounter much anti-German feeling now?' he replied from Berlin. 'It makes me think very especially of my few real friends as I know I shall be safe with them. . . . A dangerous crowd . . . has got hold of things. Individual happenings are *not* the character of the whole thing – but the whole thing has put business on a move. The western capitalist states will make a lot more of the disorder here than is legitimate in view of the veiled brutality of any capitalist state. I am sure that fear of the setting in of a revolutionary transformation of even the economic side – is one of the sources of indignation and hostility. It is here that the friends of European and world development must be careful with their criticism. I wish I could put this across to G.R. [Goronwy Rees] – but I cannot do it in a "Conspiratorial" enough manner. I hope to Heaven that the right thing is on the move as well!'

At the time I did not see the fatal fallacy in this argument. Both fallacies in fact : for what proved tragically fatal to Adam in the end was firstly his misunderstanding of what people in England, then and later, really hated in Nazi Germany, and secondly his belief that some 'right thing' could come out of it without, at this stage, halting Hitler or, later, during the war, without wiping out everything which Hitler had 'achieved' for Germany.

Although the Special Paper I had chosen for PPE was called 'International Relations', it was entirely centred on the 1919 settlement and, above all, on its consequences for Germany. The interests and safety of France or of the new countries in Eastern Europe were totally ignored. Our bible was Keynes' *The Economic Consequences of the Peace*, and as we went through the Treaty clause by clause, our indignation was aroused by the harsh nature of the terms imposed on Germany and the vindictive character of the French in demanding that these terms be fulfilled. By the time I went down from Oxford I was not only filled with a sense of guilt for all the sufferings which, so we were taught, were the direct consequence of these terms – inflation, near starvation, political violence – but even felt that consequently it was we and not the German people themselves who were responsible for the rise of Hitler. We gave them the grievances and the grievances made Hitler. QED.

At the end of the academic year of 1933, Adam left Oxford and returned to Germany. He had hoped to try for an All Souls Fellowship and thus delay for two years his return to Germany, but the second he achieved in his Finals made this impossible.

None of us wanted any more to holiday in a Nazi Germany. Isaiah suggested that Goronwy and I should meet him in Salzburg for the Festival and then get away from the conventional holiday routes by accompanying him to Sub-Carpathian Ruthenia. He wished to investigate the 'basic Slav' which he understood was spoken in that eastern tip of Czechoslovakia. We were also intrigued by reports of a miracle-working rabbi who was supposed to be in the area.

That summer (and the next) we heard the great conductors and soloists, many of whom could no longer perform in Germany on account of their Jewish origin or because of their own honourable scruples. I thought Salzburg the most charming town I had ever been in and its baroque architecture the most humane and pleasurable. I loved the fountains where prancing stone horses snorted water through their nostrils, and above all I loved Mozart's music which I had never heard played in such profusion.

Then the three of us escaped all the other Oxford concert-goers who thronged to Salzburg in those days when tickets were cheap, and travelled on via Vienna to Bratislava, where we bought a water melon which we carried along in Isaiah's hat. Isaiah, now in command of the situation, bought our tickets in his 'basic Slav'. They carried us into the Tatra mountains and on to Kosice, the capital of Sub-Carpathian Ruthenia, and Uzhorod, the terminal of this one-track eastward railway. In both towns we were hauled off to the police station, manned by Czechs from the western district of the Czechoslovak Republic, and questioned as to our exact purpose in making this extraordinary journey. Each time, having seen the hotels and, still worse, the deformed and rotting beggars on the streets, I earnestly hoped to spend the night in the spotless police station but, with wary disbelief, the officials listened to our story and let us go. From Uzhorod the only form of on-going transport, we were told, was a taxi. After we had settled ourselves comfortably, as we thought, innumerable people began to climb in, all equally anxious to make the journey. Our driver spoke English, having worked, so he told us, in one of the seasonal agricultural gangs which used to go over to America for the harvest. Shouting over the heads of our fellow passengers, he asked us what crime we had committed in England that made it impossible for us to stay there. He considered it totally out of the question that we were going to Mukacevo of our own free will. And when we arrived, I saw his point. It was then the furthest tip of Czechoslovakia; grabbed back by Hungary after Munich, it was annexed by the Soviet Union after the war and must now be the nearest tip of Russia.

Orthodox Jews, dressed in sober black robes and with long ringlets dangling to their shoulders, were the least sinister part of the population. Of the rest, like the beggars further west, a large proportion seemed to be in an advanced stage of some terrible disease which twisted their limbs or rotted them so that bits fell off, leaving ghastly stumps. Seeing my face, the driver asked cheerily whether we would like to go back with him. Isaiah firmly refused, sat down just as firmly at a table outside the one and only hotel and ordered yoghurt for us all. It was, he said, our best hope of not succumbing to minor disease. I do not believe we enquired or even raised with each other what the nature of the major disease around us might have been. Certainly there was great poverty and malnutrition. This part of Czechoslovakia, like Slovakia, had been under Hungarian rule in the old

Austria-Hungary and I remember someone saying how much better the Hungarian doctors were than the Czechs because they could diagnose and prescribe from the doorstep while Czech doctors had to come right in and examine their patients.

It was with great relief that I found a Czech guidebook in the hotel where we were staying and read of a mountain spa at a place called Uzok. Goronwy and I promptly decided to take the waters. Isaiah mocked our tourist tastes and settled down to days of happy café talk.

We went on a little train, hitched to a winding cable, up and up the mountains. Soon we were the only people travelling in it. Finally it stopped in a totally deserted spot and the guard shouted, 'Uzok!'

We stepped down onto the ground and enquired after the spa. A group of armed soldiers advanced and had some difficulty understanding our question. Ah! Springs.' they suddenly exclaimed, smiling and pleased to satisfy us. 'Springs are everywhere – all around.' We looked round. We were at the summit of a pass and there were slopes down to little valleys through which water was indeed flowing. There were two huts nearby, then some posts, then two more huts further away. 'Frontier posts,' they nodded. 'That is Poland.' Was there anywhere to stay? we asked. 'Indeed!' they cried and led us to one of the huts. It had no windows and was totally empty except for some sacks filled with hay lying on the floor. We couldn't help laughing and the soldiers joined in happily. Some Polish soldiers strolled over from their quarters and soon we were all friends, sitting on the ground drinking cocoa and trying to communicate. The Poles were exceedingly pleased to hear I was partly Scottish because they had fought against Scottish troops in the war. What a bond trying to kill each other is. We all found each other exceedingly comical.

Later we went for a walk in the valley and saw in the distance a little grey figure crossing the river over a long narrow plank. When it saw us, it turned, rushed back to the far shore and disappeared. There was no sign of any human habitation, and the whole scene seemed suddenly sinister. Though it was only a child, this little figure frightened me. As night fell, we went back and shut ourselves in the windowless hut. We slept perfectly well. Next day we returned to Isaiah who was delighted. He, or course, had had wholly satisfactory encounters not only with Ruthenians in 'basic Slav' but even with White Russians now living there who told him of the last days of the 1917 Revolution. The *Wunder* Rabbi had not turned up and we comforted ourselves that at least we had not missed that.

But who eventually laughed last was not so clear. When we boarded our little train to go thankfully west again, it transpired that Isaiah's 'basic Slav' had procured us six single tickets rather than three returns. The railway officials were adamant that it was our mistake and nothing could be done about it. We pooled our resources, travelled as far west as they would carry us and cabled our families for money. Goronwy and Isaiah continued their long philosophical discussions of which I understood not a word and against which I protested ineffectually. On our last night, we solemnly ate the water melon and Isaiah resumed his hat.

6

I was reluctant to return to Oxford for my last year. The pressure of work was increasing and the pleasure of friends diminishing. Goronwy had stayed on in Berlin where he was supposed to be researching on Lassalle; Adam had returned to Kassel to resume his training as a lawyer; Diana had gone down after one year; Peggy had left to get married and Jane was absent because she was ill. Isaiah and Christopher alone remained; much, but not enough.

What was the point of getting a degree, I wondered, of all this study in a place so obviously remote from the real world? My mother had transferred £3,000 to each of her four children. All were married now except me, and this bonus, she had said, must pay my college fees which amounted to £50 a term, the exact interest which this capital brought in. Since a term's notice had to be given if one was not to forfeit the fees, the arrangement had ensured that I continued term by term throughout these three years, since my strong impulse to leave was always cancelled by my great reluctance to forfeit £50.

In this last year, however, I was slowly formulating a resolve to get right away as soon as my Finals were over, not only from Oxford but also from the friends who had dominated my life for the last three years and still did so, even if intermittently or from some distance. I wanted to see the 'real' world on my own and decide what I was going to do with my life. I knew that I did not want, like Peggy, to marry and settle down.

Clearly it was the developments on the Continent which held the greatest interest, if also the greatest menace, for our lives. I remember one of my strongest impulses to leave Oxford came after the shelling of the workers' flats in Vienna in February 1934. It seemed preposterous to be living a useless life in this ivory tower while such things could happen. I was also deeply moved by the sight of the Hunger Marchers, England's unemployed, as they tramped through Oxford. Isaiah reproached me for my 'Tolstoyan sentimentalism' and Miss Grier, the Principal of Lady Margaret Hall, dismissed my request to go down as 'foolish'. I would have much more chance of helping people and being effective in the world with a degree, she said.

I wrote a long letter to Adam, describing my feelings and adding, 'One must make up one's mind not to have these tender Tolstoyan sympathies and at the same time cooperate in a system which by its evils evokes them. The whole question is so difficult and bewildering and I become worse at thinking every day. Economics, which is the basis of the whole question, I find quite impossible, and philosophy, which should be the ground work of one's faith, is empty and incomprehensible to me.'

In his reply Adam made no mention of all this but described a strange dream he had had :

'I was lying on my sofa in the room at Balliol reading (in a voluminous French book bound in red-brown linen) the speeches of delegates on some international conference of professors. Under a thick black line the Russian was summing up his remarks on nationalism – saying that when the work was accomplished, it would show in all its branches and forms a strong national character which belonged and could only belong to his country. . . .The young Russian stood on an elevated platform, rather idealised in his looks and rhetorical gestures – like Stalin.

'I had been looking at all this when I remember there was a long pause during which I dozed – Suddenly I heard you rushing up the stone steps – I could tell from your movements and the noise of your rather hard rain-coat flapping. You stopped at the door to listen whether I was in. I wanted to call you in – and couldn't. I tried to move and found I was completely paralysed. A few anguished seconds went by and when I at last managed to draw up my knees to rise from my sleep, I seemed to hear your steps on the gravel below, departing to some lecture or so. After that I woke up – I am afraid all this seems rather absurd to tell, one cannot convey the intensity of such dreams.

'Will we keep a relation of real persons to each other when we neither see nor hear anything of each other any more?'

It was a painfully prophetic dream and my response to it was also indicative of the response I later made to Adam's deep perplexities.

'It was a very strange dream,' I wrote. 'I hope it was not true and you are not dragged into this curse of nationalism. I'm afraid you are because even when you were here you thought in that way.'

In February 1934 Adam dismayed many people, but not really me yet, by writing a letter to the *Manchester Guardian* not only denying anti-semitic persecution in the Hessian law courts (which the *Guardian* had reported) but even asserting that 'active Storm Troopers', to whom he had talked 'again and again', 'turn with indignation from the suggestion of atrocities being committed in their presence.' Adam's Oxford friends were genuinely shocked that he could exonerate Nazis simply, it seemed, because they were Germans. Isaiah, who was a great friend to both of us and with whom I had tried to argue on Adam's behalf, wrote to me : 'What really distresses me is that by his action he should have shifted himself into a terrible region which I see in terms of sheer black and white.' And he added what indeed we all thought : 'That he was a patriotic person before everything else was patent always.'

Adam regarded criticism of his country as one regards criticism of one's family. One can criticize them oneself but does not like others to do so. Adam saw it as a humiliation and an affront and found himself trying to explain and exonerate his country and present it in the best possible light. And because all Germans had been taught to feel bitter about a lost war and the treaty which followed it, he excused, indeed was blinded to, the aims and methods of Nazi foreign policy. To the 'unpatriotic' generation of Oxford students who were his friends, this defence struck a discordant note. Isaiah's remark was not meant as a compliment.

I was now approaching my last term at Oxford and that rather harsh pre-Finals period when one feels trapped and on edge. Goronwy had returned from Germany and was much around. I was feeling more and more strongly that I had to have a year on my own in order to find out where I really stood and what I wanted to do. When Schools were over at last and term had ended, I went back to Oxford to tell Goronwy this. He agreed to my suggestion of a parting – only temporary, after all – more calmly than I had expected. The real import of my decision, I suspect, was completely overshadowed by the news from Germany.

It was 1 July, 1934 and every newspaper carried banner headlines announcing the appalling slaughter that had occurred there the previous day. Hitler, in order to rid himself of dissident elements within

the Nazi Party, had summoned all his SA leaders to meet him in conference at Wiessee under their Chief of Staff, Ernst Roehm. In the
early hours of the morning, under Hitler's personal supervision in
Munich, the unsuspecting storm troopers were torn from their beds
and shot, some at their hotel, others in the prisons to which they had
been dragged. In the meantime, Goering and Himmler had got to
work in Berlin. Some 150 SA men were mown down against the wall
of the Lichterfelde Cadet School. Two prominent Nazis, Gregor
Strasser and Karl Ernst, were also seized and executed. Himmler's SS
murdered General von Schleicher and his wife at their home and
wrecked the office of von Papen, the Vice-Chancellor, killing two of
his advisers.

Papen survived to continue his services to Hitler, and President
Hindenburg thanked the Führer for his 'determined action and
gallant personal intervention, which have nipped treason in the bud
and rescued the German people from great danger.' No protesting
voice was raised in public anywhere in Germany. Already it was
assumed that protest was impossible and served no purpose.

Many disgusted and endangered Germans had already emigrated;
many others were in concentration camps. Only two members of the
German Officer Corps, Field-Marshal von Mackensen and General
von Hammerstein, the former Commander-in-Chief of the Werh-
macht, protested personally to Hitler about the murder of their
brother officers. General Blomberg expressed the congratulations of
the Cabinet.

We had not yet supped on horror, as now we sup, and the spectacle
of the rulers of a 'civilized' European State murdering former colleagues and comrades in cold blood filled us with horror and fore-
boding.

Alarmed, I wrote to Adam, ending a long letter with the words :
'I would come to Germany if I could do anything for you.' Adam
answered : 'Unless you mean by "if I can do anything for you" that
on your own account you would not come, I would ask you very
earnestly to come now.'

In the middle of August 1934, en route once again for Salzburg,
I went to Kassel, where Adam was working in the Public Prosecutor's
office. The only train with a through connection from London
arrived at 3.41 am. As I tried to sleep on the hard wooden seat of my
third-class carriage, I wondered what on earth I was doing. I had
not seen Adam for more than a year and even on walks in Oxford I

had often felt shy. He had talked endlessly of Hegel and I had understood hardly a word. Now, for a moment, I felt as if I was going to meet a perfect stranger in a strange place at a wholly ungodly hour.

He was waiting for me on the platform when the train drew up in Kassel. His face in the dark used to take on a slightly Mephistophelian character (or perhaps he was Faust himself? I had read no German literature).

We laughed nervously and told each other how little each had changed, but both of us felt at first, I think, the great distances of time and place. In Oxford we each had primary commitments to other people. Here, suddenly, we found ourselves alone, away from those closer friends.

'I think you will like Wilhelmshöhe,' he had written to me, 'as there is a park nearby and the town rather far beneath in the wide valley. If you come in the morning . . . I can show it to you before anyone else is awake.' This he did. We drove in his little open two-seater car through the sleeping city – very fast round every corner, recklessly over every tramline. Adam pointed out the main houses. I had the impression that his family had lived in all of them. He pointed out the law courts, the theatre, the library, the Roman Catholic church. It was like a private view. There was no one else to be seen.

We drove up the broad avenue leading to Wilhelmshöhe, which was still lit up, and, leaving the car, climbed up to the palace. As we walked through the eighteenth-century arch to the terrace, the lights were suddenly switched off and there below us lay the sleeping town with one brave star hanging in the yellowing sky. Adam roared his great laugh, seized my arm and shouted : 'See how I arrange it all for you.'

This mixture of grandeur with self-mockery was Adam's most engaging quality. He liked the grandeur to be noticed but was happiest when one laughed at it with him. Really he was born out of his time. He would have been at his best as an aristocratic princeling born to power and position in an earlier century. He would have loved wielding power in a humane and liberal fashion. In our modern world, his judgement both of politics and of personalities was often at fault.

He launched at once into his own account of recent events. The official version, which Adam only half-believed, was that the Brown-shirts had themselves planned a coup d'état together with dissident groups in the Wermacht, which had thus been foiled. Adam's guesses made no more sense than anybody else's but I was anxious to hear how he saw his own position. It was, he maintained, and I noted later, 'one of unarmed hostility. He dislikes the movement, could never join it or compromise with it, but he takes his opposition as for granted; he makes no stir about it, he does not plot to overthrow the government, nor make any secret of his refusal to join the party. He is the only referendar in Kassel who has refused to join any Nazi organisation. He has been asked his reasons for not joining and answered that the leaders themselves had said no one should join except from conviction. At another time he was saved by the refusal of the older Nazis themselves to allow new and faint-principled men into their ranks. He pointed out to one of the leaders several items in the Nazi programme with which he did not agree. Though his promotion to Berlin has been refused, probably on these grounds, he has not otherwise suffered for his opinions. His work hitherto has been in Hanau, Rotenburg and Kassel, all Hessian towns and bordering on his home. It may perhaps be the strength of family prestige which has saved him in a provincial town; his name, and in Kassel his appearance, are sufficient to provoke respect for him and immunity for his views. The inhabitants of Kassel are exceedingly ugly, they are small and heavy and their faces are brutal with stupidity. Adam is very tall and thin, his features are exceedingly fine and well-distanced and immediately suggest a certain Tolstoyan nobility of character, which is slightly belied by his carelessness and frequent laughter, but these are only part of his general assurance and self-confidence. . . .

'As to the duration of the government, about that he could not say anything. He certainly seemed to think the end was not in sight, and has given up all thought of organising an opposition – it is clear that he does not think such a thing exists, and I doubt he would join it very seriously if it did. He has withdrawn pretty well from politics. His hope seems to lie in regenerating life in the country, in villages, rather than in any violent revolution. We walked through the old quarter of Kassel, formerly a communist part and there, some of the notices Ein Wille, Ein Volk, Ein Ja had been torn down. He told me how members of the Saar commission had visited the communist leader Thaelman in prison and had managed to ask him how he was treated – and he cried that he was treated disgracefully, was so treated and always would be. That had passed quickly round.'

Carefully and meticulously, I recorded everything to do with politics that Adam said. I suppose that even then, young as we were, both of us realized that we were caught up willy-nilly in the great events of our time. We talked of course of many other things too, of the book he was writing about Kleist, of *The Brothers Karamazov* which I was reading. He saw himself and his two brothers, Werner and Heinrich, as Dmitri, Ivan and Alyosha Karamazov. Clearly he would have liked to have been the saintly Alyosha, but both his character and his position in his family ineluctably drove him to take up the positions which Ivan, had Dostoievsky placed his characters in this twentieth-century scene, would undoubtedly also have adopted.

During that first week, Adam worked in the mornings while I read or tried to learn German; in the afternoons and on the long summer evenings we would set out in his car to visit scenes of his not too happy youth – Hannoversch-Münden where he was at school, the lakes in the Herzwald, the palace and gardens at Wilhelmsthal – all of which I found very beautiful, the lakes filled with swans, the gardens with squirrels, the woods with deer. It was very pleasant and gay. Adam would sing songs from his childhood, hunting songs and soldiers' songs. Even the Nazi songs, which I was hearing for the first time, I found rather stirring. At the end of the week he took me to his home at Imshausen, thirty miles south-east of Kassel.

His love of his family home matched mine for High Elms and had always been a great bond between us. But nothing could have been more different than these two country houses. Imshausen seemed like a great rock growing out of the forests and hills which surrounded it on all sides. High Elms came much later into the world and reflected the comfort and enlightenment of the nineteenth-century English upper middle classes, and their capacity to choose and mould their own environment. The fourteen thousand trees which surrounded High Elms were planted by my great-grandparents just where they wanted them, and a carriage drive swept the whole way through. Somehow the trees of the Trottenwald, one felt, were there of their own right, and the Trotts living there were an integral part of the whole neighbourhood where their ancestors had lived for five centuries or more.

Adam's father and mother were very impressive, almost alarming. His father was very old and not easy to communicate with – I could not speak German – but he was a magnificent figure and Adam told me about his distinguished career with great pride. As Prussian Minister of Education, he had served his Emperor (the hated Kaiser of my childhood) as proudly as Adam's grandfather on his mother's side, General von Schweinitz, had served Bismarck. Adam's mother was half-American. Her mother Anna Jay, was the daughter of William Jay, the American representative at Vienna. Anna had been swept off her feet by General von Schweinitz, the Prussian Minister to the Imperial Court of Austria-Hungary. Prussia had just defeated Austria at the great battle of Königgrätz and, under the guidance of Bismarck, was rapidly becoming the dominant State on the continent of Europe. In a few years she was to defeat the French Army and lay siege to Paris. Lothar von Schweinitz must have been a powerful figure at the Imperial Court when, at the age of fifty, his eye lighted upon the twenty-three-year-old daughter of his American colleague. He carried her off to St Petersburg where, as Bismark's Minister, he was no doubt also a person to be reckoned with. She bore him eight children, of whom Eleonore, Adam's mother, was the second.

It was a proud heritage for someone of Adam's temperament; I often used to think that family pride and personal ambition were the explosive emotional ingredients of Adam's dangerous patriotism – for dangerous it was at a time when Hitler ruled Germany. Dangerous because, sooner or later, Adam had to remove Hitler for Germany's sake. He paid for this with his life. A less proud and patriotic man would have waited, by 1944, for the Allies to finish the job.

Adam had talked much about me to his mother and she made a special effort to get to know me. The result was immediately disastrous. Although she despised Hitler as a vulgar upstart, like Adam she was not entirely averse to what he was doing in foreign policy. Also, like all Germans, she hated the Treaty of Versailles and did not condemn unilateral treaty abrogation so long as it was this hated Treaty which was involved. For my part, still deeply under the influence of my Oxford teaching, I sympathized with the 'wrongs' done to Germany. We fell into an argument, however, over what those 'wrongs' were. Poland, for instance, which had only been restored to existence by the Treaty of Versailles, needed, I argued, its access to the Baltic Sea and if this meant the Corridor through Germany, dividing East Prussia from the rest, this was not an ignoble price for Germany to pay. Adam's mother, every inch a Prussian for all her American blood, considered it 'unjust and un-natural, separating German from German and causing so much unhappiness and bitterness'. We argued too about Germany leaving the League of Nations, which she and Adam justified but I strongly regretted.

I cannot think now, looking back, how I presumed, or indeed dared, to argue with her. It was hardly sensitive or polite, but then, in my family, we had all been brought up to speak our minds, even to our elders. I cannot recall whether Adam removed me hastily from the house or whether the argument took place just before I was in any case leaving. My memory is only awoken by a letter from Frau von Trott which I found among my hoard :

My dear Miss Grant Duff,

I should have liked to answer your letter at once, but it reached me as I was leaving for the Schwarzwald. . . . You did not need to apologise again. We had quite 'made up' before you left. But as you *did*, I too will say again how sorry I am that I made you – my guest – feel uncomfortable.

You see, I have felt the humiliation of my country very deeply and am sore on the subject – and am therefore perhaps not able to argue coolly as to a step which the unbearability of the situation has made inevitable [the leaving of the League]. It is often hard to hear young people discuss coolly situations which were so bitter to us – and I was surprised to find that even Adam had forgotten some things which he ought to know – for instance, when I said 'at least the old regime died honourably' by refusing in the person of Count Brockdorff-Rantzau, to sign the impossible treaty – he had forgotten that fact.

In many ways you young people *know* more and are better trained, while we old ones, who went through it all, *feel* more. This is not a good basis for a discussion – though it may be and should be one for reconstruction – and I have faith in the thinking ones in the younger generation that they will devote their lives to making the world better than they found it. And for this international friendships are most valuable.

Adam has always wanted me to know you – always said we had much in common. Perhaps one of these things is a certain reserve which made it hard for us to know each other. Perhaps the little explosion on the verandah helped us more than several days of conventional conversation would have done ! But I am sorry you could not have stayed a little longer to get a more peaceful impression before you left. You will have to do that another time. . . .

. . . And I think you will agree with me in my belief that if the teaching of Christ were ever to be really applied to politics – all difficulties would be solved. It has never been done. But of course it must be realised in individual persons first – and I believe that is our only hope!

Yours very sincerely,
Eleonore von Trott

I thought about these matters a great deal, not so much in the personal as in the historical context. I told Adam I wanted to learn more about the history of Europe since the last war, 'why such peaks of idealism, hope and bravery are followed by such pits of despair, anarchy and oppression. I want to write a book about it – not the events of history but the sufferings and hopes of the people, showing the frightful price paid for every international move, for every economic change, the long-term effects of the war on freeing people and making them more hopelessly servile to fear and leadership than ever before.' Above all, I wanted 'if possible to contribute something to prevent war and bring about better peace conditions in Europe, especially in Germany and Austria.' I did not have much hope of being able to realize this ambition, 'but to attempt either and fail is infinitely better than not to attempt,' I told Adam.

Life with Adam seemed always a little grander than it really was, or perhaps I was always trying to keep it on a level where the daily problems of love and friendship would not intrude. Our private feelings were largely directed towards other people and I found it reassuring that Adam could talk to me quite openly about his love affairs, assuming in me the detachment I wished to preserve. It is not true, as his biographer, Christopher Sykes, has written, that I disapproved. It was simply that I was worried when I thought he was making my friend Diana, whom he loved and who loved him deeply, unhappy. But being both of us idealists and romantics, Adam and I sublimated our private emotions into ideas and causes which were perhaps equally dear to our hearts. The times in which we lived, and our different nationalities of which we were both so conscious, led us to elevate our friendship to a level over and above mere personal relations. 'Let's have an alliance,' I wrote to him after this visit. 'I wish it could be an alliance of a new Germany and a new England. If only our countries regarded each other as we do, there'd be greater hope in Europe.'

I was wrong. There was no hope either way, and though both Adam and I were to try to take a hand in the relationship between our countries, we each had our own idea of what was needed. Eventually each was to oppose bitterly the position taken up by the other.

On my return to England I found an anguished letter awaiting me from Goronwy in Berlin, eleven pages of misery and despair. Most of it was personal but there was a terrible reminder of the Germany I had not seen with Adam :

'Here what seems a nightmare in London is the sober everyday reality : the betrayal and death of every human virtue; no mercy, no pity, no peace; neither humanity nor decency nor kindness : only madness, shouted every day on the wireless and in the newspapers, spoken by ordinary people as if it were sober sanity : and sixty million people pleased and proud to be governed by a gang of murderous animals. The madness, the bestiality, the crude, ugly inhumanity – can you wonder that, among this, thinking of it continually, seeing it, living by it, I long for you and everything you mean to me – luxe, calme et volupte – for you and for rest, for a quiet mind, for happiness, until in body and mind I am tortured by the longing for it.'

It was not an appeal I could possibly ignore so I wired that I was coming and embarked once again on a long third-class journey across Europe. My mother was worried but would, I know, have acted exactly as I did.

Meeting Goronwy on a railway station in Berlin, whatever the hour, held no anxieties. It was still summer and we walked again in the Grünewald and sat by the Wannsee watching the coloured sails of the little boats. It was great happiness to be together again and, as so often before, his black misery left him. 'The sense of peace within and without gave me all that I longed for and despaired of during the last three months,' he wrote afterwards. And of course, being happy together, we took in as little of the horrors around us as we had taken in of Moscow and Leningrad two years before.

When I left we were both full of good resolutions about how we were going to spend the rest of the year. I still felt I needed to be on my own and Goronwy too had much to work out in his own life. His projected work on Lassalle, which he had promised All Souls, had flagged considerably and his offer to substitute a study of Marx's early works had been turned down. He was full of advice on how I should get started on a journalistic career and approved my intention of going to Paris. I do not think I confided my high-flown resolve to prevent war and save the world. He would have laughed and told me not to be so silly. I would have laughed too and continued on my way.

7

It was not as difficult in 1934 as it would seem in the more sophisticated, cynical and anarchic world of today, to seek – and be given –
advice on how to set about preventing the outbreak of a major war. I
was perhaps fortunate in putting this question to somebody as
amiable and civilized as Professor Arnold Toynbee. My two great
advantages in the world (of which I was fully aware) were a small
private income (£3 a week) and what are commonly known as
'connections'. In those days these very often went together.

Arnold Toynbee was married at that time to my cousin Rosalind
Murray, though my introduction to him was actually through
Humphrey Sumner, my Oxford examiner in International Relations.
I think the cousinship provided a cup of tea.

Professor Toynbee had no hesitation in saying that the way to stop
war was to study the possible causes on the spot and the best way to
do that was to work as the foreign correspondent of an influential
newspaper. This, at that period, was undoubtedly *The Times.*

No cousinry took me to Geoffrey Dawson who was then Editor, but
somehow or other I found myself in his office and I do remember that
a cup of tea was provided. It was one of those gifts one is taught very
early in life to suspect if brought by the Greeks. Mr Dawson was
urbane and friendly and asked what he could do for me. I said he
could send me as an assistant to his Paris office. Ah ! he said, perhaps
I should see his Foreign Editor, Mr Deakin.

As I climbed the dingy stairs of that old nineteenth-century Printing House Square to the still dingier room of the Foreign Editor, I
remembered that Harold Nicolson had written somewhere that after
splendid visits to palatial rooms in British Embassies abroad, one
climbed narrow stairs to a dirty, untidy little room to meet a dim,
unimportant little man who was the only one who knew what the

real situation in the country was and who really knew his job. Either Mr Dawson had got smartly on the telephone to Mr Deakin or Mr Deakin knew his job only too well. He explained to me at once that it was quite impossible for a woman to work on the editorial side of a newspaper since it meant night work alongside men. If, on the other hand, I was going to Paris anyway, perhaps I would like to send them some fashion notes. I was deeply incensed. To feel capable of stoping a world war and then to be asked to write fashion notes!

I still had my second advantage – my private income. I left on the next train to Paris. I had never been there before, and as I stepped onto the platform at the Gare St Lazare I experienced some of the same feelings I had had when I arrived at Kassel a few weeks earlier and found Adam waiting for me. But in Paris I knew not a soul. Moreover, I suddenly realized I could not speak French. I had studied it for more than ten years at school. I had been to French seaside resorts with my family as a child, but I was now completely tongue-tied. I had no idea what to ask for or how to ask for it. I walked with as great an air of purpose as I could muster out of the nearest exit and found myself in the rue d'Amsterdam. The street seemed to consist entirely of hotels and bars. Many of these had sinister red lights above the doors; I took them for something other than tobacconists. I chose one with the reassuring name of Hotel Britannia and asked firmly for a room as high up and as cheap as possible – the pound, even then, seemed to buy very few francs and £3 a week did not go very far.

I was shown into a small dark room; the windows appeared to be only a few feet feet from the offices on the other side of the street but the wallpaper had a reassuring pattern of large Tudor roses like those sold on flag days in England. The double bed was a little less reassuring but I supposed that all the rooms were furnished with these. At any rate the room next door to mine clearly had one which was noisily in use at almost any time of the day or night. I unpacked my suitcase and went down to explore.

The rush hour had subsided and people in the street were engaged in more leisurely pursuits than getting home from work. Though October, it was not yet cold and most of the bar doors were open. It looked lively and warm inside though not exactly cosy. The clientele in the rue d'Amsterdam seemed to be mostly working-class and middle-aged. Men stood at the bars, women sat at little marble-topped tables.

'Walk fast and never catch anyone's eye' had been the motto instilled in me as a girl for my protection and it worked like a charm in Paris. I think my appearance was a pretty stout armour too. I had a tweed coat, low-heeled sensible shoes, no hat and my face was as nature made it. French women in those days – or at any rate the French women of the quartier which I, of course, found intensely romantic but was, I suspect, louche in the extreme – had highly painted faces, very high heels and what to me seemed very smart and sophisticated clothes. The readers of the fashion notes in *The Times* would have been more grossly misinformed than even the readers of the political reports.

I found a little restaurant at the back of the rue d'Amsterdam where I could have a meal, *'pain à discretion'*, for 4.50 fr. For an extra franc, I could also have had wine. For the next three months this was the only meal of which I could be certain every day.

I had one supreme objective in Paris; having failed with the British press, I would try the American. I had been given an introduction to Edgar Ansel Mowrer, the Paris correspondent of the *Chicago Daily News*.

Mowrer was as famous in the early 1930s for his reports from Nazi Germany as Ed Murrow became a decade later for his stories from wartime London. Even before Hitler had come to supreme power, Mowrer had warned the English-speaking world what was going on; his damning indictment, *Germany Puts the Clock Back*, was published on the last day of December 1932, a whole month before Hitler became Chancellor. In 1932, Mowrer was elected President of the International Press Association in Berlin and awarded the Pulitzer Prize for 'the best correspondence from abroad'.

On 30 January, 1933, Hitler became Chancellor of Germany and all the bestialities of the Third Reich began. Mowrer continued to report them faithfully and unsparingly and the fight was on between a dictatorship and the freedom of the world press – the German press, of course, had been brought to heel immediately. In those days, so-called civilized States were still reluctant to expel foreign correspondents or to censor their scripts, so that any country which could afford a first-class correspondent knew what was going on. . . . At first, that is; later Goebbels managed to get most of the real anti-Nazi foreign correspondents out of Berlin.

So Mowrer reported the burning of the Reichstag, which let loose the terror that stifled all opposition inside Germany; the formation of the Gestapo in April 1933; the burning of the books, when 30,000 university students and schoolchildren were marched down the Unter den Linden carrying torches and shouting patriotic songs and accompanying lorry-loads of books for the *auto-da-fé*. Mowrer told the world about the concentration camps, the torture of prisoners, the beginning of the measures to exterminate the Jews, the connived-at breakdown of law and order when storm troopers could beat up and kill whomever they chose.

The German Government used every pressure to get Mowrer out. They declared a boycott of the Foreign Press Association unless he was removed from the presidency; his colleagues stood by him but when the Germans arrested Paul Goldmann, the elderly Jewish correspondent of the Austrian *Neue Freie Presse*, and his wife appealed to the Mowrers in tears, Edgar struck a bargain and offered to resign in exchange for Goldmann's immediate release. This was done. Edgar knew in any case that his editor wanted to move him from Berlin. He himself would have tried to stick it out; he was like a terrier once he got his teeth into anything. In Paris, his teeth were not really loosened.

I felt that such a man could teach me a lot and I was not mistaken. Thanks to contacts of Adam's and Goronwy's in Berlin, we met over a drink in the Café de la Paix. All the same, I was rather alarmed by Mowrer. He was not at all what I had expected. He could not, I felt, have been a character in a novel by Henry James. He had none of that suave urbanity of rich East Coast Americans. He was small and tough and wiry; his face was deeply lined and had a sun-burnt leathery texture. His eyes were of a piercing blue and his hair was dark and thick. An electric dynamo seemed to be in control of an incredibly active and forceful human being. He made constant jokes, which, to my ignorant mind, spelled cynicism on a vast scale. He asked me only one question : Did I know any economics? Remembering my PPE degree, I said Yes. He then said I could turn up for work on Monday morning. He would pay me nothing, but considering all I would learn, it was a bargain for me. Had I a rich grandmother?

I do not believe Edgar ever realized how little money I had and how little I ate. From time to time he would take me out to lunch and spend on one meal more than I spent on my food in a month. I wondered if I dared ask him for the money instead of the meal, but decided I enjoyed his company too much to risk losing it. Edgar was also something of a gourmet and I had never eaten, still less drunk, like that before in my life.

When I arrived in the office (in the Place de l'Opera and so within walking distance of my hotel), he sat me in a room which led out of his and in which his nephew Richard was already installed. Throughout the day, Edgar would burst in with some news item which had caught his fancy, or some new joke to fling at either me or Richard.

We both sat solemnly reading the papers and I think Richard occasionally even wrote something. We very seldom spoke to each other. For those first few months, I read and listened and laughed – for Richard and I, and I especially, were the butt of all Mowrer's wit and sarcasm.

England was preparing for George V's Royal Jubilee and the English newspapers were full of loyal and often sycophantic comment with which Edgar delighted to taunt me. Richard joined in too, and years later I had a letter from him starting 'Dear God Save the King!' Though married to an Englishwoman who had been through thick and thin with him and was the real and equal companion of his life, Edgar had a roving eye, loved to tease and above all to taunt the English. London was the one capital from which he had never reported and he had many fixed ideas about the British. *The Week*, Claud Cockburn's brilliant roneo-type newssheet, was a great source of fun and scandal to Mowrer. The secrets Claud seemed to know about the private and political life of everyone in high places always astounded me and I naïvely asked Mowrer how it was done. 'Oh! Claud is upper class and of course if you're upper class in England, everything's easy.'

He once asked me if I spelt Grant Duff with a hyphen. When I denied it, he said: 'But I thought it was the smart thing to have.' 'Oh no,' I retorted, 'my grandmother's maiden name was Lane Fox Pitt Rivers without a single hyphen. That is much smarter.' 'Nation of snobs,' he answered. From then on my grandmother also became a subject for jokes.

I learnt a lot about journalism from Edgar, although I mostly had to pick it up rather than be told. The things he did tell me usually had to be taken with a grain of salt and were as much an argument he was having with himself as with me. All that mattered to a good journalist, he said, was news. News came before everything. A good newspaper man would leave his bride on his wedding-night if he came on a good story. I spent much time wondering if I really wanted to be a journalist. I never confided my naïve hope of preventing a

70

world war. I thought this would also become an Aunt Sally for Edgar to hurl jokes at, but I was wrong. Edgar cared passionately about questions of war and peace, though he was very far from being a pacifist. He had very clear-cut moral and political values and for these he was prepared to die. If I had confessed my secret aims and perplexities he would, I am sure, have quoted President Masaryk's words to him : 'Follow your convictions. Live your politics. Tell the truth and do not steal. And above all, do not be afraid to die.'

Edgar had faced death on several fronts in the 1914-18 war. He and one other journalist – a Welshman – were the only correspondents to stay behind and witness the real tragedy of Caporetto when the Italians retreated before an Austrian offensive. He had also stood up to fascist thugs in Italy and to Nazi storm troopers in Berlin. He was certainly not afraid to die – perhaps for the very reason that he knew so well, and cared so much for, all the good reasons for being alive.

Edgar Ansel Mowrer was far more than a newspaper man. He was a truly civilized human being, a man of real culture and deep feeling. He never forgot that he had come to Paris in 1913 in what he called 'la Belle Epoque' to be a writer and had lived among French writers and artists. Caught up in the First World War as a correspondent, he had still continued his own tremendous self-education. In 1917 he wrote to his mother :

'I have begun a course of study which would make Methuselah sigh. Beginning with a book on the excavations of Ancient Crete, which shows the existence of a society contemporary with that of Ancient Egypt, I shall pass from the study of Egypt to that of Greece, from Greece to what is known about Etruria, from Etruria in a straight line to Ancient Rome. Afterwards one must take up theology, history, architecture and general conception of the Church with special reference to Byzance, then coming to Medieval Italy and the Great Renaissance, and so on down to today.'

It is not surprising that he had rather a contempt for a student straight from Oxford. It was lucky that he had only asked me about economics at our first interview. The rest of my ignorance was uncovered only gradually. It started with my poor knowledge of French, which he advised me to rectify as quickly as possible. He himself was completely fluent in French, Italian and German and he had a very wide circle of acquaintances in all three capitals. He made a point of knowing everyone in Paris who could give him quick and accurate

71

information and meeting anyone who went through Paris who could do the same. I once commented on his huge number of friends. 'Friends?' he said. 'I would hardly meet any of them ever again if I lost my job.'

This was another remark which made me wonder how much I wanted to be a journalist. Though I admired Edgar the more I watched him, he did not fill me with admiration for the press as a whole or newspaper men in general.

Many French journalists, he told me, and even actual newspapers, were in the pay of foreign powers. *Le Matin,* he said, was known as the Paris edition of the *Angriff.* Even the much respected *Le Temps,* the mouthpiece of the Quai d'Orsay, was known to receive Italian money. Nor was the Soviet Government exactly idle. I protested that such things were unheard of in England and he produced a favourite rhyme:

> You cannot hope to bribe or twist
> The honest British journalist;
> But seeing what the man will do
> Unbribed, there's no occasion to.

What the British were doing unbribed at the moment, in Edgar's view, was playing Hitler's game. Attacks on this front soon revealed my own feelings of guilt and my deep-seated sympathy for Germany. I am sure I produced it all, all the crimes which I felt I had upon my conscience – the treacherous armistice, the Treaty of Versailles, the post-war blockade of Germany, reparations, inflation, the occupation of the Rhineland by French troops, and now the arrival of Hitler in power, the concentration camps, Germany's withdrawal from the Disarmament Conference and the League of Nations, German rearmament and the renewed danger of war. For all this, in common with huge numbers of my thinking fellow countrymen, I felt guilty. And guilt made me pro-German. Hitler was not a representative of the German people but a spectre created and conjured up by British policies. Mowrer immediately named me 'Hitler's girl-friend' and started on my re-education.

We began with the Treaty of Versailles. 'By and large,' he maintained, 'the peace treaties of 1919-20, including the much maligned settlement with Germany at Versailles, were good treaties . . . the settlement was reasonably just and practical.'* The same could not have been said about the treaties the victorious Germans had earlier inflicted on the Russians and Rumanians. The trouble was not in the harshness of the Treaty but in the fact that the Germans had never recognized that they had been defeated. The great betrayal was not the Allies' repudiation of the Armistice terms but that of the German General Staff who 'fed the German people a diet of victory talk' and never admitted to them that they were on their backs at the end of 1918. The Allies' great mistake was to accept Ludendorff's surrender while he was still on French soil instead of driving the defeated Germans back to their own homeland. It was the German military leaders who 'suddenly ordered them to overthrow the august House of Hohenzollern and create a Republic which few of them wanted,' Mowrer said. When the Weimar Government tried to restore Germany from the ruins brought about by defeat, the German militarists, and most of the Conservatives with them, created the myth of the 'stab in the back' and turned all their guns not only against every aspect of the Peace Treaty but also against their own Government at home. 'The German struggle for Treaty revision,' Mowrer told me, 'became the fundamental fact of German national life and a chief cause of the German reaction.' I could not but remember my talk with Adam's mother.

'Then the Treaty of Versailles,' I said triumphantly, 'was responsible for the rise of Hitler. Keynes saw the appalling consequences not only for Germany but for the whole of Europe of the economic settlement alone, and the territorial clauses were still worse.'

'That book,' he spat out, 'is one of the most harmful ever written. Keynes has persuaded Washington as well as London that the beaten Germans are not dangerous, and has encouraged the Germans to think they can defy the victors with impunity. Only the French, who have had to live next door to them for centuries, have the measure of the Germans.'

I gasped. The wicked vindictiveness of French policy had been a byword in all English accounts of post-war history.

'How can you say such a thing?' I protested. 'The French marched into the Ruhr at the very moment when the Germans were completely down on their knees, starving and bankrupt, and thereby

---

* Edgar Ansel Mowrer, *The Nightmare of American Foreign Policy,* Alfred A. Knopf, New York, 1948, p. 84.

caused the most appalling inflation which any country has ever suffered.'

'It was thanks to that French invasion that the whole goddamn
stupid policy in Germany came to an end,' said Mowrer. 'Imperial
Germany had financed a lost war almost exclusively by internal loans
and currency inflation. The industrial and landed barons had counted
on winning the war and making the loser pay; when they were themselves the losers, these same interests refused to pay, and when the
Government tried to make them, they turned on the Republic.

'Year after year the Weimar Government tried to meet both its
internal and external obligations by printing money. The result was
inflation on such a scale that it no longer could pay reparations. And
when the French went in to collect the dues themselves by exploiting
the economy of the Ruhr, the Germans tried to fight them with passive resistance. It was German passive resistance, not French invasion, which so enormously increased the suffering of the German
people and produced the armed uprisings in Bavaria, Saxony and
Thuringia.

'At that point Gustav Stresemann called off passive resistance;
General von Seeckt dissolved the Black Reichswehr and dealt with
the Bavarian separatists. The "catastrophe policy" was over. Sullenly
German leaders settled down to a policy of "Fulfilment" and the
whole situation immediately improved.'

This policy of 'Fulfilment' – the Stresemann period, 1925-1929 –
was, Mowrer insisted, due to French 'toughness.' It was only because
the French had shown that they would no longer tolerate German
right-wing nationalism and open treaty abrogation, that the Germans
had at last put their own house in order, both politically and finan-
cially. The result had been the Treaty of Locarno, which had not
only put a voluntary German signature on all territorial frontiers in
Western Europe – including the de-militarization of the Rhineland –
but had also brought Germany into the League of Nations as an equal
member.

This was not the version of history I had learnt at Oxford or ever
heard advanced in England. There the French invasion of the Ruhr
had been depicted as a post-war crime undertaken against a defeated
and defenceless people. So far from bringing successful reparations
payments, it had precipitated the final destruction of the Reichsmark
and had brought the French franc tumbling after. It was only, I had
learnt, when the British and the Americans had taken a hand, when

74

Germany was given loans rather than made to pay reparations, thus enabling German prosperity to return, that a policy of détente could be pursued in Europe. Thanks to this, a freely signed treaty had been negotiated at Locarno in 1925, not only guaranteeing France's western frontiers but accepting her links with Czechoslovakia and Poland.

Mowrer made a gesture of exasperation. Did I really understand nothing about European politics? Had I lived through the last four years without even looking at a newspaper? Did I not know that Stresemann and Briand were dead? That so far from appeasing German grievances and bringing their Government as a co-operating member into the councils of Europe, concessions to Germany had served only to strengthen the nationalism of the Germans, to make them more unco-operative, more militaristic. Did I really think Hitler cared a fig for Locarno? Did I believe there was a German in the whole Reich who would not gladly see Poland crushed tomorrow and Upper Silesia reunited with Germany?

'But one of the first foreign treaties Hitler signed was a Non-Aggression Pact with Poland,' I replied.

It was a bad look-out for England, said Mowrer, if its leaders were anything like its subjects, if I represented them at all accurately. The Polish Agreement would be torn up just as soon as Germany had rearmed sufficiently to risk marching in. No treaty Hitler signed, no promise Hitler gave, no statement of fact Hitler made had any lasting validity whatsoever. Locarno was dead and gone, even though he had said he accepted it. He had taken Germany out of the League of Nations, out of the Disarmament Conference. The remilitarization of the Rhineland might take place any day and now he was demanding the swift evacuation of the Saar Territory. When the western front lay open to him, Mowrer insisted, he would turn his attention to the East, expel or wipe out its present population and colonize it with Germans. It was all written in *Mein Kampf*.

What then could I do about it all? I asked him. 'Keep your eyes open and report what you see,' he said, 'and hope that the great democracies will wake up and realize what they have to deal with in Nazi Germany.'

So far I had seen the face of Germany with Goronwy in Wickersdorf and with Adam in his own home. It had been a smiling, country face. Oxford had pleaded for a historical view. But London and Paris were filled with terrible newspaper reports of current happenings and future fears. It was time I took a straight look for myself.

75

8

The area on which all eyes were turned in January 1935 was the Saar, a district, rich in coal, covering an area of over 800 square miles. The Treaty of Versailles had given the French the right to exploit the coal resources of the Saar for a limited period in reparation for German destruction of the coal mines in northern France during the First World War. This period was now at an end and the people of the Saar were being called upon to decide their own fate in a plebiscite administered by the League of Nations. They could choose to return to Germany, become part of France, or remain as they had been for the last fifteen years, under a League of Nations Commission.

Since they were wholly German by nationality, no one, not even the French, expected the people of the Saar to opt for France. German anti-Nazis had, however, set up a United Front party, the *Einheitsfront*, pledged to a policy of remaining under the League Commission until such time as Germany was free of Hitler and had become a free and peace-loving country. They were opposed by the *Deutsche Front*, a National Socialist party who were campaigning for reunion with the Reich.

The plebiscite, due to be held on 13 January, was therefore not simply of national interest but possessed far greater and wider political importance. It was the first time since Hitler had come to power, and would be the last, when Germans were free to cast their vote for or against National Socialism. The prestige of the Third Reich was at stake.

The world tension excited by the Saar is now forgotten. The plebiscite is hardly ever mentioned in history books, so 'peacefully' did it take place and so 'foregone' was the conclusion. This is not how it felt at the time, nor should it be so regarded by historians. It was one more important step up in the military resurgence of Nazi Germany and one more step down in the development of any serious German opposition to Hitler. Those Germans who fought in the Saar against Hitler were quickly forgotten. At the time they were regarded as 'traitors' by their own countrymen and as 'troublemakers' by those who eventually had to destroy Hitler themselves by the most terrible and disastrous war in history.

At that stage it was thought sufficient deterrent to Hitler to send in a force of 3,300 British, Italian, Swedish and Dutch troops as an international force at the service of the League of Nations Commission. The local police were also strengthened by a British officer, Colonel Hennessy, and a detachment of British military police. Perhaps the greatest deterrent of all against any arbitrary act by the German dictator was the presence, from early in December 1934, of a very large number of foreign correspondents from the world press.

It was early in January that I was offered the job of reporting the plebiscite for *The Observer*. I say 'for' rather than 'by', because *The Observer* itself had nothing whatsoever to do with my appointment. I was as unknown to the management and staff of the paper as they were to me. Although the offer came when I was on Christmas leave in London, *The Observer* made no attempt to contact me and it never occurred to me to contact them. The assignment was in no way a reward for journalistic qualifications. I had never written a word in any newspaper, never reported a single event, and spoke no word of German. It was the reward of virtue.

My mother had brought her children up, by shining example rather than precept, to extend help and kindness whenever it was in our power to do so. That December, there came through Paris Sandy Rendel, the brother of my friend Jane, who has already figured in these pages as someone I had greatly treasured and admired from our schooldays together. I had also known and liked Sandy at Oxford. He was now at a loose end, trying to decide what career he should take up. Attracted by foreign journalism and finding himself in Paris, he had naturally sought me out. Mowrer was then visiting Saarbrücken, so I gave Sandy an introduction, upon which Mowrer acted with his usual effectiveness. He introduced Sandy to David Scott, who was representing both *The Times* and *The Observer* in the Saar. Scott took him on and they worked in close collaboration for both newspapers.

As the day of the plebiscite approached, *The Observer* indicated that they wished to have their own correspondent and were no longer willing to share this joint representation. Sandy, feeling that I had done him a good turn, generously thought of me as fulfilling this exalted role. David Scott, satisfied that the *Chicago Daily News* had supplied him with an able assistant (Sandy later became Diplomatic Correspondent of *The Times*), seems to have had no qualms about recommending my appointment. The knowledge of the historical background which I had gained at Oxford veiled my ignorance of how to collect and report news, and the generous help given me by other journalists veiled the rest.

I found the whole experience exceedingly entertaining as well as sadly enlightening. It was my first experience of the exciting and festive atmosphere which spreads over a town, and especially its main hotel where they drink and congregate, when it suddenly becomes the focus of top-ranking international journalists. The Hotel Excelsior in Saarbrücken was no exception, and the air of expectancy and adventure was in no way diminished by the view generally held by my colleagues that all the waiters were German police spies and (in the words of Alexander Werth) that the head porter, 'for all his suave and obliging manner, had the air of a hired assassin.'

There was much banter and mutual suspicion between the correspondents. I remember the uproarious laughter at a press conference when a German journalist asked why the *Deutsche Front* were not allowed to say *'Heil Hitler'* and give the Nazi salute, 'since they did it without thinking and it came as second nature to all Germans'. When another German correspondent complained that he and his colleagues, to whom the issue was of predominant importance, were being crowded out by this array of foreign reporters, a Dutch journalist retorted that Goebbels' Ministry of Progaganda needed only one press ticket. The commotion that followed was only quietened by a senior French journalist declaiming grandly, *'Quittons la langue elegante de Goethe pour celle de Racine.'*

There was certainly no love lost between the Germans and the French, and the latter were keeping a low profile. Except for one French bookshop and one French restaurant, gratefully frequented by the French journalists and the gourmets among the foreign press, the French were little to be seen.

Mowrer and his wife arrived direct from the Alps, resplendent in skiing clothes and with glowing bronzed faces. The nice young *Chicago Daily News* correspondent in Berlin, Wally Deuel, was already there.

But I was now a presswoman in my own right and with my own credentials; these inevitably took me among the British journalists. All the well-known names which I had heard but could put no faces to were there, and for the first time I met the leading British commentators on international affairs. Vernon Bartlett was there for the *News Chronicle,* Kingsley Martin for the *New Statesman,* Elizabeth Wiskemann, then a freelance but to become one of the leading authorities on German foreign relations, and above all, as far as I was concerned, the two distinguished correspondents of the *Manchester Guardian,* Alexander Werth from Paris and Frederick Voigt from London.

Voigt had known and liked Goronwy during his spell on the *Manchester Guardian* in 1933 and it was probably for this reason that he now took me under his wing. I could not have had a better guide, not only to the Saar but to the larger questions of peace and war which troubled me. He, like Mowrer, was one of the real aces of pre-war journalism. Like Mowrer he had been a Berlin correspondent, understood and hated National Socialism in all its works, and was determined to see that others understood it too and took steps to bring about its downfall.

Patiently he talked to me and took me with him round the mining villages. He seemed to have contacts all over the Saar and to be known and trusted by simple people and by anti-Nazis who would have been afraid to talk to anyone else. We heard at first hand about the sinister pressure and frightening intimidation which was being brought to bear on the local population. Every street, village and factory had its local '*blockwarte*' spying on its inhabitants and whispering about the fate they could expect if they voted against the fatherland, or gave any assistance to the *Einheitsfront.*

Nevertheless the anti-Nazis were waging a desperate battle. Voigt knew their leaders and took me to their headquarters. The leader of the Social Democrats, Max Braun, was a man of great personal courage and integrity. Fritz Pfordt, the communist leader, was much younger and less experienced. He had been chosen as a local figurehead, but was surrounded by old party members from the Reich, several of whom I came to know later on. The least distinctive figure was the Catholic, Hoffman, who had seen his party fade away. The Saar was largely Catholic and the anti-Nazis had set great store by this; but Hitler and the Pope, who had been on bad terms at the beginning of the Nazi régime, were both astute enough to see that each had much to gain from an accommodation before the plebiscite took place. They had therefore signed a Concordat late in 1933 and the local Bishop of Trier advised all Saar Catholics to vote for the *Deutsche Front*. This was called 'realism': Mowrer reported it as 'another example of the Vatican's unwavering support of the Nazi régime'.

It was not only avowed supporters of the Nazis who wanted to get the plebiscite over and done with as quickly as possible. It was also the earnest wish of Laval and the French Government, and it was certainly the aim of the British Government and of the British officers it had sent with the international force. The other nationals in that force, and the Swede who had been sent to take charge of the plebiscite as a 'neutral' – over the head of the resident head of the Commission, Geoffrey Knox – felt the same way.

Knox had watched the Nazis at work on both sides of the Saar border and did not like what he had seen. He knew the heavy price which opponents of National Socialism had paid in the Reich and would pay, indeed were paying, in the Saar. He would have liked the international force of soldiers and policemen to have protected these people, but was unable to use them for this purpose. They were kept firmly out of sight.

The non-deployment of the peace-keeping force was a bone of contention between many of the English and American journalists and the British military command. They were also critical of Colonel Hennessy, the British head of the international police, whom they accused of being a fascist.

This sort of talk considerably annoyed the British authorities. For English journalists to hold such views was considered 'disloyal', 'un-patriotic' and 'thoroughly objectionable'. It was in His Majesty's officials abroad that one met the nearest approach to the attitudes of the *Deutsche Front*. Just as it was 'disloyal' of British journalists to criticize British decisions, it was 'disloyal' of the anti-Nazis to have insisted on holding a plebiscite. The whole thing should have been got over without a vote.

The Saar was a powder keg, one British officer assured me, and war between Germany and France had broken out in just this area before. 'For God's sake,' he declared, 'why do you and your like stir it all up now?' A similar attitude was held by the military at home. I had asked General Burnett Stuart, who had been a close friend and brother officer of my father, for an introduction to the British officer

80

in command in the Saar. He replied : 'I hardly think it would be fair to add to the responsibilities of the Chief Command in the Saar by planting on them a young lady who wants to practise being the correspondent of a foreign rag. However, I see they have shut the place up so I don't suppose you could get in. If I was there I should have our name on the gate all right.'

It was not our name we were putting on the gate but the white flag of appeasement, and each German 'grievance' we appeased contributed directly to the growing military potential of Hitler. His opponents were our allies, had we ever known how to use them. Adam was to give his life for this; but he, like the British Government, saw it all too late.

There was never any doubt that the small, brave band of anti-Nazis would be defeated. All they hoped to achieve was a slap in Hitler's face, just a small indication, by a large enough adverse vote, than when Germans were free they were not Nazis. The United Front did not reckon with the mass hysteria of nationalism, the deeply troubled loyalty of Germans who cared more for the strength of their country than its good name. On all the advertisement pillars in Saarbrücken, the ghosts of German soldiers looked down on passers-by, announcing, 'We died for you. You should not forget.' (Nobody saw the spectre of Hitler summoning them to die themselves. Military conscription was reintroduced in the Reich immediately after the reintegration of the Saar.)

The day of the plebiscite dawned bright and sparkling over the Saar territory. Snow had fallen in the night and the whole scene looked like a German Christmas card, innocent, friendly, happy. For two days previously the great square in front of Saarbrücken's railway station had been cordoned off to allow the peaceful arrival of German voters not only from the Reich but even – in one or two cases – from the United States and South America. In all 45,000 of these voters were brought in. The snow was no impediment to the well-organized car services of the *Deutsche Front*, even post vans had been commandeered from a state service who knew who its masters were going to be. Outside the polling stations stood not the cheerful, neutral faces of the British tommies 'keeping the peace', but the stern faces of the local Nazis. The voters went to the polling booths like family parties going to church.

In the evening, the peace-keeping force at last found a role : they removed the sealed boxes to the Wartburg. We were allowed to watch the counting from the galleries. As each vote was laid out, one pile grew and grew and gradually multiplied itself down the whole length of the table.

The counting went on all night. I could not bear the atmosphere among my colleagues – the 'story' was now 'dead', I heard one say, and the crisis over. I wanted, when the result was announced, to be among the people who really cared, and so I left the Wartburg for the United Front headquarters.

News had obviously reached them already and there was a forlorn silence in the room which had so lately been full of talk and activity. The final announcement was due at 8 am and we all gathered in a central hall. The loudspeaker was playing German music grossly out of tune with the mournful and defeated faces around me. At last the announcement came. It was worse than anyone had anticipated :

For Germany	477,119	90.35%
For *status quo*	46,613	8.83%
For France	2,124	0.4%

Suddenly I felt a total stranger among these people, an impertinent intruder in their defeat. I left the hall and walked down to the banks of the Saar. The river was a cold grey mass flowing between frozen banks under a cold grey sky. It was early and totally deserted and I wept shamelessly.

All of a sudden I was aware of someone standing above me. I looked up and there was the most ragged wreck of a man I had ever seen. Though by no means old, he had a crutch under one arm and was totally unkempt and unshaven. But it was the coincidence of grief which was more important at that moment than anything else. He helped me from the ground and together we hobbled to a café which was just opening. The smell of hot milk in a thick glass still brings back to me that poignant scene when I accepted food and comfort from a beggar. It was a moment of overwhelming truth when suddenly the visible, material world, the immense discrepancy in our real fates, seemed of less importance than our shared sorrow and the shared glass of milk.

That day, the face of the Saar changed. A great plague of spiders – the dreadful Nazi swastikas – descended everywhere. Whole streets were filled with them. The green garlands which had hung so decoratively amid the snow were suddenly replaced by these tawdry flags.

It was appropriate that the snow soon turned to slush.

The interest of the international press melted as quickly as the snow. Most of the United Front leaders had no choice but to disappear across the frontiers. Max Braun, the brave socialist leader, gave a news conference declaring *'Wir kampfen weiter'* ('We fight on'). But how could they? What was left was the small fry, all the brave, humble and unimportant party workers who had tried to make their countrymen, while still free, stand up to Hitler. They were marked men.

For a period of nine weeks they were to be spared the full force of the Nazi victory. Theoretically, the international régime continued in being while it was slowly dismantled, and the old laws were still in operation. But the Saar was no longer news, and no foreign newspaper thought it worth its while to keep a correspondent in Saarbrücken. For one Sunday more *The Observer* let me fill a column with appeals on behalf of the Saar's anti-Nazi minority :

'Their position is pitiful,' I wrote. 'They have no work, no country and no money. They have no confidence in a police which is already the agent of a country for whom they are traitors. They have no faith in justice based on National Socialist law as defined by General Goering two months ago. They have no meeting places. Their leaders are exiled or driven into hiding and they themselves are isolated through the country. Already panic has begun to spread.'

While my high-powered colleagues had to earn their living and show their faces in important places, I realized that my own absurd position, above all my small private income, gave me a leeway not permitted to the established and powerful.

I at last made myself known to *The Observer* on a flying visit to London. (Actually it was a third-class train journey; *The Observer* did not offer to pay my fare and it never occurred to me to ask for it. Despite the fact that my copy had been the lead story on two successive Sundays, I had no idea how to approach the newspaper whose correspondent I had been on this dramatic occasion.) My experience with the Editor of *The Times* did not encourage me to seek out the Editor of *The Observer*. My new friend Voigt suggested I approach his friend Hugh Massingham, the Foreign Editor. Massingham greeted me without apparent surprise or disapproval, but equally without encouragement. He was clearly relieved that all I wanted was to return to the Saar at my own expense and on a freelance basis. Voigt helped me to fix the same terms with the *Manchester Guardian*.

It was hardly the continuation of a promising career, but it was what I wanted.

Back in Saarbrücken I used my position quite shamelessly to ease the escape of anti-Nazis. In all, it is reckoned, five thousand Saarlanders fled to France, where most of them lived in abject poverty. The French were glad that there were not more and, when the Spanish Civil War broke out, that many of them joined the International Brigade. Most of those who came forward for my help were German communists; many of them, I now suspect (I was very hazy about such things in those days), were Comintern agents.

That they were communists in no way disturbed me. Although Mowrer had told me frequently that there was little to choose between communists and Nazis, I did not believe him. Did I not know the generous ideas of Russian communism? Had I not been inspired by the ideals of Liberty, Equality and Fraternity ever since I had first heard them pronounced? Was the slogan 'To each according to his needs, from each according to his capacities', not the very essence of my rather Victorian, slightly Calvinistic upbringing? 'Should I not join the Communist Party?' I naïvely asked my new friends. 'Oh no,' they declared. 'You are far more useful to us as a liberal journalist.' Even this did not make me pause and think, but I am thankful now that it was as a liberal journalist that I went on.

Nor am I ashamed, on humanitarian grounds, that I then held my liberal umbrella over them. As an English journalist I was able to cross easily into France. I did so whenever asked to by the friends I had made in the United Front. I carried their typewriters and their documents over the frontier. I guaranteed them a certain immunity in that interim period by being seen in public with them. One particularly villanous-looking agent of the Comintern actually took up his abode in my house, declaring that it was the only safe place for him to be. I never thought of the consequences for my poor landlady. I had never met communist agents before and I accepted them completely at face value. They were known only by Christian names like 'Hans', 'Walter' or 'Ernst'. I went to the cinema with them and drank with them in wine cellars. The only one who spoke English had almond-shaped eyes and very black hair, and told me proudly he had been deported from England. This did not worry me. 'Do you think the Nazis now have me on their books?' I asked. 'Why not?' they answered, 'you are certainly on the Comintern's.' I clutched my British passport a little more firmly and continued on this dangerous path.

There was only one moment when a tinge of apprehension coloured my view and that soon passed. The day when Hitler was to take over in the Saar drew near. For weeks the police had undertaken arms searches all over the Saar territory. On the morning of Hitler's arrival, a young boy of my acquaintance came to me with a loaded pistol. I slipped it into my stocking drawer and went out to see Hitler, at last, in person. I stood quite near him as he addressed the crowd and was struck by his soft, pink-and-white complexion. It may have been a trick of the light for I have never heard anyone else make this comment, but to me his skin seemed to be almost that of a woman. It somehow added to the abhorrence. Goebbels, who stood near him, was, on the other hand, less sinister in real life than in his photographs. Intelligence often redeems the ugliest face. I still had a naïve belief that truth and goodness were closely associated and somehow the object and quest of intelligence. I don't think Goebbels shared my views.

As I stood there, so close and so unobserved and unimportant, I wondered why some cameraman, pointing his instrument at the Führer, had not long ago substituted a revolver and rid us of this monster. After staring closely at the leaders, I moved off to a sort of flagpost from which a loudspeaker was relaying their speeches. I had learnt some German in the previous weeks while I had been on my own in the Saar and proceeded to take notes of what was said. Then suddenly I realized that all the people around me had moved away and that I was surrounded by uniformed storm troopers. They asked me what I was up to. I said I was taking down the speech. On what authority? On what authority, I asked them in return, did they presume to ask me questions? (Possession of a British passport still made one feel perfectly safe.) Let them call the police if they were worried. At that point a policeman conveniently arrived and I handed him my press card. As he gave it back to me, after showing it to the storm troopers, I saw my address in large letters and remembered the pistol in my drawer.

At the risk of missing the speeches for *The Observer* and being thought cowed by those who had witnessed the scene, I waited for the storm troopers to clear off and then dashed for home. I quickly put the pistol in my pocket and took it down to the river.

As I threw the pistol into the coal-black water, I remembered Mowrer's amusing story of how the Albanian police had once urged him not only to carry, but in case of emergency, to use a pistol. 'In this country no matter whom you kill,' they told him, 'you are sure to have done someone a favour.' There was no one left in the Saar to whom I wanted to do much of a favour, so shortly after, I too left the territory. The Germans had voted overwhelmingly for Hitler; it was, I felt, time to see to our own protection.

9

Seeing to their own protection was, of course, what all the Great
Powers seemed to be doing in the early months of 1935. If for me the
episode of the Saar did not end until Hitler actually took possession
on 1 March, for the Great Powers (and this was how we still thought
of Britain, France, Italy and Germany) it was over and done with in
January.

They had turned instead to intense diplomatic activity; a con-
certed effort was being made to sort out the conditions of peace in
Europe. Clearly, if I was to understand what was going on and what
was being discussed, I must get back to a listening post in one of the
European capitals.

Adam was always suggesting Berlin, to which he had now moved
and where he had persuaded Diana to join him. Voigt, when I met
him again in London, suggested Rome where, he said, there were no
good English correspondents. I hardly felt qualified to attempt such
an assignment. Alternatively he, and Massingham of *The Observer*,
proposed Warsaw or Prague, where there were not even bad correspondents. I consulted Mowrer. 'Exploitation of kids,' he muttered
angrily, adding in his usual teasing way, 'Now if Voigt is suggesting
going with you. . . .' Voigt was equally scathing about Mowrer's offer
to continue teaching me my job in Paris. That, he said, was not the
way to become a foreign correspondent. Now I had started on my
own, why didn't I continue, and report the news myself? I dared not
confess that I disliked news as such : the coming and going of statesmen, the meetings, the talk, the intrigue, the speculation left me both
bored and confused. I wanted guidance to understand these meetings, not the opportunity to report them. I wanted to know why
France was so afraid, Germany so dissatisfied, how peace could be
kept and justice done.

So I abandoned *The Observer*, and they abandoned me, as casually as we had taken each other up, and returned to my desk at the *Chicago Daily News*.

It was the end of March 1935 and Mowrer was angrier than ever with the feebleness of the Western Powers in the face of German military resurgence. Governments had long been aware of the secret German rearmament and its intensification as soon as Hitler came to power. Now Hitler felt strong enough to bring it out into the open. On 9 March Goering declared that a German Air Force was already in being and fully up to strength, and six days later the German Government announced its intention of reintroducing military service. Both had been forbidden under the Treaty of Versailles, and Mowrer asked me sarcastically if I still thought these clauses were more unkind to the Germans than their revocation was now going to be for Germany's neighbours.

Mowrer spoke contemptuously of Laval, the French Foreign Minister, who, he said, saw himself as the one man in France who could prevent a war between Germany and France (which, indeed, he eventually helped to do in 1940, leaving England to fight on alone). Laval had talked of disposing of the Saar because 'it was a red rag to the Hitler bull'. Perhaps now, said Mowrer, he realized what the Hitler bull, encouraged by victory, was like. Laval's predecessor in office, Barthou, had taken the more realistic approach (according to Mowrer) of preventing Hitler from even thinking he could engage successfully in war, by showing that Germany would once again have to fight on two fronts if she attacked either in the East or in the West. Now Laval half-heartedly picked up Barthou's negotiations with Eastern Europe. That summer, France signed separate agreements with Russia and Czechoslovakia, by which both would come to her assistance were she attacked, and she would come to theirs. The Soviet Government stipulated that Russian assistance to Czechoslovakia would be dependent on France first honouring her own agreement.

Poland opted out altogether from this defence system, having signed a bilateral non-aggression pact with Hitler in 1934. Mowrer pointed out that Poland was not a democracy like France and Czechoslovakia. Her Foreign Minister, Colonel Jozef Beck, admired and envied rather than feared and disliked the sort of régime which now existed in Germany. He would no doubt see in good time what Hitler had in store for Poland, just as England would.

Mowrer, like the French, was highly suspicious when the British Foreign Secretary, Sir John Simon, accompanied by Anthony Eden, visited Hitler in Berlin at the end of March. His suspicions were confirmed and the fire of his anger stoked, when two months later the British signed a bilateral treaty with Germany agreeing to German naval rearmament up to 35 per cent of British naval strength. This made a farce of the joint declaration condemning German treaty violation which Britain, together with France and Italy, had made at Stresa, and inevitably sowed deep suspicions in French and Italian minds as to where Britain really stood.

It was not possible, because of the censorship, to discuss these matters openly with Adam, and yet I longed to do so. Was German policy really so malevolent? Was British policy really so short-sighted? Was the future really so dark?

'I quarrel on your national behalf,' I wrote to Adam, 'and only half believe my own side. I wish terribly to speak to you, being shaken in all my beliefs. . . . I start fresh and happy every morning and end every day jumpy and on edge.'

I do not know what Adam answered, for though I kept most letters in those days, not only from Adam but from all my friends, there is a short gap on his side in this period. Sheltered as all Germans were by the tight Nazi censorship of the press, I expect he thought me alarmist and absurd and was himself glad of any Anglo-German rapprochement, whoever signed it. It was probably now that he began to think of me as the victim of the 'foreign press' whose 'lies' were constantly denounced in every German newspaper.

He came increasingly to hate my profession as a journalist, seeing in journalism, rather than in the rapidly deteriorating international situation which it reported, the origin of my anger. In so doing he misjudged the growing climate of opinion among many of his contemporaries in England, a failure that was to bring increasing uneasiness into some of his relationships there.

I was by no means alone in my anxieties: similar fears come up again and again in Goronwy's letters.

'Whenever I begin to think seriously now,' he wrote to me, 'the thought of war breaks in and makes everything futile. The sickness, a physical sickness of being dirty and disgusting and imbecile which the thought of war arouses, makes one certain that somehow you and I and others must do things that are better and new and something which is not just giving in to old and stupid passions. . . .

89

'The world is decaying not even slowly now but fast : war will be the last sudden disruption. I think of Germany, of Italy, of our own country, it amazes me that we can walk with our heads upright, not ashamed when such things are happening in Europe. For we are responsible. Surely these politicians, our own as well, are remarkable only for their imbecility. It seems to me by now that a Europe ruled by such people is condemned to destruction. Nietzsche says that justice is a terrible thing and a war seems to me very like a terrible but just punishment for Europe.'

It was precisely to try to find out how to avoid this punishment that I had set out on this road, but where was I getting to?

When I returned to Paris, Mowrer had given me an assignment to look into the Fascist Leagues which had successfully brought down the Daladier Government in the Paris riots of February 1934. I went to their meetings, read their propaganda and their newspapers, interviewed their functionaries and their supporters, all with growing distaste. They reminded me of the uniformed bands which Goronwy and I had seen in the streets of Berlin before Hitler came to power. Their ideals, narrow and nationalistic, offered nothing for humanity. At least communism was a universal creed, an ideal for mankind : the Soviet Union was not yet identified with imperialist goals but preached of world peace and the need to support the League of Nations. Fascism, whether French, German or Italian, spoke only of its own nation, presaging international anarchy and war.

Even Mowrer, who hated all totalitarian régimes, was becoming less critical of my soft approach to communism. He even went so far as to find me a room in the house of his old friends the Vildracs, who were both ardent supporters of the French Communist Party. Charles Vildrac was one of the leading French poets and playwrights of those days and his wife kept a picture gallery. The panelled walls of my large room in their beautiful flat on the rue de Grenelle were hung with exquisite Impressionist pictures. But thanks to my shyness in speaking French and my difficulty in paying for the large and expensive meal the Vildracs cooked for themselves in the evening, I did not meet their impressive artist friends and escaped all indoctrination at their hands. Looking back, I much regret missing this opportunity to enter, if only modestly and timidly, a genuine and admirable part of French life.

I did, however, make one brief incursion into it. That summer, the first-ever Writers' Congress for the Defence of Culture was held in Paris under the aegis of great names like Gide and Malraux. I was brought in by my German communist friends to help with letters to and translations for the English delegation, which was headed by E. M. Forster and comprised, unlike the French, German and Russian delegations, very uncommunist writers like J. B. Priestley and Aldous Huxley. Forster made a characteristic speech, gentle, timid and moderate, full of *mea culpa* not only about the limitations of British freedom but also of his own attitudes : 'I am not a communist,' he said, 'though perhaps I might be one if I was a younger and a braver man, for in communism I see hope. It does many things which I think evil but I know that it intends good. . . . Fascism does evil that evil may come.' Gide was more positive and his reception by the Congress considerably warmer. He still thought of Russian communism as 'an unprecedented experiment . . . which fills our hearts with hope . . . an impetus capable of carrying forward in its stride the whole human race.' He looked forward to the day when, under communism, 'great literature could be made, not as till now out of men's sufferings but out of their joy.'

It was noble and inspiring and I was proud when one of the German writers procured a copy of *La Condition Humaine* for me in which was written '*Avec la sympathie intellectuelle d'André Malraux.*' Unfortunately he had neglected to add my name, so the volume was smartly lifted from me by one of my literary-minded English friends.

My chief contact, since it was they who had brought me in, was with the German writers and the German members of the organizing committee, one or two of whom were those same German communists whom I had befriended in the Saar – my friend Hans for instance, who, haunting the office of the *Chicago Daily News*, had earned the name of 'Old Pop Eye' from Mowrer. The writers whom I remember best were Gustav Regler, Ernst Toller and Johannes R. Becher. With the last I made special friends, and he told me his extraordinary life story – from Reichswehr officer to proletarian poet. Surely, with such people, Germany would throw over the Nazi régime before it could once again unleash war in Europe? But Becher said he had been condemned to death in Germany and it was clear that he, like all the other German emigrés in Paris, was living in great misery and despair. I still have the pencilled note he sent me :

Ich habe allerdings vermieden, in letzter Zeit mit Dir zusammen

zu kommen, da ich Dich nicht in all dies Elend einbeziehen wollte.
Ich denke viel und mit grosser Freude an Dich. . . .

Du warst gut zu mir, sehr gut. Du hast mir viel geholfen. . . .
Vergiss mich nicht ganz.

There was sorrow as well as hope surrounding the Congress. René
Crevel, a young writer on the French organizing committee, actually
committed suicide. I remember Becher saying, 'It is not he who is
mad, but we who live on who are mad.' Nevertheless, I'm afraid I
enjoyed the Congress very much. I was not sure who attracted me
most : all the grand writers or the handsome young men in their shirt-
sleeves who organized everything.

I made a good friend among the latter, a young Swiss medical
student who was a member of the French *Jeunesse Communiste.* I
was to meet him again later that summer when he was working
underground in Berlin.   He told me he had been asked to give up
his medical studies and become a full-time agent of the Comintern.
I strongly advised him against it, not out of anti-communism but
because, naïvely, I thought that a doctor could do more for the cause
than an agent. With his blood transfusion unit in Spain during the
civil war, perhaps he did. Perhaps also this sort of advice, tendered
with sympathy and conviction, saved me from receiving similar proposals myself. 'Moles', as we were to learn after the war, had to be
quite tough and sophisticated. I do not know, since he did not keep
my letters, what I told Goronwy of all this, but what he wrote to me
about this time is interesting in view of the strong stand he was to take
later about both Guy Burgess and Anthony Blunt :

'Nothing is really valuable but integrity : but it is very elusive and
once you have lost sight of it, I think you will never see it again. I
think that is what happens. One is born with integrity and keeps it
when young, but then compromises for some advantage or other,
promising oneself to be honest again when one can afford it. As if
integrity wasn't exactly something which one can only keep by dis-
regarding the cost.'

In another letter written during that period, Goronwy said : 'It is
vitality and desire which make it impossible to be a communist.'

Goronwy had visited me in Paris that spring. Strictly speaking, this
was breaking our compact to live this year on our own, but Goronwy
had finished his novel *A Bridge to Divide Them*, had parted company with *The Times*, for which he had been working since the

autumn, and had applied for a job with the BBC. While waiting for their decision and Faber's reaction to his novel, he came to Paris. It was Easter and I was able to leave my desk for a few days and go with him to the country, where we were always happiest.

After the harsh loneliness of much of my life as a journalist, it was a great comfort to be with Goronwy again. We took a train to Mont-fort l'Amaury, a place I have never been to since and could not find now. It had a dreamlike quality, like the scene in Barrie's *Dear Brutus* where the characters walk out into a wood meaning to relive their lives differently. Such a wood lay below the windows of our hotel and the nightingales sang all night. We sat on our balcony, listening to the birds in silence, and each time I awoke in the night they were still singing.

When we returned to Paris I was unprepared, after the wet autumn, for the city's radiant beauty in the spring. Although I had to go back to my work, we met every lunch-hour and walked along the Seine, watching the swallows flying under the bridges and the fishermen sitting idly beside their rods.

Mowrer was delighted with Goronwy. He feasted us both in all his favourite restaurants and laughed and talked. He had never quite worked me out or understood what I was doing all alone in Paris, leading so frugal and dedicated an existence. He was now quite sure that what I needed was what he called 'a poky life' and to marry 'Ap Gwilym'. This was what Edgar called Goronwy, presumably after Dafydd, his fourteenth-century forebear who wrote such beautiful love and nature poems and was also a great womanizer. This last Mowrer tactfully did not divulge, for I wanted not to believe it of Goronwy, particularly if marriage was contemplated.

But from this I still shied away, for I was still seriously concerned with the task I had set myself and abhorred the thought of turning aside to something so demanding and final as marriage. I had been a bridesmaid at several family weddings and heard the promises made at them. 'Forsaking thou all others, cleave thou only unto him,' stuck in my throat; not because I was promiscuous – on the contrary, in those days sexual taboos were very strong – but because friendship meant so much to me. 'For better, for worse . . .' seemed to me the definition of loyalty in *all* human relationships. Yet it was more com-plicated than that. Rather inadvisably, I thought aloud in a letter to Adam :

'Do you remember that last summer I said I thought loyalty was the capacity to reconcile, inside oneself only perhaps, all the important things of one's life, and if one loved someone, one could be loyal to them only if that love made such reconciliation possible. You never said what you thought of that. I still want to believe it and yet there are such conflicts one doubts whether they can ever be reconciled and one can only have one thing by sacrificing another.'

Marriage with Goronwy was not really a feasible possibility at that time. The job at the BBC had fallen through. His connection both with *The Times* and with All Souls had come to an end. Tentative approaches from the *Evening Standard* filled him with disgust: 'I could not pimp leader writers for Beaverbrook at any cost.'

'I often think you must get tired of my shiftlessness,' he wrote after leaving Paris for Spain, '[my] poverty, inability to give you what you should have – house, animals, certainty, safety: I'm very sorry, I want terribly to give you them, you make me so happy: but I must try to write and it isn't easy to do that and give you things. . . . But everything depends on that damned book. . . . My novel is in every way better than my last, but I bet they are very disappointed and dissatisfied.'

'I will learn to write from the very beginning,' he wrote from Madrid. 'I will use no adjectives till I've learnt to use nouns and verbs properly. I will not try to write about anything ambitious. I try to describe very complicated things when I can't even describe a man walking down the street. I have made a plan of all I have to do. I will be very good one day.'

'You see I am frightfully excited: I can't think why. I think really it is your saying you love me. It is like finding out one is very good after believing, on the best evidence, you are very bad. . . .'

On returning from Spain, he decided to spend the rest of that summer with his sister in Wales and work on a series of lectures on the Renaissance for the Workers' Educational Association. For my part, I felt that my job in Paris had come to an end. I had completed my report on the Fascist Leagues for Mowrer and there was no question of my being taken on to the staff of the *Chicago Daily News*. I wanted to go to Russia, but an enquiry to *The Observer* elicited a fatherly letter of refusal from Hugh Massingham, ending, 'I really must say how profoundly I disapprove of this desire to go into journalism. It is no life for a nice person.' Goronwy was suggesting I leave journalism to work for the Labour Party, who needed people interested in foreign policy, but as a last fling I decided to take a holiday job in the office of the *Daily Telegraph* in Berlin. It was purely secretarial, a job I was even less qualified for than journalism, but I was glad to see an English newspaper office in a foreign capital and had long wanted to visit Berlin again.

The two correspondents at that time were Eustace Wareing and Hugh Carleton Greene, later to be a wartime colleague of mine in the BBC's European Service and eventually its Director-General. Greene was patient, correct and distant; he was pleasant to work for since he immediately grasped what I could do and what I could not. Wareing, on the other hand, was emotional and explosive; he was bewildered by the many mistakes I made both in German and on the typewriter as well as with the many buttons I was expected to press on the telephone. I was also unpunctual, which was anathema to him. After a few days, his anger turned to sarcasm, which made me laugh, and this seems to have endeared me to him. When, with relief all round, I completed my term, he gave me a lecture, embarrassing to us both, about taking my work seriously. Life, he said, came too easily for me.

It had not been a very serious episode and I had been enjoying myself too much in Berlin to be an altogether dedicated secretary. Adam was no longer there, but through Gerry Young and Ingrid Warburg, both contacts from Oxford, I met many people who, unlike the Parisians, seemed easy to please. It was all, however, on a very shallow basis. Though I visited a Nazi labour camp, wandered with my Swiss communist friend round the working-class district of Wedding, and stayed a weekend with a socialist worker's family in their tent at Wannsee (they were friends of Voigt's), I did not feel I had penetrated the brittle and ingratiating surface of Nazi Germany.

International concern in September 1935 was concentrated on Italy rather than Germany, and the uninformed minor officials and journalists I met treated European anxieties with slightly smug self-satisfaction that they, at least, were no longer the bad boys involved in betraying the League of Nations. I found their attitude disingenuous, especially as in this same month, September 1935, Hitler took his first lethal steps against the Jews. The Nuremberg Laws deprived German Jews of their citizenship and forbade intermarriage between Germans and Jews.

When Goronwy sent me a poem whose last verse began with the lines

Come back from that country
Whose heroes are hangmen :

I was already preparing to leave. I decided to return home via Hamburg, where Adam was now working. It was a year since I had stayed with him in Kassel and Imshausen, a year in which, in my life at any rate, much had happened. We had corresponded intermittently and he had more than once suggested that I should visit him again. This was obviously the moment to do so.

Adam had been invited to stay for the weekend at Count Albrecht von Bernstorff's great domain at Stintenburg, and decided to take me with him. We drove there in his little car. Stintenburg seemed a place apart, huge and ancient and still untouched by the Nazis. Bernstorff was a pre-1914 Rhodes Scholar who had befriended Adam. He had resigned from the German Embassy in London out of hatred for Hitler. Apart from myself, the gathering was entirely male, but I was getting used, in journalistic circles, to finding myself the only woman. My fellow-guests were both Englishmen, the historian John Wheeler-Bennett and Basil Newton, Counsellor at the British Embassy in Berlin. I was to meet him again in Prague. I do not know whether it was Bernstorff or Wheeler-Bennett who described Newton as 'bone from the collar-stud upward', but both were equally eager to find out from him what was afoot in Anglo-German circles. He divulged little, however, and after-dinner conversation was boringly confined till late into the night to the ancient pedigrees, as witnessed by their tombstones, of the Trotts and the Bernstorffs.

On the Sunday we boarded a boat and steamed for hours on a lake entirely contained within the boundaries of the estate. Bernstorff, who insisted that he was a socialist, certainly hated Hitler with all his might. He had no reason to conceal this from Wheeler-Bennett; Basil Newton, however, dampened all our spirits, and I was not sorry when the party came to an end.

For the next weekend, Adam took me to Travemünde on the Baltic coast. There an extraordinary incident occurred.

In the evening, after walking together along the sand, we returned to the little sitting-room in the house where we were staying, Adam asked me what my plans were, and when I answered, 'To marry Goronwy,' he flung himself down beside me and said, 'Marry me !'

I was completely flabbergasted. Admittedly, some of our letters

1 High Elms in 1930

2 The author in 1938

3 *Left to right*: Christopher Cox, the author, Diana Hubback and Adam von Trott. Cornwall, 1932.

4 The author, Douglas Jay and Peggy Garnett in 1931

had been written in highly exalted tones. I had expressed the warmest possible friendship for him, but in so far as I had written about love, it was primarily of his problems I was thinking : my own I did not confide in any detail though occasionally they intruded, as in the letter I have quoted above. I assumed he understood about Goronwy, since he had written only a few weeks before : 'I know that anything I have ever asked which might possibly impair Goronwy has turned you against me right away.'

Why was I not turned against him now by this preposterous proposal? My reaction should have been one of righteous indignation at the suggestion that I, and still more he, should betray the two people, Goronwy and Diana, who cared for us most and had also been friends to both of us over many years. But instead of anger I felt concern. I remembered my mother telling me that no man ever proposed without expecting to be accepted; if one had so led a man on, she insisted, one had behaved most cruelly. I did not think I had done that, but my whole concern was somehow to restore the situation as if the question had never been put. Neither Goronwy nor Diana must ever know of it and the question must never be raised between us again. At the same time, I did all I could to preserve Adam's pride from hurt or humiliation and our friendship from damage.

As soon as I was able to, I left for Paris. On the long train journey, across many frontiers, I tried to read *The Trial of Socrates* to give myself courage. But from Cologne onwards, left to myself by the seven other people in the third-class compartment and little troubled by passport control, I mostly slept.

It was early when I arrived. Paris is charming at seven o'clock in the morning, the bars already open and the streets still and empty. I climbed to Sacré Coeur and looked down on the awakening city. It was Sunday, one of the last Sundays of summer, and I stayed all day alone on the hill. It was like being in a country village : no pavements, just the cobbled, tree-lined square where the cafés put out their tables, old people slept and the children played. I found a room, high up, looking out onto a steep corner bounded by a house with blue shutters.

The next day I wrote to Adam :

'Partir c'est mourir un peu – never before has it been so true. Not only are we parted and a little bit dead but the world in which we were is split and divided. That is the difference between love and friendship.

'Friendship is something which two independent lives can share and create from two different worlds. Love is making one life of two lives, one world of two worlds. Perhaps in talking with you I have minimised the difference between love and friendship, fearing the gravity of my answer. If I have seemed insensitive to that gravity, ungrateful for the honour you gave me, unaware of the consequences of my answer, it is only from the impossibility of expressing all I have thought and, if you can understand, from the respect in which I hold your feelings.

'I know that in offering you friendship for love, I am offering something which you have not asked for, and refusing something which should be an honour to give – but let me give you what I have to give, which is deep affection for you, a real desire to share in your work and always to be a warm and steadfast element in your life.

'I have meant all I have said. Friendship goes very far – all the way [–] while loyalty to oneself and the life one has chosen, remains.'

My feelings were in great turmoil, though basically nothing had changed. 'You have been constant and beautiful and considerate in your attitude to me,' Adam wrote to me later. 'I could not help admiring you for it even though it was but a reflection of the new life you have set your heart on. It was very moving to see how brave and simple you are and yet capable of the further sincere desire for a friendship as you want it with me. That if nothing else would call for my truest efforts.'

I valued Adam's friendship perhaps even more highly for the confidence he had shown in me, but it was Goronwy I loved. Nevertheless, all my doubts and fears about marriage were stirred up once again. I wanted to marry nobody. It was a cage I did not want to enter.

I wrote to Goronwy but do not now know what I said, certainly nothing of what had happened. But he had great tenderness and intuition. He wrote back :

'Nothing of mine has come between us. How could it? I am too much in love with you and you are so beautiful and so lovely. I wish I were with you in Montmartre. I want you home terribly : but stay in Paris till you are not tired and see your friends : but I want you here all the time.'

Next day I descended to my old base in the Place de l'Opera. I saw Mowrer and felt again all my amused admiration. The office was transformed with maps and papers, no longer the brandy-drinking, joke-bandying place of my time. Mowrer was excited, pleased with the English for their toughness with Mussolini, angry with the French, which was unwonted. All the newspaper kiosks carried screaming headlines about the Abyssinian war. 'I'm glad the Abyssinians are savages,' Mowrer said. 'It makes it crystal clear that what all this is about is the League of Nations and its preservation.'

In his letter Goronwy had also written :

'It is terrible to see newspaper bills with War. Italians bomb women and children. 17,000 casualties at Adowa. I hate all these sanctions : I hate that England should perhaps have to fight again : but I think it is necessary. It is terrible that such things should be necessary. . . . But I don't think Europe is done yet and it will recover. Things will become easier one day : it will be lovely if they do and we are together. That is what I hope for. I think these next few years will be hard and perhaps terrible : if it were possible, I would like us to work and learn to know each other and love each other, and then when things change we shall be fit for a better world. It is something of this sort I think about Dürer's *Ritter mit Tod und Teufel*. The Knight is in a dark wood, with death and the devils around him, on each side : but he rides straight on, over skeletons and serpents and he is smiling. I think the world today is like that wood but that people can be like the Ritter if they want to and if they are, will come out of the wood, and so should you and I together. One thing that frightens me is this : that one day the world will change and become lovely and there will be no one fit for it and I should like to be.'

10

It was a good moment to return to England. The causes of war and the conditions of peace were in the forefront of British politics in the second half of 1935. The Italian war against Abyssinia, threatened all summer, had now been declared. British public opinion had been alerted by a campaign organized by the League of Nations Union as a 'Peace Ballot', in which $10\frac{1}{2}$ million householders voted for collective security and the League of Nations Council had voted unanimously for economic sanctions against Italy. The lessons I had learnt from Mowrer were being demonstrated before my eyes. The aggressive nations were fascist Italy and Nazi Germany, and the way to deal with them was by collective action through the League of Nations.

Parliament was dissolved at the end of October and a new election called for 14 November. Here was an immediate chance to work for the Labour Party as Goronwy had suggested. The constituency in which I lived, and now for the first time had a vote, was Chelsea. The sitting candidate was that same Sir Samuel Hoare who had made such an inspiring speech at Geneva. My doubts about opposing him were firmly quelled by friends like Douglas Jay and Jane Rendel, who insisted that one voted for parties not individuals; they also pointed out that the Labour Party Conference in October had pledged support for the League Covenant by 2 million votes to 100,000 and that the TUC had voted for sanctions against Italy even at the price of war.

In the election campaign, these issues were pushed into the background and the Labour Party was once more soundly defeated. It increased its seats in Parliament, but the 'National' Government still had an overwhelming majority. There was no question of a paid job with the Labour Party, but thanks to Eva Hubback, Diana's mother, and no doubt to Douglas Jay, who was one of his younger advisers, I secured an honorary post as secretary to Hugh Dalton, the Labour spokesman on foreign affairs. Diana herself was taken on by Ellen Wilkinson, a left-wing firebrand and one of the few women members in that Parliament.

There is no need to confess again my shortcomings as a secretary and I strongly suspect that Diana was no better qualified than I, but we both greatly enjoyed our free access to the House of Commons, and the insight we gained into the work of its members and into the political and economic problems of the country. Both Hugh Dalton and Ellen Wilkinson represented North Country seats, Barnard Castle and Jarrow respectively, where the depression had hit hardest and poverty was far more grinding than in the South where Diana and I had been brought up. For us, it was a valuable experience; our employers, however, must have been thankful when paid professional secretarial services became available to all Members of Parliament.

Hugh Dalton was a very vigorous and powerful member of the Labour Party; he probably did more than anyone else to steer it away from the pacifism of Lansbury and the appeasement which became so general in the later 'thirties. I learnt a great deal from him about the inner workings of the party and the views of his colleagues. In Parliament itself, I heard the views of the leading spokesmen of the other parties. The greatest shock was to discover that the naïve faith I had formed about the principles of British foreign policy after Hoare's speech at Geneva, was totally unfounded.

Once safely back in Parliament with their large majority, the Tory 'National' Government cynically decided that they no longer needed to pay even lip service to the policy of 'collective security' through the League of Nations. They not only steadfastly refused to introduce oil sanctions against Italy, the only hope of halting her armies, but even proposed, in defiance of League policy, a joint plan with France whereby Mussolini was to be confirmed in possession of all the Abyssinian territory he had conquered and the Abyssinians were to be bought off by territorial concessions in British Somaliland. This was the famous Hoare-Laval Plan which created such an uproar that Hoare was immediately disowned and dropped from the Government. The British and French Governments, whose one hope it was, had virtually destroyed the League of Nations as well as all hope of finding in collective security an effective alternative to an old-fashioned alliance system with which to deter German aggression.

All my dissatisfaction with Mowrer's analysis of the causes of war and his policy for the maintainance of peace returned. This time, however, my doubts were fanned not by German communists but by anti-imperialists of a very different colour. Once again it was willingness to help a friend rather than any deliberate intention on my own part which took me onto a totally different road than the one I was following as Dalton's secretary.

Ellen Wilkinson had asked Diana to give assistance to the India League, which was arranging a visit in January by Jawaharlal Nehru, President of the Indian Congress. Diana agreed, but as Christmas approached and with it the Parliamentary recess, she longed to visit her beloved Cornwall. She asked me whether I would take her place. I was shamefully indifferent to Indian affairs and had little idea who Nehru was, but since I was staying in London, I naturally agreed.

Certainly at this stage I had never met or heard of V. K. Krishna Menon, the founder and secretary of the India League, to whom I was to report. Later he was to be Indian High Commissioner in London and eventually Minister of Defence in Delhi. He was already an impressive and rather frightening figure. A South Indian from Malabar, he looked as if he had stepped out of the tomb of Tutankhamun, saturnine, emaciated and limping heavily on a tall walking-stick. But he had considerable presence and a fiery command over the numerous hangers-on, Indian and English and mostly from the London School of Economics, who thronged the drab and dingy premises of the India League in the Strand.

Krishna received me very graciously and treated me as if, unlike these others, I had a real function to fulfil. He sat me in what I supposed was meant to be his office; it had bookshelves filled with files and newspapers, several tables used as desks and a telephone. For some reason he seemed to think that telephoning was my forte and for the next few weeks he used me to fix up Nehru's appointments.

My first and most difficult task was to find somewhere suitable for Nehru to stay. Krishna politely asked my advice, and when I had none to give, produced a list of service chambers and flats. In making my enquiries I was to be sure to state not only how important Nehru was and that many people would be calling upon him, but to make it plain that he was a coloured gentleman. This shocked me : colour, like class, was a strong taboo word, and indeed, subject. In the 'thirties, young people of progressive views would not even admit to noticing such human differences; actually to mention them out loud was in very bad taste. We thought it liberal and generous to consider people of other races as good as ourselves and to recognize no differences. Such was the measure of our class and colour prejudices.

To the landladies I telephoned the differences were all too real, but pleasant chambers were eventually found in Artillery Mansions just south of St James's Park and not far from the underground station. As I lived in Chelsea and my duty was to call on Nehru each morning, tell him his programme, deal with his letters and generally act as his bodyguard, this was convenient for me too.

In the two or three weeks I worked with Krishna before Nehru's arrival, I underwent an intensive course of indoctrination. Krishna must have known of my imperial background; James Grant Duff's *History of the Mahrattas* was still a textbook in English and Indian universities, and Krishna had studied in Madras where my grandfather had governed for the British. And he must soon have discovered my profound ignorance of Indian affairs, which he tried hastily to amend by giving me Nehru's *Autobiography* to read. This had recently been published by the Bodley Head, with whom Krishna had collaborated closely.

Krishna was a formidable teacher. He often read manuscripts for the Bodley Head and was shortly to be asked by Allen Lane to become the first editor of Pelican Books. He was also, incidentally, a member of Middle Temple, a Borough Councillor for St Pancras and, having degrees in Arts, Science, Economics and Law from Madras, London University and the LSE, had been at one time or another a teacher, barrister, journalist and publicist.

Krishna represented a very different aspect of the Labour Party from Dalton; Krishna's contacts were people and organizations whom Dalton referred to as 'the lunatic fringe'. Nehru was to meet members of the Socialist League in J. F. Horrabin's house in Hampstead; while Bridgeman and the League against Imperialism were definitely regarded as communist and subversive. Ronald Kidd for the National Council for Civil Liberties looked very wild, I noted, but talked very mildly; Harold Laski was feared but respected. George Lansbury, who was to chair Nehru's parliamentary meeting, was honoured and revered but was a total pacifist. Stafford Cripps, who was to preside at a great meeting at Friends House (or was it Caxton Hall? he had meetings at both), was regarded widely at this time as a crank. Dick and Naomi Mitchison, who were to give a party for

Nehru in their Thames-side house, were noted left-wingers.

Krishna Menon himself was well to the Left, though strictly inside known boundaries. He had a didactic mind and through his eyes I saw the Hoare-Laval Pact not as a terrible betrayal but as the typical act of imperialist Powers bargaining away territories as if they were their own property and people as if they were slaves. It was pointless for me to shed tears for the League of Nations, which was simply a league of capitalist Powers out for their own interests. All that I hated in Nazi Germany was at this very moment going on in British India : censorship, imprisonment, dictatorship, military rule for military purposes.

Three days before Nehru was to arrive, George V, the British King who had reigned throughout the whole of my lifetime, died. His death produced a great surge of patriotic feeling, not least under my own roof where my beloved sister Lulu and her soldier husband, Robert Boyle, eventually to be Colonel of the 'Loyals', were staying. Robert had served in India and was highly incensed with me. To his disapproval and contempt for my 'revolutionary' support of an Indian 'renegade', I opposed the mockery and scorn I had learnt from Mowrer for manifestations of royalist adulation in England. The tributes and dirges on the wireless, the preparations for the great State funeral, all produced tension in our house and there was no question of the Boyles being present when my mother so demeaned herself as to give a luncheon party for Nehru and Krishna Menon to meet Dalton, the Toynbees, Sir Neill Malcolm and the Editor of *The Round Table*. I invited Geoffrey Dawson, but Nehru received even shorter shrift at his hands than I had once done. Dawson's secretary telephoned a curt refusal. Christopher Cox, who was to become Educational Adviser to the Colonial and Commonwealth Offices, also refused, but he at least was sorry.

The train which brought kings and heads of state to the funeral also brought Jawaharlal Nehru. The stiff representatives of the British Raj were gathered at Victoria Station at one end of the platform, neatly carpeted and cordoned off. At the other end, in some confusion and disarray, were the humble friends and followers of a man who was one day to rule a sub-continent, but who was then regarded as of little consequence. Most of those there to meet him were Indians, but several old English friends were also present. Gentle old ladies from philanthropic backgrounds, like Agatha Harrison, or fierce red-headed militants like Ellen Wilkinson.

104

Krishna Menon was in command, and I drove with him and Nehru to Artillery Mansions where the rest followed and were refreshed from enormous teapots. Pushed inevitably into a corner, I tried to take in this totally unfamiliar scene and above all the personality of Nehru himself.

I had been moved by his *Autobiography* and deeply impressed that, though it was written in prison, it showed no sort of rancour or bitterness against the British. This was not another fierce Krishna with all his angry condemnation of British rule, but rather a philosopher king who showed why that rule should be changed, how this was happening and what should take its place. It was the work of a really good man : brave, temperate, understanding and humane. And now, as I looked at him, it seemed, above all, goodness which radiated from him, goodness and serenity, for he was the quiet still centre of that excited gathering. He was very beautiful, with not only the beauty of form and feature but also that of expression. A Kashmiri Brahmin, he was golden skinned, and though he had the same dark sorrowful eyes that haunted me at the India League, I felt his was the sorrow of outward compassion and not the suffering which so often weighed me down with Krishna.

Thereafter followed one of the most absorbing and moving weeks of my life, in which whole days were spent with Nehru, looking after him to the best of my ability, fulfilling his needs and doing his bidding. My duties could not have been easier, more pleasant or indeed more mundane. Every morning I had to present myself at his chambers in Artillery Mansions, and with him go through his appointments for the day. At whatever hour I arrived, the hall would already be full of his countrymen, striving to have a word with him or even just to set eyes on him – a replica, somehow touchingly out of place in a small mansion flat in London, of the crowds milling round his father's house in Allahabad. Usually he had letters to write and, unlike Dalton, he let me write them myself once he had given me the gist of what he wanted to say. He had a formula I greatly liked and which I adopted wherever possible : 'It is very good of you. . . .' The goodness was his, not theirs, I felt, and to me the formula expressed just that. He was always courteous, patient, firm and unhurried, and listened as much as he spoke. But when he did speak in his low, quiet voice, no one interrupted.

When the letters were finished, I would often accompany him to his appointments. Being a Londoner, I knew what buses and trains

105

went where, for Nehru seldom took taxis unless there was a real necessity. The first morning we went together to the Chinese Exhibition at the Royal Academy. Afterwards Ellen Wilkinson presided at a press conference he gave in a room in the House of Commons and later she took us through to Westminster Hall where the King was lying in state. From the top of the steps we looked down the great dark hall where the coffin lay on a lighted dais, guarded at its four corners by magnificent guardsmen in full regalia. We watched the hushed and sodden crowds who had waited long hours in the pouring rain, some of them all night, slowly passing the draped coffin. It was very moving and impressive, and I was a little ashamed to walk in and out in this privileged way.

Nevertheless, in my new role as the daily companion of a revolutionary who was challenging the British Empire in all its dignity and strength, I gazed next day on the visiting potentates, the marching soldiers, the gaping crowds, more in anger than in sympathy. I felt strongly that it was this might that had put a man like Nehru in prison and forbidden him the right to serve his country. Nehru was, I think, more far-sighted, more generous and proud. It was acceptable as well as conceivable to him to think of meeting the dead King's heir, man to man and equal to equal, and shaking him by the hand. These people mourning their sovereign were in no sense enemies. It was imperialism that was the enemy, not people, not governments, not even the gaolers who guarded his prison, but simply the system to which his own people were subservient.

This system, he told me, was wrong not only because it was British and therefore alien, but because it was capitalist and therefore exploited the people in the interest of private profit, the many in favour of the few. Capitalism in India, he told the Socialist League, would not survive if the prop of British rule were removed. He believed it and I believed it. What I heard now tended to reinforce not only Krishna's teaching but all I had heard in Paris from my German communist friends, indeed from Adam himself. 'You must make up your mind about your imperialism,' he had told me, 'and I about ours. Perhaps I am a little clearer already about mine than you are about yours and therefore less committed to mine than you are to yours. . . .'

Adam refused to see the danger of war as coming exclusively from Germany. Was it then this international anarchy, created by rival imperialisms, by capitalist competition, that led to war? Was it not

106

some dreadful flaw in the British system that led to the imprisonment of people like Nehru? And was it perhaps true that the British worker lived off the backs of Indians and all the other colonial peoples? I thought seriously of shifting my search for world peace in Europe to searching for world justice in India and elsewhere, by studying conditions on the spot.

Nehru himself warned me against this in a letter he was to write to me after he had left :

'I have thought of our conversation on the day I left London and of your desire to go to India. It is difficult to advise anyone in such a matter; one must be clear in one's own mind and follow one's bent. Often a quick enthusiasm leads to an equally rapid disillusion and India is a country of extremes. I have felt sometimes the desire to run away from India and when, rarely, I have been away, the pull of the country has been great and impossible to resist.

'But whether it is India or some other place, it is not worth while merely to drift, Micawber like, waiting for something to happen. One has to find one's own niche in life where it is possible to fit in – a terribly difficult job in this world of ours. Again the niche may become a rut and then it is worse than ever. So you see I cannot give you any helpful advice. Still, do not hesitate to write to me and tell me what you are doing and propose to do. If I cannot be helpful, I am at least interested and that is something.'

It was a very great deal indeed, but I wanted more. I had felt a growing conviction, day by day, that Nehru was no ordinary man but a spiritual leader, a mystic perhaps, and someone who was himself good and true and beautiful and could tell me what goodness was. I had made up my mind to ask him if ever the opportunity presented itself. It came at last.

I had taken him on the Northern Line to dine with the Henry Nevinsons in Hampstead. It was his last evening, and as we went up in the old slow station lift, I had wondered if I would have time for my question. I did not, but when I collected him later in the evening to take him home, he suggested a walk on Hampstead Heath. The moon was shining and the lights of London could be seen in a haze. We talked about mountains, about Badenweiler (the health resort in the Black Forest where his wife was lying mortally ill), about India, about skiing and climbing, till I felt brave enough to ask him whether he thought man was naturally good or naturally evil. 'Good heavens!' he exclaimed. Then he laughed and asked me, 'What is

107

Good and what is Evil?'

I carefully recorded the rest of the conversation :

'He seems to doubt absolute standards and said "good" men and pious men are often covetous and narrow, and different societies have different ideas of "a good man". I said that goodness was something one recognised immediately. He admitted there was the old individual religious test but for him the test of a good man was his goodness for the community, adding, "But this is all very high-brow." I said it was the fundamental problem of life. He repeated "fundamental" to himself – and then said, "The fundamental thing of life from which all else springs is the relation of human beings to each other."

'I asked him if he really thought it futile and foolish to think about goodness. He said that as a pure discussion it was, but as a means of knowing how to be good it wasn't. Not knowing what is good and what not is the characteristic of a transition stage.'

I was terribly disappointed. I had expected some absolute answer. Now, on re-reading his *Autobiography*, especially those parts where he deals with religion, I see that I could have expected no other answer than the one he gave me. 'It is the *Tao*,' he writes there, 'the path to be followed and the way of life that interests me; how to understand life, not to reject it but to accept it, to conform to it and to improve it.'

My disappointment lay in the relativism of his reply, the modesty of its claim, its almost basic Marxism. Years later, Nehru himself was to be disappointed. When, after the war, he came to England as the Prime Minister of an India whose independence he had won, he asked me to breakfast in the hotel where he was staying. As we were walking towards the lift and were saying goodbye, I remembered another lift and another goodbye and reminded him of my question. Eagerly he asked, 'And what was my reply?' When I told him, he sighed, smiled rather sadly and said, 'How banal.'

I did not tell him the whole conversation because I had not then come upon the record I had kept of it. I remembered just my question about goodness and his defining it in terms of value to the community. I remembered the lift but the memory of that moonlit walk, so precious to come upon now, had totally faded.

11

The threads of my personal life had not been flowing very smoothly all this time. Goronwy had resented my complete absorption in Nehru's visit and the continued demands made upon me by Krishna Menon even after Nehru had gone. Nor had the path of true love been very straight even before this, for Adam had inadvertently brought everything into the open. The confusion and distrust engendered all round darkened the shadows already falling between Goronwy and me.

The first time I heard the bell actually toll was when Adam asked me to meet him again in Germany. I asked Goronwy if he would mind. He answered : 'The terrible thing is that I do not mind.' I did not go but the shadows lengthened.

For me, part of that shadow was Guy Burgess. Goronwy tells us in his autobiography, *A Chapter of Accidents*, how Burgess came back into his life at this stage and how great a part he now began to play in it. (Actually Goronwy gets the dates wrong. Unlike me, Goronwy did not keep letters, so he had only his fickle memory to go by. I do not appear in his book.)

I was instantly repelled by Burgess and remembered how alienated I had felt at Oxford by some of Goronwy's friends; they were all brilliant and clever, but also somehow cynical and amoral. I knew he needed them, and deserved them indeed, because of all they had to give him. For Goronwy had the most receptive mind of anyone I have ever known. He assimilated the books he read, the pictures he looked at, the music he heard, the conversations he took part in, with more pleasure, intelligence and feeling than anyone else I have known, and he contributed richly to the pleasure of others. The 'spring of crystal water', which the name Goronwy means, was, so a poet friend told him, his 'leaping thought and lucid mind', but it was also the clear pools in which he stored all the treasures of the human spirit which fascinated him, suffering as well as joy, evil as well as good.

He loved the poetry of Baudelaire and I have a letter from him, written about this time, in which he describes Baudelaire as 'one of the most innocent of poets' :

'The whole of *Les Fleurs du Mal* is based on the clear distinction of good and evil which he sees as a child might see them, black and white : and it is an innocent state of mind to like and love things which you know to be bad : as a child likes doing things which he knows he ought not to : and Baudelaire is like the child in deriving an extra pleasure from the knowledge of the evil of what he likes.

'The sophisticated point of view is either a) to deny any difference between good and evil or b) to convince yourself with sophistries that what you like is not evil but good, that is to confuse the boundaries of good and evil. But Baudelaire does neither and I think perhaps one reason for the wonderful clarity and objectivity of his poems is that he sees things as if being good or bad were an integral property of theirs, like their colour or shape, and not something added by the observer : and because their natural and moral properties are thus so crystallised together the emotion they arouse is perfectly pure : Baudelaire sees and feels with a naked eye because the moral quality of objects appears to him as an absolute and objective one, fixed by forces outside himself : and because the fact that an object is good or bad does not control his pleasure in it.

'I think this perhaps explains why his poems, though they appear to refer to a diseased and decadent world, give one such a feeling of joy and pleasure.'

Goronwy should have been a Catholic, with a Catholic's acceptance of the great richness and variety of the world, tolerance of all the flaming imagery of heaven and hell, and acknowledgement of sin and forgiveness. This was not my world and my narrow path was not his. For three years at Oxford we had shared a simple childish world entirely encompassed by our affection for each other, our happiness in each other's company. For a brief spell we each had a 'private' income (his from All Souls), and therefore no necessity to take account of the 'real' world in which one must earn one's living and decide what one is really going to do with one's life. I remember I just laughed when my old nurse, Nunn, who was still living with us as housekeeper, complained : 'Is Mr Rees ever going to do any work instead of always reading and writing?'

Now for the last year, both of us had been trying to find what this 'work' was. Goronwy wanted above all to be a writer, not the writer he became but a novelist who would write 'about what really happens inside people today; . . . turn all the doubts, conflicts and desires inside them into a real world of people and events.' But the great problem of an artist who creates what he wants to create and not necessarily what somebody else will pay for, is how to earn a living and still be able to do his own work. For Goronwy the means was obviously journalism and, after several abortive attempts at freelance and daily journalism, he now became Assistant Editor of the *Spectator*. The new job provided security, as well as an opening-up of his life, for his salary of £500 a year meant that for the first time he could afford a flat of his own instead of a single room in Blooms-bury or Chelsea. The flat was in Ebury Street, just round the corner from Guy Burgess.

Most entertaining of all for him, he was now being taken up by writers and publishers, and above all by a publisher's lady and by lady writers. It was over the publisher's lady that I decided we could go no further together. I knew perfectly well that she counted for nothing with Goronwy and that the affair would be over in a matter of weeks, but it was a watershed on the other side of which I did not wish to live.

The publisher was giving a great party and she invited us both to go. I was unwilling but Goronwy insisted I should. The evening was pleasant and uneventful and Goronwy behaved impeccably. Under the influence of wine, Goronwy always became increasingly gentle and affectionate. *In vino veritas*, I said erroneously to myself, and out loud said some testing word to him. In the silence that followed, the tolling of the bell was sonorous. There was no mistaking for whom it tolled.

The party had gone on late and there was every reason to leave with no more being said. I knew that I was leaving for ever and that Goronwy would not call me back.

It was growing light and the dawn has always given me courage. As I walked home from Ebury Street to Mulberry Walk, I felt both a lifting and a sinking of the heart; wounded but free. I was convinced that all wounds heal, even those of amputation. And since our parting had been without recrimination, friendship at least could survive. But constant companionship, constant sympathy and tender-

111

ness, were gone for ever. After four years, I was alone.

Filed away with the letter which Goronwy wrote me after this, was my answer. I do not know whether it was a copy or whether I never sent it but as it truly expressed what I felt then and felt again forty-five years later when he was dying, I reproduce it here :

'Thank you for your letter. It is difficult to answer because, as you say, you must learn in your own way and yet I want to stand between you and all pain and suffering. Only I want to ask of you, never to prefer the second rate, never to deceive yourself and not to confuse suffering with sin. Perhaps you are right that you will only become stronger and braver through suffering and unhappiness, but I love you so much now, it is not necessary for you to suffer in order for me to love you wholly – only not to be afraid and to be strong.

'Forgive me that I find it difficult to understand you. I do try and I think I do, but we think of life so differently. You think of evil as something to be known and learnt from and almost made part of your life. I think of it as something to which one must give nothing and one's life should be like the Roman boy carrying a white bird through the market place. Our life together was not like that of your friends. . . .

'. . . I cannot believe we will ever come together again. But I will grow up and try and understand the world. You must not be unhappy for me or ask me to forgive you. I am happy in a way and have infinite hope in a life of beauty and splendour, and peace and sanity. I wish we could have had it together, but you are right that you must make it for yourself. . . .

'Take care of yourself and do not harm yourself.

'I love you.'

12

In March 1936, when all this was taking place, Hitler took another crucial step towards war: German armies entered the Rhineland and took up positions eight miles from the French frontier. The re-militarization of the Rhineland was not only a strategic move of the utmost importance but another blatant affirmation that Hitler felt himself bound by no treaties, not even those which, like Locarno, he had himself reaffirmed only ten months before. Here was inter-national anarchy, the debasement of all public morality. If the national leader of one of the leading Powers in the world could not be relied upon either to keep his word or speak the truth, how could problems be sorted out or agreements made?

At the time I did not see it so clearly; what I saw was the horrible spectre of war. I typed letters for Hugh Dalton which began: 'We have been nearer to war than most people realize', and I listened with alarm to the debates in Parliament. 'This latest news is ghastly,' I wrote to Adam. 'I have just come from a debate in the House of Commons. The Government seems to regard war as inevitable – now the object is to win it. It was heartrending to hear the Government jeers when Morrison and Cripps said there was only one way out – only one hope for peace – a just and equitable world system based on a sharing of wealth and not the competition system. Of course it's not realism – realism now is just to do with guns.'

Adam answered: 'My trouble is rather that I cannot take very seriously that soulless monster "Europe" which is agitating you so much. I can and want only to work for the new order of labour which I know will come about whatever our bad fate will be in the near future. I know also that my country has a very essential if not the most vital contribution to make in that order, whatever its facade is now. To share in this contribution has been the object which I have

113

never quite lost hold of all these years and though it may look like fatalism, it makes me certain and tranquil in view of the dangers which shatter people's nerves so much. . . . I think that Cripps is more realistic than he knows himself. In the meantime one must hope the other side will consider the bloody thing too costly for all and themselves.'

Whom did Adam consider 'the other side' and which side was his? And why was Europe a 'soulless monster'? Were German grievances so great, not just against Versailles but against Locarno too, that they justified these aggressive acts of treaty violation? Was it only the postal censorship which stopped Adam from ever criticizing these great coups which Hitler brought off for Germany? Was he totally unaware of massive German rearmament and the strategic significance of this move? I believe he gave no thought to it. Like Lord Lothian and the other would-be appeasers, he saw this drastic move as no more than 'the Germans walking into their own back garden'.

Instead of mobilizing and demanding instant withdrawal, the French were persuaded by the British to attend a League of Nations Council Meeting in London. Mowrer arrived to report it and I eagerly sought him out. He told me how he had lately been on the Dutch-German frontier, by official Dutch invitation, to report on German military preparations in that area. He had motored up and down the border in the company of a Dutch Staff Officer, and through their binoculars they had seen formidable German military establishments – new soldiers' quarters, fifteen new airfields and many new roads mysteriously ending just short of the frontier : in fact nothing less than part of a German 'Van Epp Plan' to overrun the Netherlands in a first attack. To achieve this, German forces first had to re-establish themselves in the demilitarized Rhineland zone to the south. This they had now done. 'Mark my words,' he said. 'The present push is not likely to cause war. But unless something is done to change the situation, the next one, or the next after that, surely will.'

'And what are you doing now?' he said abruptly.

Under the influence not only of Adam and the pacifist wing of the Labour Party, but above all of Nehru and my anti-imperialist dream, I answered boldly : 'Disrupting the British Empire.'

He looked at me aghast. 'You would,' he said with the utmost contempt.

These words detonated the same explosion in my mind as the 'toll-

114

ing of the bell' I have described above detonated in my heart. All my convictions were in disarray. I no longer knew which paths to follow, either emotionally, professionally or politically. In every sphere there was conflict between ideas and people and purposes I held in esteem. I knew I must make a choice and strike out on one particular path but now, perhaps for the first time, I realized that to choose is to sacrifice that which is not chosen, and that this applies not only in the sphere of personal satisfaction but also in that of faith and ideals.

Although I was profoundly disturbed I continued for several more weeks trying to help my Indian friends. I did not think I was achieving much in the way of destroying the British Empire but I did seem to be bringing a little human warmth into some of their lives. I made especial friends with an Indian writer called Iqbal Singh, who has remained a good friend all my life. I also went on working for Hugh Dalton in a desultory way that was unsatisfactory for both of us. I remember asking him at some point whether I should work for the Labour Party or go round the world; sensibly but discouragingly, he replied : 'Go round the world.'

In fact I went to Paris to talk once more to Mowrer. I went for a walk with him from one side of the Bois de Boulogne to the other. 'I find him infinitely admirable,' I wrote to my mother. 'I think it is because he is honest and clear minded and intensely vigorous. We talked mostly of peace and war, of education and the sort of things we wanted. He asked me why I wasn't happy and I tried to explain the mixed reasons of my personal life and my political bewilderment. He was a little crude about the former and said I needed a man to order me about; and about the latter he also condemned outright a great number of my rather tentative hopes. He is strangely rough in a way and yet sensitive and I am devoted to him. It is easier to be with him than it used to be because I feel older and braver altogether.'

He gave me Ibsen's *Brand* to read because he thought it would cure me of my 'all-or-nothing fanaticism'. Instead it made me ashamed of how hesitant and doubtful I really was. Nehru had told me that doubts are perhaps never resolved, and all we can do is to choose that which we know to be less evil than the alternatives.

Mowrer was absolutely clear that the greatest evil at the moment was Hitler and that the next victim on his list was Czechoslovakia. Plans for her destruction were already being put into operation. The remilitarization of the Rhineland would cut her off from France.

Her allies in the Little Entente, Yugoslavia and Rumania, were already being wooed vigorously by Hitler. The antipathy of the Poles and the Hungarians was constantly being fed and everything possible was being done to portray the Czechoslovakian alliance with the Soviet Union as a danger to Europe. And not least, the country's large German minority, which had lived side by side with the Czechs in Bohemia since time immemorial, was being incited to make demands which would totally destroy the Czechoslovak Republic. If I wanted a cause, what better one could I adopt? T. G. Masaryk, the ageing Czechoslovak President, was the finest leader of any country in Europe, indeed the last leader of any stature whatever, and his country was the last surviving democracy east of the Rhine.

Arnold Toynbee, I found, was of the same opinion. Hitler's Germany, he wrote in the 1936 *Survey of International Affairs*, was 'one of those modern régimes of the Napoleonic type that did not know how to maintain their hold at home without gratifying their subjects' vanity or distracting their minds, by presenting them with a continuous succession of exhilarating successes abroad. The constant care of a Government in this uncomfortable plight must be to keep a look out for the least dangerous possible next foreign adventure.' And he proceeded to give cogent reasons why Czechoslovakia would be just such a target.

Why, Mowrer asked, did I not take up Voigt's and Massingham's suggestion of the previous year and go to Eastern Europe with the aim of making it as dangerous as possible for Hitler to attack Czechoslovakia? No one in England, as far as he knew, was even aware of the country's existence, perhaps I could put it on the map before Hitler did.

This was not how, in June 1936, I presented my case to Hugh Massingham, and still less to J. L. Garvin who, as Editor of *The Observer*, was already pursuing what later came to be called 'appeasement'. Fortunately it did not seem to be considered necessary for Garvin to meet his minor correspondents. The letter I was given for the Czech authorities carried his signature, but I strongly suspect it was a rubber stamp. My interview with the Foreign Editor bore out Mowrer's remarks. 'I think we've got a correspondent in Prague,' he said. 'Oh no! I think he died, but if you should happen to meet him, just say you're *a* correspondent and not *the* correspondent of *The Observer*.'

I asked what aspects of Czechoslovakia particularly interested his readers. 'Oh, cows with five legs and that sort of thing,' he replied.

Dalton, who knew Czechoslovakia well and much approved of its leaders, welcomed my decision and gave me letters of introduction to Masaryk and Benes and several others. Krishna Menon, whose work at the India League I was now abandoning, was less enthusiastic and Iqbal Singh was even sad at my departure.

I felt I owed an explanation to Nehru and after I had arrived in Prague I wrote to him:

'. . . In one way I feel I have deserted you and in another I want you to think I am right because I trust very deeply your political and human judgements. . . . Do you remember the day you went away I told you that what I really wanted to do was to stop war. I think you did not answer; but listening to you, reading your book, made me believe the way to stop it was to destroy imperialism and to make a worldwide socialist system. I believed it hesitatingly but tried to work for it last summer. Then week by week the European situation grew worse and worse and the necessity to stop war more and more immediate.

'Even if the root causes of war are imperialism and capitalism, and I still believe they are, there is no time to remove them, only to allay the immediate causes and give time to work out a system in which the root causes are also removed.

'But war is probably your chance of freedom and you have to take it; yet for us it is the threat to the whole of European civilisation which, for all its political evils in other continents, has evolved a European system which is not entirely bad and a culture which one wants to defend. I know that, in a way, all wars are imperialist and certainly all wars are harmful; and yet to a Nazi Germany and Fascist Italy and perhaps now Fascist Spain, how can one answer with pacifism or even revolutionarism which plays into their hands?'

As always, and to all my letters (for this reason, alas, I wrote very sparingly so as not to burden him), Nehru answered immediately in his very beautiful handwriting:

Dear Shiela,

Your letter was welcome. . . . Why should you imagine that I might accuse you of desertion? The idea never struck me, for you had not tied yourself down to anything and had made no promises. It was obvious that you were puzzled and perplexed and searching for some solution which would satisfy you. It was because

117

of that, do you remember? that I discouraged the notion of your coming to India. But even apart from that there could be no question of desertion in my mind for the work we care for has many aspects even as the problem we have to face is many sided. I work in India for Indian freedom because I feel that this is my proper field of activity and I can work most effectively here. But always I try to think in terms of the larger world problems and try to fit India into them. If you have that in view, it does not matter much where you pitch your tent – in Prague or London or India.

I agree that we must try to stop war. I would even go so far as to say with you that it is important to allay the immediate causes and thus gain time to root out the ultimate causes. But how is one to do this? War will not come from us but from those who oppose us and we cannot control them. A Liberal democratic Spain is attacked by Fascists and reactionaries and even in England there is a great deal of sympathy for the rebels. I think that if England had the kind of Government that France has today and the two joined hands with Russia, war would be unlikely. But the tragedy is that England flirts with Germany and thus encourages fascism.

I do not want world war even for the sake of Indian freedom, or perhaps it would be more correct to say that I do not look forward to any real freedom for India as a result of a devastating conflict all over the world. I do not know what the result of such a conflict will be, except that it will destroy a great deal of what we value. But then we are back to the question : How are we to stop war? Mere pacifism is not enough and often the revolutionary plays into the hands of the reactionary.

It is all very complicated and we are really forced to look deeper down and examine the roots of the evil and try to remove them, avoiding as far as one can, the destruction of the good that we have. . . .

Yours,

Jawaharlal Nehru

13

Before I had actually taken the decision to work in Prague, I had been very reluctant to return to Germany. To meet Adam there, I had told him, was 'impossible, both in time and place. The biggest problems we have to work out, we must face alone. I think each would complicate the problems of the other. I admit I could not bring quite to your conditions the sympathetic understanding which you need. I am an alien enemy to it, you see, not one of its children, and I could make it not easier but more difficult for you.'

'Perhaps, Shiela,' Adam had answered, 'you are right about time. But to think that you hate this country so much that one cannot see spring in it together is a little painful. Meeting might have called back to you that being attached to it has nothing to do with the things that it is natural to hate from Paris.'

It was not true that I hated Germany. What was 'natural to hate from Paris', and would no doubt be even more hateful from Prague, were the Nazis' aims in Europe. It was clearly important to find out what these were and to know what Adam was thinking. Now that I had made up my mind what I was going to do and it entailed crossing Germany in order to reach Czechoslovakia, there was every reason for us to meet. I arranged to visit him in Kassel on my way to Prague.

Adam now lived in the Mozartstrasse, in a spacious first-floor room with a balcony. He had found a charming, newly painted attic for me on the fourth floor, whose two windows were like eyes looking out over the rooftops to the park.

I was thankful with all my heart to be once more away from England and with a definite task ahead; thankful too for the long quiet hours on my own while Adam studied for his final law exams. He had bought me a ticket for the library, telling me it was where the

119

Brothers Grimm had worked. I read and wrote letters and struggled over the German newspapers with a dictionary until Adam fetched me for lunch (usually a picnic in the park) or for a drive to those little palaces and gardens, river banks, woods and village inns we had visited so happily two years before.

Adam fully lived up to the promise he had made in one of his letters to 'be very careful with you and leave you to cope with the things you['d] better not tell me. I promise not to bewilder or frighten you.' Adam knew what it was to part with someone very close : all one's 'inner habits were shaped by communication' with that person. He thus respected my continued attachment to Goronwy and did not consider it an obstacle between us.

'In a sense,' he wrote later, 'one can never, and must never, part with the person one first loved. Their memory and person, even if actually gone away, seems to be in itself what love means to one and there is a strange and important presence of them in all the new things that matter. Perhaps learning to be alone adequately is to realise that one keeps them and yet lets them go to lead their own different life. . . . It is very important for us both to learn to be alone, in a sense it means the very supposition of our friendship.'

Gradually, the charm of each other's presence took over. I loved Adam's alternate moods of gaiety and solemnity. Today, more than anything else about him, I remember his laugh; I can still hear it. I think gladly not only of the light-hearted days we spent together but of what our friendship really was. 'We remind each other,' Adam wrote to me after I left, 'that life must be lived simply and bravely, and that it can become ordered and even beautiful. We share, I think, the essential ambitions of what man should still be in this present world and we share the smaller gaieties of life.'

Those two brief weeks made me feel whole and strong again and brave enough to face the lonely assignment I had taken on. Adam reproached me for being like a bird which allows itself to be caught only when its wings are tired or hurt, but when they are strong again, does not take long before it 'prefers to fly alone and perhaps mock me from the branches of some slightly hostile tree'.

There were occasional hostile trees around us even before I went to Prague – where they grew in forests. I remember one evening in Kassel when I dragged him to the 150th anniversary of the Kyffäuser-bund, which a friend of mine in Reuters had asked me to cover. The whole city was beflagged for the occasion – those horrible spiders which had filled me with such loathing in the Saar. I expressed my loathing now and though Adam shared it, he retaliated by saying there was no sympathy or support abroad for the non-National Socialist Germany. I protested that there had been little evidence of the existence of such a Germany; it would have been better to have died in the streets than let the Nazis take over. This hurt Adam very much : he thought that I was reproaching him personally as well as condemning the whole of Germany to be this thing that he hated. I was able to persuade him that I thought neither, and in the midst of all that crowd, with its flags and uniforms and songs and bugles, we felt a strong, defiant, civilian nucleus of something which would triumph. We immunized ourselves with jokes and laughter, pretending to be chauvinists, but when, towards the end, the whole crowd stood up with raised arms for a hymn and Adam would not raise his, I was afraid for him and we left.

In the park on the way home, we sat on a seat by the lake and talked. Venus and the moon were still together in the sky as we had seen them on our way to the stadium; symbols of peace, we said.

But was peace possible? Adam insisted that it was : that Mowrer's diagnosis (Nazi Germany's will to war) and his remedy (encirclement, which Adam called 'the lid theory') were wrong : that conditions inside Germany were such that there could and would be developments that would change the policy and the character of the régime. His Germany, he said, was the Germany of himself and his friends; he tried to make me understand the position of one who both loved and hated what he belonged to. If only I could accept that, he said, then things between us would change.

We discussed the question of marriage with the candour and coolness which is only possible perhaps when the prospect is a distant one. Both of us knew it was out of the question at that moment, both for ourselves and for each other. Other loves burdened each of our hearts and, in any case, our practical lives made it impossible. Adam had his law exams to get through and was planning to leave Europe for America and the Far East. Neither the work he wished to do there nor the third-year scholarship he hoped to get from the Rhodes Trustees would encompass taking a wife with him. I had my assignment in Prague and was determined at least to explore whether this, as Mowrer said, was the focal point at which Hitler would strike to gain his ends and beyond which, if he were not stopped, the holocaust of war would inevitably follow. Adam reminded me that there were things for which he cared more than for any personal relationship, and the same was true for me.

For our last weekend, we went to Imshausen. My relationship with his mother was much easier this time; one could always find her sitting somewhere quietly and be welcomed to sit beside her and talk. She was reading Nehru's *Autobiography*, so we had much better things to talk about than the Polish corridor. In any case I hope I had grown a little bit more tactful. I had forgotten that Adam had told her he wanted to marry me, so nothing of this passed between us, but I was touched when Adam wrote that he had told her again after my departure and she had said that 'it would not break her heart.' Touched too that he said I had even won his father's heart.

Adam's younger brother, Heinrich, and his sister Vera were also there. Adam had always spoken of Heinrich very affectionately and I saw why. He was troubled and unhappy at this time; his boy-scout admiration for the Nazis as a schoolboy had turned to total nausea and disgust, and his public apostasy from the Party had already cost him dear. He was living in a forester's hut in the Trottenwald, so beloved by all the Trotts, and dreading the moment when he had to leave for one of Hitler's youth camps or for military service.

After the war, when the rest of the family were scattered or dead, Heinrich and Vera were to keep the Trott demesne going : Heinrich caring for the forests and timber and the deep values he had shared with Adam; Vera carrying on and expanding the Christian spirit and works of her mother. In memory of Adam, they erected a huge wooden cross, high on a hill, looking down on the forests to which, he once said, he confided all his thoughts and feelings.

He loved to show them to his friends. We went for long walks in the forests together and tried to approach unheard the grazing deer. The smell of the warm pine needles under the trees and the soft mossy clearings were so beautiful. All we felt together endured on into the winter, as Adam wrote to me in November from his home :

'I was happy to remember you saying you would like to walk with me in these fields here [and] when I stopped to tie the laces of my shoes and smelt the peculiarly winterly smell of the wet and smeary ground and saw the dead yellow leaves, [I felt] all that was more part of me than any philosophy in the world and that that was quite easy for you to understand. . . .'

This was indeed a different world from the 'one which it is natural to hate from Paris'. 'I have been so happy here,' I told my mother.

'They are very admirable people and it is a great thing to realize that such people were once the rulers of Germany and may be again.' This was how Adam saw himself and his friends. He had noble ambitions but his roots were deep in the earth of Germany.

When it came to leaving, Adam said he would take me on my way. He looked up the route the train would take to the Czechoslovak border and drove me to an inn near some wayside station. We talked long and late into the evening and when I went alone into my little room I could not sleep. I heard Donne's tragic lines :

> Stay, O sweet, and do not rise,
> The light that shines comes from thine eyes;
> The day breaks not, it is my heart,
> Because that you and I must part.

It was not my heart, or either of our hearts, which was breaking, but a very fragile, ephemeral bridge, perhaps no more than a rainbow, which, that night, we might have crossed. For me the bridge was never there again. It was the bridge which makes one life out of two, the bridge from friendship to love. Perhaps it was always only a rainbow and it faded as swiftly and as inevitably as a rainbow must.

14

I had no premonition as I left Adam on that wayside station that this could be the parting of ways. We had come so close together, not only in our mutual enjoyment but in the ambition that we both had to make something of our lives and, at that very moment, to get on with our own immediate purposes. I felt no grief at leaving but, on the contrary, a renewed strength to go forward, and renewed happiness which I urgently wanted to share.

'At moments,' I wrote to him from Prague, 'I wish almost unbearably that you were here – and this is one of them. I am eating my supper on an island and the river is glistening. A brass band is playing lovely music rather aggressively and people are dancing under the trees. How much I like pleasure and want to connect it with you! Prague is really wonderful and I long to show it to you. At sunset it has an almost perfect skyline and there are houses and streets in it almost indescribably beautiful. I love towns built about rivers, and of all architecture, baroque is the most humane and splendid. I would like to visit a thousand new places and all with you. Must we discover all the world first by ourselves? Well let us, if the rest of the world is as desirable as this, it is intrinsically to be discovered whatever way one discovers it.

'I live in a kind of Kurfürstendamm which, like the Kurfürstendamm, grows fascinating and horrible at night – but my room is remote. It has walls of rose-pink Regency silk, except for one of glass. I have a blue bathroom all my own and white painted furniture. I am very happy but I think I shall move and live in the skyline that is so beautiful at sunset. It will mean leaving the hot sausage stalls in the street where I live, the milk bars, and even, darling Adam, the old women selling radishes which remind me of you every fifty yards I walk. What could make me think of you with so much feeling in the perfect skyline?

'I am very happy and very fond of you and miss you very much. What a wise man Turgenev was when he made the girl in his story write that the pain of parting was itself a pleasure. The brass band is a military band which accounts for the aggressiveness. You will have to look out for the Little Entente!'

In Prague everyone was relaxed and smiling. Under the bridges over the Vltava, peasants in brilliant national costume sold their wares. I loved the Czech and Slovak pottery, rough and crude as it often was. I loved the huge rounded forms of the peasant women as they sat behind their stalls. I loved their flat Slav faces and their strange incomprehensible language. It always seemed to be the men who played the music, sometimes so gay, sometimes so melancholy, on small, vibrant violins. The sun was warm and brilliant and all the world was shining. Prague was one of the most beautiful and happiest cities of Europe. Although a tiny city to which peasants carried their baskets of fruit, vegetables and pottery, Prague was also a true European capital. The history of Europe was written on its walls and they breathed the air of European civilization. Its music was magnificent : there was not only a first-class opera but the most marvellous concerts were given by its own composers, conductors and players, men of international repute. A great network of international railways linked Prague with the whole of Europe, and music lovers came from far and wide.

Another link was the literacy and enquiring spirit of its population, many of whom spoke several languages; the Republic itself embraced citizens speaking five different native tongues. This was held against it, but in time it could have become its great strength. Books of all nations were translated into Czech, and in the cafés were stands from which one could take and read not only all the local papers, Czech and German, but the leading newspapers of every European country. The Czechs were proud to be the bridge between East and West; they thought of themselves as the hub of Europe. Now, as the darkness of fascism and dictatorship descended on the countries around her, Czechoslovakia became the refuge of exiles. People were not frightened in the first Czechoslovak Republic. No police came knocking at the door in the early hours of the morning, and one could walk alone in the streets and in the countryside without fear. There was no rioting, no vandalism, no terrorism, no pornography. People were free to attend what Church they chose or to declare themselves of no

125

religion. There was a variety of political parties extending from the far right to the far left. There was equality before the law and equality of opportunity.

Of course, it was not all idyllic. In the industrial districts, many of which were German, there was much poverty and bitterness in the wake of the terrible economic depression of the early 'thirties. There was also anger and bitterness among the Bohemian nobility, who were much more Austrian than Czech. Many of them had owned beautiful palaces in Prague which were now Government offices. Though they had for the most part retained their castles in the country, their huge estates had been diminished by land reform. Prague was a less German city than it had been in the three preceding centuries, and many Germans felt themselves to be second-class citizens where before they had been the rulers. Nevertheless, they had their own university, their own newspapers, their own theatres, their own restaurants and meeting-places and much else besides. Prague also had old Jewish traditions and a great German Jewish literary culture. Now there were many young Czech and Slovak writers and artists, and the new film studios at Barandov were making a real contribution to the European cinema.

I had brought with me from London a whole box of introductions to well-known people. After forty-five years it is still almost full. The same diffidence which cut me off from the French society of the Vildracs now prevented me from pushing myself into the society of Prague, from presenting letters of introduction either to the established or to the famous, like the young Firkusny in the world of music, Kokoschka among the artists or Capek among the writers. I had come to Prague with a purpose and felt at ease only on my own political ground; also, it must be admitted, speaking my own language or my still schoolgirl French. Hyka, the head of the press department of the Czechoslovak Foreign Office, spoke English and gave me armfuls of books and pamphlets – history, politics, art, culture, statistics, maps – all in English and all produced by Orbis, the state publishing house.

On my arrival in Prague I had been dismayed to find I was to be the only resident British correspondent. I found no band of helpful newspapermen as in the Saar, no established office like the ones where I had worked in Paris or Berlin. All the British Central European correspondents were based in Vienna and relied on 'stringers', mostly German emigrés, in Prague. *The Observer* had given me nothing but the single sheet of paper I arrived with, stamped, if not signed, by Garvin. I had no office and no expense account. All *The Observer* paid for was what it cost to communicate with them and the space my copy filled. Nevertheless, I had my small private income and a free pass on the Czechoslovak railways. I was not rich but I was free; I was often entertained by journalists and diplomats, and girls did not, in those days, pay for their own meals when invited out. The Czechs entertained me in the Spolecensky Club, of which I was made an honorary member, and minor diplomats took me to the French Restaurant. Major diplomats, like Ministers, provided more sumptuous entertainment.

The British Minister at that time was Sir Joseph Addison, who was just on the point of retirement. The Czechs did not like him very much, knowing how much he disliked them. I wrote my name in the Legation book and since two of my uncles had been in the diplomatic service it must have been familiar. Or perhaps it was a letter from Oliver Harvey, Permanent Private Secretary to Anthony Eden, whom I had known slightly in Paris, that caused me to be summoned into Sir Joseph's presence. As our talk was bright and amusing and he, no doubt, was bored, he invited me to stay for a tête-a-tête lunch in the beautiful garden of the Thun Palace, which housed the British Legation. I described the scene to my mother : 'I stayed four hours which seems rather rude but it was very pleasant. It was so nice in his garden and I felt so much at home that I found it hard to leave. He is a funny old thing and we had lots of jokes. He refused to tell me anything about this country but from his very refusals I learnt a certain amount.'

One refusal told me a great deal. 'Have you many Czech friends?' I asked him. 'Friends!' he exclaimed. 'They eat in their kitchens.'

Later he invited me to eat in the elegant Legation dining-room with the friends he had made, Bohemian noblemen. My neighbour at dinner solemnly assured me he was heir to the throne of Ireland. I laughed and said I hoped he was not adding a Habsburg dimension to the troubles of that already troubled land. He frowned and turned away. The potential restoration of the Habsburgs was still dear to many noble hearts, a small but possible cause of trouble. The Bohemian nobles were, of course, all Austrians, but I do not think they felt a strong allegiance to the little rump state of Austria. They were Europeans, in the sense that the Holy Roman Empire was Europe. Since it no longer existed, their allegiance was to the

Almanach de Gotha. They viewed the Czechs with the same snobbish distaste as their English host.

If Sir Joseph was beginning to have his doubts about me – as being unsound both on class and on national hierarchies – I was equally disillusioned. Next day I wrote to Adam :

'. . . Yesterday I had a great lecture on British interests from our Minister here, and I felt really bruised and hurt by the cynicism of it and by my own silence towards all that he said. When I did say that for me it was not enough to be British because there were other things I believed in and other things I cared for, he said I was the sort of person who was ruining England by my anti-patriotism and that women should never have anything to do with politics because they introduced sentiment into them. It doesn't seem to me that politics suffer from sentiment but from just the very cynicism that Sir J. suffers from himself.

'We had all this again about the ruling classes and about Government being a capacity learnt after generations and not possible to the ordinary man unless he be a genius. What truth is in it? Is it not again a matter of interest? To the Austro-Czech nobles, the Czechs govern badly because they pass land laws against the nobles, but is that bad government? It is true what Owen Lattimore said, that to understand a country one must know in whose interest it is governed. This country is governed in the interest of small people. . . .

'I should not complain of my Minister. He gave me a beautiful lunch and was nice to me. He lives in a wonderful house and we had lunch in his garden which looks over the whole of Prague. That was lovely and he was interesting even if he was provoking.

'I do not think diplomats have been the best servants of the League of Nations and it may even come out one day that it was they who wrecked it. The new world will have to be built with new stones.'

That weekend, 11 July, 1936, saw the signing of the Austro-German Agreement which signalled the end of the Austrian Republic. I sat all day in my hotel bedroom reading newspapers and trying to work out what it meant. The rain poured down my windows, the streets were empty and shuttered, everything looked grey and mournful. 'I have reached such a depth of international despair,' I told Adam, 'that I suspect everything that happens of sinister designs and ominous consequences, and this rather more than most, though the official note is cheerful and calm. To-day I must find out what they [the Czechs] really think, but it is difficult and I do not

128

5 Goronwy Rees, *c.* 1933

6 The author in Oxford

7 Imshausen, the home of the von Trotts. Adam's room is indicated by an arrow.

8, 9 Adam von Trott in 1935

yet know how to do it.'

I turned again to the diplomats at the British Legation and this time found an attaché called Taylor who was slightly lower down the social and diplomatic scale and rather more explicit. 'The Czechs know they are doomed,' he told me, 'and will be fools if they resist. The French will not help them and neither will we.' The Poles, he said, were sitting on the fence and doing it extremely well. They knew that Poland would be the battlefield of a German-Russian war, and therefore they would do their utmost to avoid it. Earlier, I had asked the Minister what British policy was in Eastern Europe. Once again he had scoffed. 'British policy! You flatter them.'

I found myself terribly depressed by the cynical and uncaring attitude of my fellow countrymen and felt lonelier in their company than I did when alone. The implication that we were the English and they were the Czechs was so apparent in every word and gesture that one felt totally isolated. I knew that I must somehow make contact with the people in whose country I was living.

The American Legation put me in touch with a woman – I cannot remember now whether she was British or American – who, they said, 'knew everybody and the country inside out'. I found that she spoke not a word of Czech – as did none of the diplomats – and that 'everybody' turned out to be all the diplomats of Prague and such Bohemian landowners as invited them to stay. 'It really isn't good enough,' I wrote to my mother, 'and I shall have to "know everybody" all by myself. I don't think it will be very difficult because they are very nice to me, the Czech officials. I also belong to a nice Czech club where people are very kind and friendly and bow to me. I am told I ought to ask the secretary whenever I go there to introduce me to anybody whom it would be interesting to meet. When I protested, they told me that shyness did not go with my profession.'

Then suddenly the situation was transformed. Into my life came not only the best possible person to inform me but a real and lasting friend.

This was Hubert Ripka, diplomatic correspondent of the independent Brno paper *Lidové Noviny* and *homme de confiance* of President Benes himself. (A. J. P. Taylor has described him as Benes' successor designate.) I had been told to get in touch with him by the handsome Slovak press attaché in Paris, Dr Safranek. 'Ripka,' he said, 'knows everything and is as clever as a bag of monkeys. He speaks German, Russian, French, Serb, but no English, has written a book about Yugoslavia and knows all the countries of the Danube Basin like the back of his hand. Even before he had a French wife, he was at home in France and on terms with all the French politicians. So,' Safranek added, 'you really don't need to know anyone else – except of course, my boss, the admirable Hyka.' And then he made the most endearing and the most prophetic remark of all. 'Ripka is the Mowrer of Czechoslovakia.'

Timorously, on account of my schoolgirl French, I rang him up in his office; he said he would come round. I was beginning to hate my hotel. It had eight porters who were all too ready to open doors and hand me my key and letters and air their bad English. Its entrance was on the first floor where there was a noisy café. On the ground floor was a cake shop filled with large and luscious cakes. Behind its counter worked a kind, smiling woman who greeted me in the mornings with a glass of milk and put extra sugar on my cake. Ripka preferred to meet in the café and I waited there nervously.

But when I saw him, every anxiety fell away and I only wanted to laugh : he had such an absurd face and such a mocking, friendly smile. Well over six feet tall and with broad shoulders, he must have been in his early forties. Like Mowrer, he made constant political jokes at the expense of all and sundry, not least his own countrymen. Yet this was something different from the cold cynicism of the English. For Mowrer and Ripka it was merely a mask to disguise their political commitment, their fighting temperament. Both knew what it was they had to fight if the values they cared for were to survive in Europe.

I was delighted with this new friend; from the very first I was at ease and unafraid. I even found myself babbling French. It seemed quite natural, a toy we shared but which belonged to neither of us, so we could do what we liked with it. Prague was still in a holiday mood, and like everyone else Ripka was ready for enjoyment and pleasure. He immediately suggested a 'bombe' with his good friend Jan Borovicka and 'your friend Hyka', as he called the press chief.

I had no idea what a 'bombe' was, but as soon as I had experienced one I was wholly in favour. It started with a tremendous meal in a garden overlooking the river at Barandov, the Hollywood of Czechoslovakia, and continued in the nightclubs of Prague.

Borovicka was Professor of History at Bratislava University. He had white hair and a nice boyish face, though I suppose he was probably approaching his sixties. He could read English and had even read some of the works of Sir John Lubbock – a great inital bond between us – but unfortunately he could not speak English or understand it when I spoke it, so we somehow got along in German.

Heaven knows what common language we all spoke that evening, but there was not much need of language. It was a rollicking affair where heady Yugoslav wine flowed like water, followed by the fierce local slivovitz. The band played intoxicating gypsy music and heart-rending Slovak songs. As the evening went on, Hyka grew more 'official and bourgeois' while Borovicka laughed protestingly and indulgently as Ripka became more and more outrageous. He mocked at Hyka, teased Borovicka and flattered me in terms nobody could have taken seriously. He made wild declarations on all subjects, scoffed at prejudices dear to Hyka's official heart, and ended with a plea of passionate patriotism which I suspected was put on for my sake. I was amused and touched, but I could not help wondering why he kept repeating that he would save Europe from the decadent Western Powers.

Later, when I questioned him, he just smiled and denied having meant it seriously. It was only when we had started working closely together that he admitted his anxieties about France. Of England he knew nothing : but France he knew very well, both because of his French wife, a highly intelligent and courageous woman from Alsace who taught French Literature in the French Lycée and Institute in Prague, and through his own and Benes' contacts with French politicians.

Through Ripka's eyes I began to see the whole Allied settlement of Eastern Europe, from the Baltic to the Aegean, in a totally different perspective from that which I had learnt in Oxford. There – and this view permeated the Foreign Office too – the post-war settlement was described as the 'Balkanization of Europe', and the dissolution of the Austro-Hungarian Empire was deeply regretted. But to those living in the area, the 1919 peace settlement was regarded as a great liberation, not only of subject peoples but of submerged classes. Vigorous young states had risen from the ashes of the fallen empires, and democracy had triumphed not only within but between States. The League of Nations was both their charter and their protector.

On the shores of the Baltic, liberated from the Russian Empire of the Tsars, arose Finland, Estonia, Latvia and Lithuania. Poland, which for more than a century had been partitioned between Russia,

Austria and Germany, was united and independent again. Czechoslovakia, created from the historic lands of medieval Bohemia together with the Slovak districts which had been under Hungarian rule, was established afresh. Yugoslavia was the old Serbia with Croatia added to it. A new world had been called into being to redress the balance of the old, a world dominated neither by Germany nor Russia but inspired by its own vigorous national entities. These threatened nobody and were themselves protected by the principles for which the Allies had fought in the First World War and which were embodied in the League of Nations – respect for the independence, integrity and freedom of all nations, the condemnation of war as an instrument of national policy, the peaceful adjustment of such conflicts as did arise by negotiation or arbitration and the collective guarantee of every country's security.

Czechoslovakia, Ripka told me proudly, was one of the main pillars of this new order. Benes had been not only one of the most active participants at the Peace Conference but, from that day to this, one of the chief upholders of the League of Nations in Geneva. Nothing Ripka could have said would have engaged my sympathies more ardently for his country.

As Ripka was talking, I suddenly remembered a moment when Benes had come up in my studies of the Peace Conference at Oxford. In his book *Peacemaking, 1919*, a somewhat critical account of the Paris Peace Conference, Harold Nicolson had singled out for praise Sir Eyre Crowe and Edward Benes, two men who were to be much in my mind in the coming months. 'Benes taught me,' he wrote, 'that the Balance of Power was not necessarily a shameful, but possibly a scientific thing. He showed me that only upon the firm basis of such a balance could the fluids of European amity pass and repass without interruption.'

What, I asked Ripka, was the Balance of Power in Europe now? 'The one war Hitler will not fight,' he said, 'is a war on two fronts. Bismarck laid this down for Germany in the nineteenth century, and it was because Kaiser Wilhelm II ignored it that Germany was defeated in the last war. Hitler actually says this in *Mein Kampf*. But there is only one Power in Eastern Europe which could stand up for any length of time against the military power of Germany and that is the Soviet Union. That is why we have always worked systematically for the establishment of the friendliest collaboration between the Western Powers and the Soviet Union. The Franco-

Soviet and the Czecho-Soviet Pacts of 1935 complete our long-standing alliance with France. If this axis is strong, Hitler will not move.'

This was how Mowrer saw the situation from Paris; it was now confirmed by Ripka in Prague.

15

On my way through Paris Mowrer had stressed that my most important task was to discover Czechoslovakia's capacity to stand up to Hitler. This was dependent on four factors. Firstly, her will to do so. 'The Poles, after all,' said Mowrer, 'chickened out and have signed a bi-lateral treaty with Hitler and are just waiting for him to fall on Czechoslovakia so they can have a bite.' Secondly, the strength of Czech alliances with France, Russia and the Little Entente. Thirdly, the state of the Czech military defences; and finally, the relevance to all this of the three-and-a-quarter million Sudeten Germans living in Czechoslovakia.

I put all this to Ripka. He laughed and said I had a lot of work to get down to and he would help me when he returned from a holiday with his family in France. He would be back in September for the conference of the Little Entente in Bratislava and he suggested I went with him. He had surely convinced me already of Czechoslovakia's will to fight, and he really did not advise me to go round asking questions about military defences. A very stiff Defence of the State Act had been passed that spring, and one of the stiffest of its clauses dealt precisely with people wanting to find out such things. As for the Sudeten Germans, this was indeed a key question, but a very complicated one.

First of all I should read the history of Bohemia and see how for centuries Germans and Czechs had lived together and struggled for power within its historic frontiers. By examining the natural contours of the mountains on large-scale maps, I would understand why these frontiers had remained unaltered for so long. I should study economics and see the links between the highly industrialized German areas and the agricultural Czech districts behind them. I should study the negotiations leading up to the peace treaties and why the decision had been made at Versailles to leave so large a German minority within a Czechoslovak State. I should then read the history of the last eighteen years and see how, gradually, up to 1933, the Sudeten Germans had become reconciled to the Republic. After 1926 two, and after 1929 three German parties actually joined the Czechoslovak Coalition Government, and these three 'Activist' parties were still in the Government, although the enormous swing to the crypto-Nazi Henlein Party in the 1935 elections meant that they now represented only a third of the Sudeten German electorate.

Ripka advised me to get in touch with these parties and talk to them myself. Wenzel Jaksch, the young Social Democrat leader, was a good friend of his and he could make an appointment for me. I told Ripka I had met one of the Henleinists, a man called Rutha, when I had been visiting a friend at the House of Commons. He raised his eyebrows slightly at this, but said that in that case I would find it easy to make contact. What he did suggest was that I should visit the German districts myself. President Benes was shortly to make a tour of them and it would be interesting for me to see the reaction. Incidentally, the summer manoeuvres were also going to be held there soon, so I could wave at the soldiers. He did not advise doing more than this.

I met Jaksch shortly afterwards. He became a friend and talked very openly to me. If all Czechs were like Ripka, he said, there would be no problem. Czechoslovakia was a democracy and freedom was guaranteed to all its subjects. The Germans had their own schools, their own university, their own newspapers. There were some German officials, though not enough of them proportionately, and more and more Czechs were settling in German areas. Really intolerable, however, was the petty discrimination practised by local Czech officials, and what was worst of all, of course, was the terrible hardship and unemployment caused by the depression. There was real economic suffering in the Sudetenland; although this was because it was heavily industrialized and it was here that most of the export industries were based, the Germans could not help comparing their plight with better-off Czech districts and blaming the Czechoslovak Government for the difference. There was undoubtedly a very strong mood of resentment in the Sudeten German districts. If there had been no depression and if exports had not been hit so badly, the whole situation would have been different. It would have been totally different too, Jaksch told me, if Hitler had never come to power in

135

Germany.

Was Henlein a Nazi? I asked Jaksch. He frowned and said it did not really matter whether he was or wasn't. With the Nazis in power in Germany, it was inevitable that a right-wing nationalist 'movement' in the Sudetenland would collaborate with them. Certainly Henlein's followers behaved like Nazis, as I would see for myself, but if only the Czechs would make genuine concessions to the Sudeten German Activist Parties – his own Social Democrats, the Agrarian Party and the Christian Socialists – he felt the situation could still be saved.

I must admit that I disliked the atmosphere in the Sudeten area very much when I went there. I visited Bodenbach, Reichenberg, Gablonz, Karlsbad and Herrnskretchen, and had introductions to people in all of them. The most impressive man I met was the socialist mayor of Bodenbach. He was much older than Jaksch and came from the old school of social democracy, which put the ideals of socialism so firmly above those of nationalism that one felt a sound and integrated community could exist. Elsewhere, the disruptive forces of Henleinism were so hard at work that crude chauvinism took over on both sides, Czech and German, with the added hatred and fear between (Henleinist) Nazi and anti-Nazi that I had seen in the Saar, the same whispering of the fate which would be meted out when the day – *der Tag* – came.

Konrad Henlein, who was not available during my visit, was the 'export' model of his party. Though leader since 1933 when the party was formed from the dissolved National and National Socialist Parties, he never stood for Parliament, preferring to remain outside, as Hitler had done. Despite the restrictions then in force, he always had funds available for trips abroad and no shortage of foreign currency. He obviously looked more to outside help and pressure than to parliamentary endeavours to improve the situation of the Germans in Czechoslovakia. In this period he was still strongly denying that he had any links with Germany or that he was in any way a Nazi or following Nazi policy. In fact he and his party had been subsidized since 1935 by the German Foreign Office to the tune of fifteen thousand marks a month. Henlein became an overt National Socialist, who took his orders openly from Hitler, only after the Austrian *Anschluss* in March 1938, and in 1936 his non-Nazi pose was still convincing to some people. I remember Arnold Toynbee visiting Czechoslovakia and being much impressed with Henlein

136

(as were many in England, including another anti-Nazi, Vansittart of the Foreign Office). Toynbee denied hotly my suggestion that Henlein was a Nazi. 'Oh no!' he said. 'He himself assured me he wasn't.'

My chief contacts in the Henlein Party were the press chief, Wilhelm Sebekovsky, who was pleasant enough, and Karl Hermann Frank, then a member of the Czech Parliament but later to be Reichsprotektor of Bohemia and to become notorious as 'the butcher of Prague'. With such people around in large numbers, and being adjacent to a country thirsting for confrontation like Nazi Germany, the Czechs had everything to fear. It was a Catch-22 situation. If they gave in to the demands of the Sudeten Germans, they would render totally ineffective their already vulnerable defence system. The measures needed to make this system less vulnerable, necessarily pressed hard on the local population and exacerbated their grievances. The external danger which forced this situation upon them was not yet the open threat of German invasion (Czechoslovakia was still protected by her alliances with Russia and France and the obligation of the League of Nations in minority questions) but the danger of alienating public opinion and support from those in the West on whom the Czechs relied.

This, in fact, was the danger to which Czechoslovakia eventually succumbed. In one fell swoop at Munich the Czechs lost both their military defence system and their Sudeten German fellow-citizens. But as I travelled round the Sudetenland in August 1936, trying to gauge the reaction to President Benes' firm but conciliatory speeches in Reichenberg and Gablonz, no such outcome seemed remotely on the cards.

I was fortunate once again in running into two fellow countrymen well-versed, I presumed, in the problems with which I was wrestling. These were the British military attaché, Colonel Daly, and the British consul in Reichenberg, Peter Pares. Both were maddeningly discreet, but it was not difficult to see where their sympathies lay.

Colonel Daly could not be drawn, of course, on the effectiveness of Czechoslovak military precautions, but I did gather that both he and Pares were primarily concerned about the restrictions of civil liberty which were taking place under the law for the Defence of the State. Toynbee described this law in the *Survey of International Affairs 1936* as 'the most striking example of the organization of all the resources of a nation for the purpose of defence' and 'perhaps the most comprehensive and drastic of all the measures that had been and were being taken in various countries in preparation for a state of war. . . .'

It was not this aspect – whether the Czechs could actually hold off a German invasion – that seemed uppermost in the minds of the British representatives, but rather the grievances of the local population and the use being made of them by Nazi Germany to further German expansion. Czech defence was not considered. I heard later that Britain was even urging Henlein to take up the Defence Law at Geneva, so that the League could bring pressure on the Czechs to put internal security in these areas into Sudeten German hands. Fortunately nothing came of this, so that when the two test cases of Sudeten German 'revolt' were attempted in May and September 1938, both were easily and swiftly put down by the Czech authorities.

I reported my findings in the Sudeten districts to *The Observer*, writing a piece both on Benes' conciliatory tour and the negative attitudes of the Henlein Party. Neither was published. *The Observer* was increasingly taking a line of appeasement towards Hitler, and was strongly criticizing Benes and Czech policy generally. An innocuous piece I sent on the Czech manoeuvres was published. It carried the headline STRIKING POWER OF THE CZECHOSLOVAK ARMY, as if Czechoslovakia, and not Germany, was the would-be aggressor.

This new tone in *The Observer* put me in a difficult position. The enthusiasm with which the arrival of a permanent British correspondent had been greeted in Prague was wearing thin. Some argued flatteringly that I myself was the initiator of the paper's new line, others that I was not really a journalist at all. I was now writing for the *Spectator* too, but since the articles were unsigned, no one was to know.

It was inevitable that I should confide in Adam the anxieties I was feeling, although, in common with the great majority of his countrymen, he felt no affinity with the Sudeten Germans.

'Your countrymen even over the border drive me dotty,' I wrote to him. 'How can your country hold two such opposites together as the stillest and most beautiful country and the most disordered and almost, if you would not be hurt, ugly-minded people. Just sometimes one meets somebody as still and peaceful as the woods and then there is nobody better in the world – but how many and many one meets who seem to drive all beauty and stillness away. I am depressed. Reichenberg is hateful, I decided suddenly to leave, it set all my nerves on edge.

'I miss you and want so often to talk to you about the things which drive me dotty. It is the whole atmosphere, a sort of intensity which Germans have. It is almost as if they feel, rather than think, with their minds. Perhaps I am writing nonsense and you will say I am a journalist again. I want really to understand Germany and Europe. I will learn German until I can read your literature and history without faltering. . . .

'I ought to try and sort out all the stories I've been told and what they mean and what the solution of the Sudeten German problem is, but I feel so hopeless about it. It is always the same problem. What is the future of Europe? I wish we could solve it together. Alone it unbalances me very much. You are the only bridge I have to this unknown, rather feared and often hated world. Stay close whatever happens.'

'Thank you for your letter from the train,' he replied. 'My God, how often I think they are dotty and how true it is that their number is very many, and how much more awful it is to be dependent on them for something very serious that must be dealt with and cannot be dealt with by the lid theory which I'm afraid you subconsciously followed by running away from them. These psychological incompatibilities which are so painful for you and me (in the singular) will, if they are not dealt with rationally, no doubt stew up to the same kind of plural incompatibility that our fathers did not prevent and left to us in the shape of a messy deteriorated Europe.

'The point is we cannot stay close whatever happens because if that happens again, all Duff-Trott coalitions are going to be torn asunder.'

But I did not see the danger of war coming from 'plural incompatibility'. It was from one side and one side only that it threatened. One of the most disturbing encounters I had in the frontier districts was in Herrnskretchen, where I had decided to have a peaceful day by the river, reading *The Idiot*. As I was lying in the grass, a pleasant young man came along and sat down beside me. I tried to freeze him off, telling him I was Czech. Rather than leaving, he plunged into a political speech, telling me, 'England is finished; France is going under; Jews, Christianity and Communism are the three united enemies of Europe. The German race alone is *ehrlich* and must rule.'

For the first time in my life I felt nationalistic and wondered if it was not time to count my soldiers. I wrote angrily to Adam. We had

139

often argued about the 'lid theory' – that the only way to stop Hitler was to surround Germany with such a strong ring of defensive alliances that he would not dare to break out – Adam always pleading for a deeper understanding of the problem. Now I told him what Mowrer had said to me : 'If a man stands at your door with a pistol and says, "I want what you've got and if I cannot have it, I will kill you," you do not give it him and go away and think what is the cause and what is the cure of crime. You call in the police.'

Adam replied that his 'rational respect' for the 'pistolstoryman' had diminished considerably; he attacked me for 'the insufferable habit of journalism to pick up impressions of everyday life and elaborate on that substance an equally unbalanced and painful wrath by which nothing but the general confusion is furthered.'

This seemed to claim that everything which so horrified me was not the very essence of Nazi teaching, that the Nazis were not the rulers of Germany, that Germany was not rearming night and day. Why couldn't Adam see it? Did he feel no 'painful wrath'? Did he really think that what was happening in international affairs was simply 'general confusion'? If I continued, he said, to make myself 'the mouthpiece of our dear neighbours all over the place', I would 'bring on . . . the Spanish state in all Europe'. This really angered me. The Spanish Civil War was a deeply emotive issue for our generation in England, a *'Farbenkenner'*, as Isaiah Berlin had said, by which one could tell immediately where people stood politically. What did Adam mean?

'Remember who started the Spanish war,' I replied. 'Are we just to stand still and let them win over the rest of Europe, because if we do not let them, they will commit the same sort of atrocities here?

'I deny absolutely that any of the neighbours of Germany are a danger to her. Everyone is ready for peace and for the construction of some sort of European system. The only things they are not ready for are bilateral pacts which leave a very strong spider talking to a very weak fly.

'In the realm of spiders and flies, England is still the largest spider, though we don't seem to know it, and I think it is our job to look after the flies. This is why what I am trying to do is very remote from Spain. If it brings on the Spanish state in all Europe, it is the fault of the spiders. . . .

'I don't want to be made hostile to you, and am not made [so] because I am not a spectator and you an actor, as you believe. We are both spectators and actors at the same time and not so very much divided. If I were ever to become only a spectator, I would not watch this particular play. There are nicer ones to watch, wiser and more peaceful. I would have children and live in the country somewhere very remote and read books and bathe and have a farm.'

There were many times when that really was all I wanted, and after the war I achieved it. But it was not possible in the 'thirties. If I had thought it was, I would never have taken up the work I was trying to do; I would never have come to Prague. Adam reacted to my genuine perplexities and anxieties chiefly in terms of our relationship, almost as if my real desire was to quarrel. This was far from being the case.

No doubt I was tactless in my formulation of the problems and certainly when I got angry, my tone was quarrelsome. But 'It is not quarrelling really . . . ,' I wrote at the end of one of my tirades. 'I do beseech you to be determined and firm. When I am hysterical and stupid, the thing is to say so and not be distressed. And above all you must realise I am in deadly earnest about all this and it is important for us too. . . .'

And Adam, always responsive and generous, replied : 'Sorry to write distressed letters. I promise I won't do it any more. . . . But there must be a way out of the "world civil war" that is threatening to break out, with either side of which we are profoundly out of sympathy. . . .'

I let this pass, but it was not true for me. In this 'world civil war' I felt deeply committed to the side of freedom. The issue was not, as perhaps Adam was thinking, and certainly the appeasers in England were seeing it, a struggle between fascism and communism. Both were dictatorships. I believed in the democracy of the Popular Front, and in the loyalty of communist co-operation in it. If this was the parting of ways, I did not yet see it like that. We were on different paths in the dark wood but we still called to each other across the darkness, separated but not yet divided.

Our tragedy was that it was just what each of us most valued and most admired in the other that set us so painfully apart. We both felt that we must live our lives for a cause greater than ourselves, that we had an inner purpose to which we owed allegiance, and to which all else must be subordinated. Mine at that moment, as I had made it perfectly plain to Adam, was to frustrate Hitler and prevent war. These were exactly the purposes for which Adam was to give his life.

141

But because we were born in different countries and reared in different historical perspectives and with different philosophical attitudes, we had totally different conceptions of how this could be achieved.

Adam felt all this could be sorted out if we got things straight between ourselves on a personal level. But I suspected him of holding a view sometimes uttered in those days: 'He for God alone and she for God in him,' and I was far from convinced that that was where my God was.

In one of the letters he wrote to me in Prague he had said: 'Do you think that women too have a sort of primary inner purpose for which they must live and to which they must relate their relationships as something decidedly secondary? I don't think that in complete comradeship (as I have told you once before) that there can be any distinction between primary and secondary, because the very purpose is common. But is it not that the woman must to some extent recognise the purpose that works in the man and which, by a natural partition of their labours later on, must have a certain predominance in their life together? Of course she must have her entire sovereignty and independence in *judging* and sizing up that purpose and she will continually share in its elaboration, but must she not to some extent, if the thing is to be a success, *accept* it. . . . What troubles me still more is of course the intrinsic Germaness of the purpose I could offer for our life. . . .'

This of course was the crux, and perhaps at that moment in history there was no way out for two people such as ourselves. At least friendship, we thought, would transcend all national differences, and certainly it would eventually have done so, had Adam survived; but while this terrible confrontation with Nazi Germany was taking place, our 'primary purposes' had totally to coincide or else our personal relationship had to remain 'decidedly secondary'.

At this point, each of us was bent on pursuing our own path, and the paths were leading away from each other. That summer, as we walked in the woods of Imshausen, they had come very close. Soon after I left for Prague, Adam had written: 'What you say of emotional and political life is true enough. Who else could help me better than you? Clearly the root of both these concerns must be in one's own single heart and it seems as if God has sent you to me as the one chance of a true, single love.' The moving vision we had shared for one moment had flashed through the sky and was gone.

16

The summer of 1936 was now coming to an end. Ripka had returned from France and I was eager to check with him all the information, impressions, ideas and opinions I had collected during his absence. I waited anxiously for him to call me, and eventually he did so. He had found out a little about me from several of my press colleagues in Paris and especially from Mowrer, who had assured him that, naïve as I still was in many ways, I cared deeply about the political issues of the day and saw them very much as he and Mowrer did. It seemed that he was prepared to carry on Mowrer's job of turning me into a serious political journalist and, even more than Mowrer, to keep an eye on me in the rougher seas of Central Europe. In the terminology of Oxford, he became my tutor not only in politics and journalism but my moral tutor as well, protecting me, no doubt, from all sorts of dangers of which I was still unaware, and steering me towards the norms of conduct acceptable in Czechoslovakia.

Ripka had never been to England, had no contact with the British in Prague nor any conception of how English minds worked. I often saw a look of comical amazement on his face as I babbled away about my life and thoughts. He called me 'ma petite' and treated me like a child, but at the same time he took my work seriously and urged me to do the same. He expected a great deal from me.

A very hard worker himself, he practised what he preached. Like Mowrer, he drew his contacts from all the corners of Europe, and checked and counter-checked all his information. 'Il faut s'imposer,' he advised again and again. People, I found, stood in considerable awe of him.

That September he took me with him, as he had promised, to the Conference of the Little Entente – Czechoslovakia, Rumania and Yugoslavia – in Bratislava. Without his help I could not have attended, since *The Observer* refused my request to report the conference in favour of Fodor, their older and more established Vienna correspondent. Having no responsibility, I set out to enjoy it – and succeeded. In my romantic eyes Bratislava became another *Congress Dances*, the film of Vienna in 1815 we had all enjoyed so much at Oxford. Though none of the Danubian politicians or foreign correspondents had the looks or glamour of film stars, they were amusing enough to watch or talk to, and the flamboyant security arrangements added a strong theatrical atmosphere. The journalists were all lodged in Bratislava's two largest hotels which, conveniently placed back to back on two parallel streets, became one large complex with heavily guarded entrances back and front. This heightened both the hilarity and the tension which, as I had found in the Saar, surrounds any large assembly of the international press. The principal negotiators arrived for the sessions to the roar of sirens and hooters, with noisy outriders ahead of their fast, bullet-proof cars.

This was not the style of state events in the democratic Czechoslovak Republic but was in honour, I was told, of the much-hated Yugoslav Minister Stoyadinovitch. The latter, together with Prince Paul, was rapidly taking Yugoslavia into the Nazi camp, both in its foreign policy and in its internal police measures. When the lights went out at a great state banquet, where we were celebrating what was in fact the failure of the conference from the Czechoslovak point of view, we all fully expected shots to ring out. But when the electricity was restored, there sat Stoyadinovitch, annoyed but unharmed, and surrounded by his security guard, brandishing their pistols. The British journalists laughed.

The Little Entente was an alliance of the so-called Succession States, who had benefited from the dismemberment of the Austro-Hungarian Empire at the end of the First World War. Each member country had a sizeable Hungarian minority, and had pledged to help the others should Hungary try to seize back territories which had previously been hers. Each was also strongly opposed to any restoration of a Habsburg to the throne of Austria.

On these points the three countries were still united, but in 1936 they were no longer the real issues. Hitler was certainly not going to allow any Habsburg to return, and his plan for Austria was not that it should rejoin Hungary, but that he should annex it for himself. He also had his eye on the old Austrian province of Bohemia, especially

144

that part of Czechoslovakia where the Sudeten Germans lived. These were to be the bases of the great German empire that he planned to create in Eastern Europe.

At Bratislava the Czechs had hoped to extend the treaty obligations of their allies to foil this Hitlerian project, but neither Rumania nor Yugoslavia had a common frontier with Germany and they were too short-sighted to see the danger. They were foolishly reassured by Hitler's anti-Habsburg and anti-Austro-Hungarian postures. The doctrine of 'appeasement' was spreading fast throughout Eastern Europe, isolating Czechoslovakia from her neighbours as dangerously as the remilitarization of the Rhineland had isolated her from the West.

On the last day of the Conference, Ripka and I walked up the little hill outside Bratislava from which one can look down on three countries, Austria, Czechoslovakia and Hungary, each lapped by the disappointingly grey Danube. Intently, Ripka surveyed the whole scene.

I sat down on a rock and, watching this tall, silent figure, I thought how glad I was to have met him on my path; indeed how grateful I was for all those who had guided me on my way: my mother, through whose loss I understood so young the terrible evil of war; Douglas Jay, whose stern insistence on the 'real world' had taught me that one can and must do something about it; Edgar Mowrer, who had told me so clearly what it was that had to be done; and Nehru, who had shown me the great vistas that lay beyond. Even Goronwy and Adam, from whom I differed so deeply but whom I loved so kindly, had given me the lesson of this contradiction. And now Ripka, a passionate European, whose country was the exact point at which Hitler had to be held.

I thought of another small, far-away country where the imperial hordes of Xerxes had to be held in a mountainous pass. Was this then 'the noblest Kingdom of them all' and Ripka 'the most valiant of men'? I was proud to be at his side and waited for him to speak.

As he sat down beside me he said: 'We are the key to the Danube Basin and to the whole of South-Eastern Europe. We are your eastern fortress on the flank of the enemy. We must hold this fortress, come what may.'

I asked him if he thought war was inevitable.

'No, not inevitable,' he replied, 'but there is an irreconcilable conflict. Either Europe must submit to the domination of the Third

145

Reich or Germany must submit to Europe and become culturally and socially a member of the European community.'

'How does she do that?' I asked.

'Only by ridding herself of National Socialism,' he answered. 'It is a revival in a still more deadly form – because it is revolutionary – of the old militarist pan-Germanism against which Europe fought in the First World War. If the tradition of German humanism cannot reassert itself, then Europe must do it for them. That means to oppose, not to placate.'

I told him about Adam von Trott, of our great friendship and our mounting discord and fear of war. He listened sympathetically and said: 'If Europe is to be saved, the German nation must also be saved. The situation would not be improved by a war which could only lead to the defeat of Germany. It is not only the other European nations but above all the German nation which must be liberated from the yoke of Nazi oppression. Only after the destruction of Nazism will Europe be able to organize itself freely and to found, on the basis of the free federation of nations, the structure of a lasting peace.'

I told him that Adam would soon be coming to Prague and that I wanted very much for them to meet and talk; he said he would like this.

Unfortunately Adam's visit in October 1936 coincided with that of King Carol of Rumania. After the failure of the Bratislava Conference, the Czechs were particularly anxious that this visit should strengthen their ties with Rumania, which were vital for the implementation of the Czecho-Soviet Pact. Ripka was constantly occupied and even I got caught up in various state occasions. Worse still, perhaps, was the departure of summer. In Bratislava, well to the south, summer had still been there in all its joy; now, under the leaden skies of winter, Prague was engulfed in the dreadful grey darkness of Central Europe. All the gaiety and pleasure I had longed to share with Adam, the bright colours of the peasant women with their huge baskets of summer produce, the ceramic market with its colourful wares, the whole summer scene by the river and the shaded gardens and cafés on the hills, all these were gone. Under such unfriendly skies, I found it hard to recapture my original delight or even that of my friendship with Adam.

The meeting between Adam and Ripka was disastrous. Worn out by serious discussion all day, Ripka and Borovicka arranged another 'bombe' for late in the evening. I had seen much of Borovicka all that summer and written indiscreetly to Adam of the effect on me of his views concerning the opposition between Europe and Germany. 'I understand your professor friend hating us,' Adam had answered, though I had never mentioned hate. 'I respect it : but there's no use for the future in this whole source of political reflection.'

Fortunately Adrienne, Borovicka's wife, had now become a close friend, and I knew Adam would love her. She was the most beautiful woman I have ever known, not only in her classical features and shining brown eyes but in the gentleness and sweetness of her expression. I loved her and her little teenage daughter very much; they were the gentlest part of my life in Prague. I was very glad she was going to be there that evening of the 'bombe'. I knew Adam would respond to her beauty and she to his : but the men did not like each other. When Borovicka took his wife from Adam on the dance floor, Adam danced with a call-girl and brought her back to our table. The reception was frigid. Adrienne alone saved the situation.

Much more important from Adam's point of view was his meeting with Otto Strasser, founder and leader of the anti-Nazi *Schwarze Front*. I had met Strasser with Wenzel Jaksch and had been favourably impressed. They both came to my room to meet Adam. This was very brave of Adam, for Strasser was feared and hated by the Nazis. Until 1930, he had been one of their leaders, and his brother Gregor had been murdered on Goering's orders on 30 June, 1934. Jaksch was undoubtedly the most active and effective of the Sudeten German anti-Nazis. Both were well-known in Prague.

Of what use it was to Adam to meet them, I never knew, but he wrote afterwards to me : 'I think you know how good old Neill [we had agreed to refer to Strasser and Jaksch by the names of my brother and his wife] was very important for me to meet, for whatever his detail [*sic*] qualities are, his will is determined and he will not make mistakes out of fear, though perhaps out of lack of thought. I am thankful to you for being my link to him.'

Perhaps Adam's visit was not the disaster I thought. Nevertheless, I felt contrite when he had gone. 'You are quite right to reproach me,' I told him, 'and I am very sorry I do not help you or give you any impression that I am near and strong and solidaric. Yet it is not true that I underestimate you. I admire you very much and especially lately and if you win through this crisis alone, you will be glad in the end you were able to do it and I am nearer than you think. . . .'

147

Was I, I wonder? Perhaps I was further away than I thought at the time.

We met twice more before Adam left Europe. (He was going first to America and then on to China.) In December we both stayed in Berlin with his and Diana's friend Wilfrid Israel. One of the bravest and noblest of the Jewish leaders, Wilfrid was a man of great grace and culture. I liked him very much. Then in early February 1937, just as we were planning where and how we would spend our last week together, Mowrer sent me a telegram asking me to undertake 'an important assignment in Western Europe'.

I knew at once that it must concern the Spanish Civil War, and that here was a direct choice to be made between 'primary aim' and 'personal relations'. I tried to reach Adam by telephone to discuss it, but he was in transit between Berlin and Leipzig and, if I was going, I had to leave at once for Paris. My mother, who had been staying with me in Prague, was the bearer of the news when she left next day for Imshausen; she carried a letter of explanation asking him to meet me in Paris.

I felt I had little option over accepting the assignment, though Adam, I knew, would not agree. He had challenged me earlier when I had written : 'I'm afraid I love the world very much just in the way Christians were always taught not to love it. It is so beautiful and moving even when it is terrible and wicked. This Spanish thing moves me terribly. Every newspaper is what Malraux says Art should be, "an attempt to give man a consciousness of his own hidden greatness". I hate the killing and suffering even of the side with which I do not sympathise, and it makes me love all the more my baroque streets and the flower markets and the river.'

To my generation the Spanish Civil War appeared as one of the great battles of human history and its mythic quality moved us all. It touched, as Arthur Koestler has written, 'the collective archetypes of human memory . . . and caused the last twitch of Europe's dying conscience'.

In Paris I discovered that my mission was even more directly related to the struggle than a straight newspaper assignment. Malaga had fallen to Franco and no newspaper correspondent had yet been allowed in. Koestler, representing the *News Chronicle*, had been caught there and arrested as a Republican spy. The Spanish Government wanted a report on how Republican prisoners were being treated, whether the fascist Powers were fortifying Malaga harbour,

148

and information about what had happened to Koestler. Mowrer was prepared to cover this mission with a *Chicago Daily News* press card but he could not send any of their staff correspondents because of the paper's well-known anti-Franco line.

He thought of me, not altogether flatteringly, as someone who might slip in unnoticed. The intermediary with whom all this had been arranged, and whom I met for a short briefing in Mowrer's car as we drove round Paris, was introduced to me as André Simon. Mowrer had spoken of him highly as 'a Jew with a duelling scar', exactly the combination Mowrer would admire. In fact he was Otto Katz, a Comintern agent later executed after the Stalinist trials in Prague in the 1950s. It was he too, I learnt later, who had been responsible for sending Koestler into the Civil War.

I protested my total ignorance of both Spain and its language and made the point that I had never flown in an aeroplane or been outside Europe. I was told that I had to take a circuitous route through North Africa and approach Malaga from the south. Tickets would be provided for me as far as Tangier but then I was on my own; all I had to do was to get to Malaga. 'How?' I asked. 'Oh, stand by the side of the road with a bunch of flowers in your hand and an Italian officer will give you a lift,' said Mowrer sarcastically, and more reassuringly, 'Once you're there all you have to do is to contact the American consul. He is a stout supporter of the Spanish Government and will tell you everything we need to know.'

I reached Malaga, unaided I am glad to say, in a bus from Algeciras. To find the consul was more difficult, since there were no taxis, the streets were deserted after nightfall and when I reached his house, it was protected by a huge garden wall which I had to climb. The maid who came to the door would not let me in till the consul himself appeared. He invited me in to dinner, but my fellow guests were Nationalist staff officers and it was clear, from the few moments that I was alone with him, that this was the side that had his sympathies. Conversation at dinner was exclusively about the horrors of Red rule, and when my fellow guests conducted me back to my hotel, which turned out to be Franco's staff headquarters, they insisted on producing photographs of the horrors they had been describing. One of them became angry when I showed unwillingness to look at these pictures, but the other two were bright and friendly. On their part it was more a flirtation than a political encounter. Suddenly one of them looked at his watch. 'Good heavens!' he said.

'Twenty minutes to midnight! Do you want to come to the execution with us?'

Silence fell and all three looked at me. I felt confronted, as I had never been confronted before, with a stark choice the consequences of which would stay with me for ever. For a young journalist it would be a sensational coup; for a spy it was precisely one of the things I had been sent to find out; for a human being, it would be to stand and watch people whom I regarded as friends and allies being put to death in cold blood. I knew I would never be able to live with this. I did not go.

I awoke to spring sunshine and went down to the terrace. Little orange trees in tubs had been rolled into the garden and the fruit was warming in the sun. There were swallows flying low over the water and the sky and the sea were shades of the same deep azure blue. The young men were having their breakfast. Still in military uniform, they now had revolvers at their belts. I thought of Prague with its leaden skies, the snow piled in sodden heaps in the gutters, the ill-clad Czechs shuffling along with their shoulders hunched against the cold. I turned to one of the officers and said: 'How can you have a civil war when you have a country like this where the skies are blue and the sun is warm in February and the swallows are here already?' 'You are talking like a Red,' said the angry one of the previous night. 'May I see your passport?'

Mowrer had made me ask the British Consulate in Paris for a new passport because my old one had a Soviet visa in it. The effect of this three-day-old passport was dramatic, and immediately raised the questions of who I was and what I was doing so near the front when no journalist had yet been given permission to come there. Luckily they were due at the front themselves, but the angry one said he would be back that evening and would have me sent to Seville for a full investigation.

I had no intention of going to Seville or being investigated, so I had only this one day to find out what Mowrer wanted. I bluffed my way through the juvenile guards on the harbour gate and ascertained that no fortifications were being built. I attended a summary court trying Republican prisoners and learnt how the sentences carried out at midnight were reached. The British consul told me that Koestler was probably in Seville, awaiting investigation.

That evening I went early to bed and next morning I caught the first bus to La Linea. I strolled past the long line of cars held up at the frontier and walked, trembling but safe, into Gibraltar.

As instructed, I cabled my findings to the *Chicago Daily News*, then crossed over to Tangier, took a train to Oran and flew back to Paris. Adam had been waiting for two days but was enjoying his first visit to the French capital. He did not understand or agree with my passionate commitment to the cause of Spanish freedom, and even questioned on which side it was to be found. But any hard feelings he may have had soon evaporated. We travelled to London together and I took him to my home. We parted in mutual confidence, aware that our relations had stabilized on a lower level but were still hopeful and strong.

On the boat carrying me back to the Continent, I wrote to him: 'It seems so very final getting off this boat and returning to the depth of Europe – that I must write. . . .

'Bless you, dear Trott – I am pleased with you and think you not in such need of blessing as you and I have been during the last year and a half. We are getting stronger to deal with this hard world, and we will be happy and good allies.

'I thank you for all you have done for me, and it was very much, for without your encouragement and kindness I don't think I could have been brave, and one has to be jolly brave.

'The boat's engines are stopping, and we are in the dark harbour. I feel a little like going into a dark jungle and you across the open sea – but we will cut the European trees down, and make it a fine place to live.'

And Adam, who was about to leave for America, replied:

'Don't have that final feeling. Europe is not the world and the world must belong to us and support our bond as Europe did. You are splendid and brave and I will try and be the same. In all this haste and turmoil here, your memory has stood out clearly as something very special and very precious to me. We will not lose each other. We will not be captured by the fatal round of things. . . .

'Your country has been very kind to me. I am glad you belong to it and yet are so free and so strong to be away.

'Well, Duff, the rush and sweep of the big waves of your Atlantic will soon lie between us. But it's all right. I, too, am pleased and content and I know there's nothing fatal or final to divide us.

Love always,

A.'

17

My visit to London had been useful if somewhat salutary. I had called on *The Observer*, to find not my sympathetic friend Hugh Massingham, but Mr Harmer, the news editor to whom I had sent my copy from Czechoslovakia, so little of which had ever been printed. He expressed himself satisfied, but I tried to explain the difficulty of my position in Prague. The increasingly pro-Hitler and anti-Czech line being taken by *The Observer* was causing some apprehension, and as their correspondent, suspicion could not fail to fall on me. I told him that the local Foreign Press Association had in fact questioned whether I was really a *'journaliste de profession'*. Harmer showed little sympathy : correspondents did not dictate editorial policy and the Editorial Board had been joined by Lord Lothian who, after his meetings with Hitler, was convinced that appeasement was the right policy and that carping at Germany must stop. I also learnt that Henlein was a frequent visitor to London, and that Sir Robert Vansittart, Chief Diplomatic Adviser to the Government, had taken him up and was making sure that he received the maximum publicity not only in the British press, but also in influential circles.

From Thomas Balogh, always a well-informed source, I heard that my position in Prague was much worse than I had outlined to Harmer. I was widely considered to be in the pay of Germany : my visits there had been watched, my meetings with Germans in Prague had been taken note of and special enquiries had been made in London as to who I was and what I was doing.

This was corroborated when I visited the Czechoslovak Legation. Kraus, the nice press attaché I had seen before going to Prague, was rather solemn on the subject but said the matter was now closed. Jan Masaryk, the Czechoslovak Minister, with his great charm and genial dismissiveness of anything embarrassing or unpleasant, pooh-poohed the whole affair.

Tommy Balogh, however, gave me a stern warning to mend my ways : 'Never meet a German in Prague, suspend all correspondence with Germany. Be good, and if you can't, be very careful. Don't forget you are almost a war correspondent.' Even more helpfully, he commissioned me to be the Prague correspondent of a new paper being set up in New York, *The Financial Observer*. Gerhard Schacher, the Prague 'stringer' for the new *Manchester Guardian Economic Weekly*, would write on economics, while I was to cover the political scene and to correct Schacher's Germanic English. Since I strongly suspected Schacher of being the source of the calumny against me, I was delighted with this arrangement. Alas! it did not last. After two issues the paper closed down. All the same, my appointment had shaken Schacher and convinced the Press Association that I was after all, a *'journaliste de profession'*. By then, however, I was more interested in a new commission which my old Oxford friend Jane Rendel had arranged for me : to write a pamphlet for the New Fabian Research Bureau, of which she was now the Secretary. I wanted to write about the political and strategic importance of Czechoslovakia in Europe but the Fabians, like everyone else in England in those years, were more concerned about the Sudeten German minority. We compromised on *'German and Czech: A Threat to European Peace'*.

It was with hopeful purpose but also a little dread, therefore, that I returned to Prague in the early spring of 1937. It was only to Ripka that I could tell the whole story : of my experiences not only in London but also in Paris and Spain. Mowrer had forbidden me to mention the latter to anyone, either in London or in Prague. Ripka was exceedingly angry – not about the aspersions against me, which he dismissed contemptuously as mere tittle-tattle (*'Ce sont des idiots'*) – but about my foolhardy involvement in the Spanish Civil War. He berated my 'imprudence' and Mowrer's irresponsibility. Not only was Mowrer risking my safety quite unnecessarily but he was actually damaging the cause which all of us cared about. Spain was a dangerous and perhaps deliberate distraction from the real thrust of Nazi aggression in Central Europe. It was Spain that was frightening the French Government, who thought they might be encircled on the Rhine, Alps and Pyrenees, and preventing them from concentrating on their only hope of security : Hitler's fear, because of

France's Eastern alliances, of having to fight a war on two fronts.

Furthermore it was grave 'imprudence' on Mowrer's part to involve himself, never mind me, with an agent of the Comintern like Otto Katz. Fear of the Bolshevik danger was one of the strongest weapons Hitler was using to terrify the French, the British, the Czechs and the whole of Eastern Europe. Co-operating with undercover agents fed, and even appeared to justify, this fear. The only way to combat it was by an open and avowed policy of co-operation with the Soviet Government at Geneva and by strengthening the military clauses of the French-Czech-Soviet defensive alliance. These alone could implement the collective security obligation of members of the League of Nations.

Ripka had told me before, and he repeated it now, that the real reason why the Czechs could co-operate with the Russians (which neither the Poles nor the Rumanians dared to do) was because of their strongly democratic social and political system. Czechoslovakia had no powerful bourgeoisie or aristocracy frightened of losing their privileges, and its large Communist Party, though not represented in the Government, strongly defended the independence and integrity of the country.

I asked about the Czech Agrarian Party, whose leaders were always being quoted as opponents of Benes and sympathizers with Henlein. Ripka shrugged his shoulders contemptuously. 'They're members of the Government, aren't they? Our Prime Minister, Hodza, is not only one of them but a Slovak to boot. Of course Nazi propaganda is rife among them as it is rife everywhere else with the twin arguments about the Bolshevik danger and the "rights" of the Sudeten German minority.' Henlein was the Nazis' tool for both purposes. If he could persuade either the Western Powers or the Czech Agrarian Party that his 'rights' entailed either membership of the Government or autonomy for the Sudetenland, the Franco-Soviet defence system would be in ruins : in the first eventuality, because Czechoslovak foreign policy would be redirected towards co-operation with Nazi Germany and in the second, because Czechoslovakia's entire defence system would fall into German hands.

I told Ripka of the commissions I had brought back with me from London. He was specially interested in the pamphlet for the NFRB and hoped it would mean that I would 'at last' settle down to some serious work.

This I did. Although I was still writing occasional pieces for *The*

Observer, my difficulties with the paper had in no way lessened.

It was in the middle of May that an article by Garvin finally provoked me to resign. I did so in a three-page letter to the Editor, in which I argued not only against his presentation of the problem of the German minority but against his assertion that the pacts with Russia signed by France and Czechoslovakia threatened to drag Europe into war.

'Chronologically,' I wrote, 'these pacts followed the refusal by Germany to take part in a pact sponsored by Great Britain, which was to guarantee peace between Germany and Soviet Russia as well as the independence of the sovereign states of Germany's Eastern frontier.

'It was and still is the intention of the Czech Government that their pact with Russia should be neither aggressive nor exclusive, and Germany's adherence to it (which would be a safe and certain way of breaking through what she considers encirclement) would be most warmly welcomed. I agree this is not "realistic" but probably no country desires this more fervently than Czechoslovakia.'

I ended with the famous quotation from Sir Eyre Crowe's Memorandum on British policy towards Germany before the First World War : that England must be the natural enemy of any country threatening the independence of others and that as a great empire we had obligations as well as rights. 'To pass the leadership of further Europe to a country which denies the ideas which Europe stands for, is gravely to shirk these obligations,' I told Garvin boldly. He, however, was not going to argue with a junior correspondent.

'After considering in the light of long experience, the points you put and a good many others as well, I differ most deeply though in perfect friendliness with the view expressed in your letter,' he replied. 'In resigning your connection with the Observer you do what you think right. For more years than I care to count, Czechoslovakia and the regions and races now included in it, have been a close study of mine.' On this letter the signature was undeniably a rubber stamp.

It was in the early summer of 1937 that relations between Germany and Czechoslovakia took a sharp turn for the worse and a major hate campaign was launched in the Goebbels press. We now know, thanks to General Moravec, the head of Czechoslovak Military Intelligence, that vital breakthroughs had been made by both the Czechoslovak and German Intelligence services. Inevitably this produced considerable tension on both sides of the border and especially, of course, in the highly sensitive Sudeten German region. The campaign in the German press was largely devoted to the alleged ill-treatment of German nationals arrested by the Czechs as spies. Its aim, I pointed out in an article in the *Spectator*, was simply one of intimidation. Both Czechoslovakia's allies, the Soviet Union and France, were badly weakened at that moment by internal crises – Stalin's terrible purges in Moscow and acute economic and social upheaval in France – and if England could now be alienated Czechoslovakia would be isolated and at the mercy of Germany.

Ripka urged me to do something more to alert opinion in England. Could I not get into direct contact with people who had some influence? I sat down and wrote to three leading Members of Parliament: two whom I knew personally, Hugh Dalton of the Labour Party and Wilfred Roberts of the Liberals, and one whom I did not know except from his constant warnings against the dictators, Winston Churchill.

It was in Churchill that Ripka was primarily interested. Ripka knew Dalton already from his visits to Prague and Geneva, but it was Churchill who represented to him, as to all those on the Continent who wanted to stand up to Hitler, the authentic voice of a country which – they still thought – stood for freedom and justice, the protection of the weak against the strong, peace against aggression. So, on 19 June, 1937, I wrote boldly to Churchill :

'I believe I am a cousin of Mrs Churchill's so I hope you will forgive the liberty which it is to write to you when I do not know you, but the matter is so important that I think it should justify itself.' Describing at some length the unusually acute tension between Germany and Czechoslovakia, I continued : 'Information has reached this country that our foreign office is hesitating. I am writing to ask you to do everything in your power to make our attitude firm and unfaltering. The crisis has never been so great and I am convinced that only a stand on our part can overcome it. Czechoslovakia is, for the moment, almost entirely dependent on us.'

Churchill replied : 'Thank you so much for your letter which I have read with great interest. Both Mrs Churchill and myself hope that when you come to London you will let us know as it would be very nice if you would come down here to luncheon one day.'

I don't think I was offered a meal by Dalton or Wilfred (the latter was another of my mother's seventy-two first cousins, so he did not really need to), but both replied that they would do what they could.

156

18

It was on a beautiful summer's day in July 1937 that I went to luncheon at Chartwell and began an association, lasting fourteen months, which I hoped would save Czechoslovakia from destruction and Europe from war.

I believe Churchill would have summoned me whoever I had been, for his unremitting endeavour at this time was not only to amass all the information he could about the dangers that threatened us, but equally to 'procure allies and associates for what could before long become again the common cause'. I hoped that both Czechoslovakia and I myself were such allies, and my hopes were not disappointed.

Churchill had no prejudice and no snobbery about whom he saw or where he got his information. I was surprised at some of the people I met in the grandeur and elegance of Chartwell, but who they were I have forgotten since I never thought to record it at the time. I may have owed my first invitation to lunch to the fact that I was a kinswoman of Mrs Churchill's (we were both descended from the Ladies of Alderley, but had never in fact met). I am sure that Churchill cared not a fig about such matters, but I think it made a difference to Clementine Churchill that I came from the realm of family life, could be friends with her daughter Mary (who was then sixteen years old and kept goats, one of which she gave me), and could laugh at family jokes and at our eccentric relations.

Our families were in no way close, even though Chartwell was less than twenty miles from High Elms. I used to motor over from there, but until I took my mother (whom Clementine had not seen since they were girls together) there had been no visiting between the houses. I have written enough in my first chapter to show that there was little reason why there should have been, and a letter in my

157

possession from my grandmother to my mother on the occasion of Clementine Hosier's engagement to Winston Churchill reveals every reason why there should not have been. There was only one mutual relation who frequented both houses and this was Sylvia Henley, a great friend of my grandmother's and Clementine's, but no go-between.

None of this counted for anything with Churchill. He wanted to see me simply and solely because I had lived for a year in Czechoslovakia and could perhaps give him useful information. He sat me beside him at lunch and I did my best. As I have already said, I cannot remember who else, apart from the family and Horatio Seymour who lived on the estate, was there. I know from Martin Gilbert's biography who was not. This was Sir Ian Hamilton, who wrote to Churchill a few days after this luncheon : 'I am rather glad I missed Miss Grant Duff because I should have differed from her too violently. Except the Masaryks, there are no distinguished persons among the Czechs. They are, in fact, a most harsh and disagreeable lot and to put those 3,000,000 *Sudeten* Germans under them has been a very bad business indeed.'

This was typical of 'informed' British reaction in those days : class snobbery against the Czechs and the idea that the Sudeten Germans had been 'put under' them. Czechs and Germans, as I had to keep repeating, had lived side by side in Bohemia for centuries, behind exactly the same frontier that still separated them from Germany. Admittedly, in Austro-Hungarian days the Sudeten Germans had felt themselves superior because theirs was the State language and it was they who enjoyed all the privileges which accrued therefrom, but if they were now a 'national minority', at least they were equal citizens of a democratic State. Churchill was less concerned with their grievances than with their disaffection and how far this could cripple Czechoslovak defences. The Czechs, he said, must 'pander' to them to the greatest extent possible without impairing the security of the State or its power to defend itself. 'They are in a very dangerous situation,' he told me. 'Heaven knows whether in a year's time the country will still be there.'

I do not know whether at that stage I had told Churchill of Ripka, or revealed that it was Ripka who had prompted me to write to him. Churchill nevertheless gave me advice which Ripka wanted, and obviously expected, me to hand on. 'They have a sporting chance,' he told me, 'if they arm well, build fortifications, behave circumspectly, be careful of getting too left and involved and hold tight to the League of Nations.' This advice, I am sure, Ripka made full use of in his political struggle inside the country.

For someone as young and inexperienced and unknown as myself, this meeting with Churchill was a great privilege, and as the whole party strolled on the lawn after lunch I felt tremendous elation and hope. As we walked through the gardens to feed Churchill's beloved black swans which floated on the lake he had spirited into existence, I remembered that great expanse of water at Blenheim which his forebears had created and where we had skated that day in 1933 when Hitler came to power. 'An explosion of some sort is inevitable in Germany,' Churchill said. 'If Germany is sufficiently tightly encased by a strong alliance system (call it Geneva, nobody minds about that), the explosion will be inside Germany and get rid of this gang. A military revolution would at least put people in power who could be spoken to, who would understand what they could do and what not, and who would hesitate at crime.'

If Britain was strong, he went on, we could discuss on even terms the redress of grievances. Without a firm stand on our part and with our allies, we would be driven 'helter skelter across the diplomatic chessboard until the limits of retreat were exhausted'. I said this was how the Czechs felt about the grievances of their own Germans. People like Ripka fully recognized these grievances, but while Hitler and a rearmed Germany threatened their very existence it would be disastrous to give way or make any real concessions.

Churchill saw this point immediately, but the British Legation in Prague still interpreted delay as 'Benes' bad faith'. The 'Czechs are an obstinate people,' Basil Newton, the British Minister in Prague, wrote in October 1937, 'with whom fear may more easily breed hatred than readiness to yield.' And yet, from this point on, it was the weapon of fear which the British Government used, in addition to the growing intimidation from Germany, in order to coerce the Czechs.

As I drove back through the Weald of Kent that afternoon, I tried to memorize everything Churchill had said and to get clear my feelings about him. There was a long backlog of prejudice against him in the country, from which I was not altogether immune. I had never heard him praised either in my family or by any of my Oxford contemporaries. The latter condemned his part in the General Strike of 1926 and the former regarded him as erratic and unreliable. Even

159

before my meeting with Nehru and my total conversion to his cause, I had accepted the general view that Churchill's attitude to India was archaic and impossible. Now, having met him face to face, all this fell away. Admittedly we were allies on a quite different front, but there was something more than this. He did not have the charismatic effect on me which Nehru had had. Churchill was to produce that for all England, myself included, in 1940, but he did not produce it now. I did not see him as a great leader, but rather a strong and curiously noble man, totally without spite or rancour or pettiness of any sort.

In the years since I had grown up and gone out into the world, I had not been very impressed with my own countrymen. Mowrer was an American, Nehru an Indian, Ripka a Czech. But here, suddenly, was a great Englishman, someone who actually made one proud to be English and who set a standard to live up to. I thought of the reaction in the Legation in Prague when I had said that there were things I put higher than British interests. Here was the proudest, most assertive Englishman we had, and yet I was sure I would never have had such an argument with him. His whole concept of what British policy should be was related to those higher interests, to the vision of a world order based on the freedom of nations and the freedom of individuals, on the rule of law, on the principles of mutuality and reciprocity, where the security of nations would stand on a much higher foundation and where Great Powers would be concerned with their duties and obligations and not their petty 'interests'. I saw him thinking of Czechoslovakia not as a small, tiresome and artificial State, but as part of a great whole, of a great community of States large and small, where each had a part to play, where each had rights, to which all contributed, and where bullies were kept down. 'We must all fight our own corners as well as we can,' Churchill was to write to Lord Linlithgow, 'each in his station great or small.'

I knew at once that he and Ripka would see eye to eye and be able to communicate; in spite of the vast disparity of their relative positions in the world – Churchill a great patrician in a great imperial country : Ripka, a forester's son in one of the smallest, newest and most vulnerable States of Europe – they were both loyal representatives of their countries. As human beings, dedicated to a great purpose above and beyond their personal concerns, they were worthy to stand side by side. I was very proud to be the mediator between two such men and in such a cause.

When I left Chartwell that afternoon, Churchill shook me firmly

10 Edgar Ansel Mowrer in 1970

11 Hubert Ripka, *c*. 1946

12 The author at a press conference in Prague, *c.* 1936

13 Hubert Ripka in Bratislava, September 1936

by the hand and told me to keep in touch, and Clementine and Mary said they hoped I would come again.

19

Although Adam was now far from this scene – he arrived in Hong Kong in August 1937 – the flow of letters between us continued. The will to communicate was there, but both of us found writing more difficult over the immense distances of space and time and the intruding disparities of experience.

Adam had arrived in the Far East just as the Sino-Japanese war had broken out. Experiencing at first hand the suffering caused by war, he became a little impatient and angry with the rumours of war in Europe, of which, he felt, I made too much. I had told him of my fears in mid-summer 1937 and, very briefly, of my visit to Churchill.

'I know Churchill is "nearer the thing",' he replied, 'but isn't he a war monger? And isn't the "lid theory" as unsound as it always was? Your intended "internal explosion" will blow the lid up – a cynically conservative attitude cannot take it on to educate the explosive forces : a paternal, or better, a fraternal conservatism might. Don't make yourself a wire in a cynical game of Central European power politics . . . don't get bitterly and peacelessly involved in a conflict which must, if you are to remain yourself, be outside your reach.'

Had this letter arrived at a moment of stress, as later letters from Adam were to do, I should have been angry, but at that moment, the autumn of 1937, all was relatively calm and I was chiefly worried about the bombs falling around him. I myself had had a beautiful holiday with Jane in the Western Isles and with François, my communist Swiss friend, near Camaret. After meeting Isaiah and Stuart Hampshire at the Paris Exhibition, I had travelled home joyfully with Isaiah to be met at Victoria Station by Goronwy. The brief re-emergence of this gentle world to which both Adam and I had belonged, made me nostalgic for the past and critical of my present life and the role I had taken on.

'You are right,' I wrote to Adam, 'and I must not get bitterly involved in all this. . . . I care awfully, but sometimes it all seems a mad, dangerous game in which one only has to be braver than everyone else and dare them out and I get excited instead of religiously wanting to save the world. There is no saving. I can't save myself or Diana or Goronwy so why did I suppose I could save crowds? Only a little of life is political and we try and make it all political. It is waste and wicked.'

Waste and wicked? That was not what I had learnt from Nehru. 'Politics are not the whole of life,' he had said to me, 'but the groundwork of life. Today one is forced to take part in them : at every turn one is threatened or hurt so that the natural reaction is to try and prevent this through politics, or at least try and alleviate the evil.'

So there was no turning back from the path I had chosen. This time I really was committed – to Ripka, to Churchill, to Mowrer, to all those I had met on my way who cared about the struggle, all those now threatened and who could be so terribly hurt if the evil of Nazi Germany were not checked. I was even committed by the NFRB pamphlet, now published, which had brought sympathy and support and requests for articles, as well as reaching a public, I hoped, beyond those normally associated with foreign affairs in England.

I went back to Prague and Berlin that autumn and, as I had promised, reported to Churchill about the two most significant developments, the visit of Lord Halifax to Goering and Hitler and that of M. Delbos, the French Foreign Minister, to France's erstwhile allies in Eastern and Southern Europe. The message of both was the same : Germany was inexorably turning the tables on the Western Powers. 'It is now Eastern Europe which is frightened to commit itself in a West European quarrel,' I told Churchill. 'Poland, Yugoslavia and Rumania are trying to pursue an equivocal policy which will allow them to come in on the winning side if there is war. If only we could prove to the Eastern neighbours of Germany that we are the winning side, the war might be prevented altogether.' This, however, had not been the impression we had created, or indeed wished to create, during Halifax's visit to Germany.

'I was there just after Halifax's visit,' I wrote to Churchill, 'and was told by British diplomats that the purpose of our foreign policy was now to "get right on our side". This they said we could do by giving way as much as possible, primarily in Central Europe. The Germans, they said, would not enter into any general settlement about Central Europe because they are so certain that time will bring it into their hands in any case. They are convinced that we would be neutral if they attacked Czechoslovakia.' 'I don't believe they are quite convinced,' I added, 'nor had they better be.'

'To read again,' Churchill noted on the letter as he left for a month's holiday in the South of France; to me he wrote : 'Pretty bleak !'

It was to get rapidly bleaker. I was in Yugoslavia in February 1938 when the news came of Eden's resignation. 'It is widely believed,' I reported to the *Manchester Guardian* from Belgrade, 'that German and Italian influence played no inconsiderable part in Eden's downfall.' The resignation was received joyfully in Balkan Government circles and without much sign of mourning in the British Legations. These Little Entente countries, who had once placed their faith and their security in the League of Nations and their French alliances, were now using British policy as an excuse for coming to terms with the dictators. 'Pro-British' was an alibi for 'anti-French'.

Nor were they unduly disturbed when Schuschnigg, the Austrian Chancellor, visited Hitler at Berchtesgaden and promised to introduce Nazis into his Government. Back in Prague at the beginning of March 1938 I found the Czechs watching with alarm a preview of what they could expect if, yielding to British pressure, they took Henlein into their Government.

They did not have long to wait. Alarmed by the tremendous crescendo of Nazi activity, desperate to preserve the independence of Austria, and certain that this was what his people wanted, Schuschnigg suddenly took a decision which at any other moment in history (except when Hitler ruled in Berlin, Mussolini in Rome, Chamberlain in London and no one in Paris) would have been accepted as the right and rightful course for a Head of State. He declared a plebiscite, to be held on Sunday, 13 March, in which the Austrian people simply had to answer Yes or No to the question whether they were in favour of a 'free and German, independent and social, Christian and united country.' The voice of the Austrian people would be heard. Surely it would be respected?

It was then 9 March and the Czechs held their breath. They were certain that Hitler would never allow a vote on this issue which he had not stage-managed himself, but how would the Stresa Powers (Britain, France and Italy), who, only two years before, had pledged themselves to uphold the integrity and independence of Austria, react?

In those two years a great deal had happened. Mussolini had joined Hitler in the Rome-Berlin Axis. Chamberlain had informed Hitler, personally through Halifax at Berchtesgaden and through his ambassador in Berlin, that the British Government was sympathetic to his aims in Central Europe, especially in so far as they concerned people of German blood (neither the Austrians nor any of the minorities had ever been German citizens). France was in the throes of deep social and political conflict and had no Government. Hitler decided to invade Austria, 'if other measures proved unsuccessful', and knew he could do so with impunity.

Ripka had left for Paris at the start of the crisis. Benes had to know how his French allies were reacting and, since the Chautemps Government had fallen on March 8 and no new administration had been formed, official channels were hampered.

I decided to go to Vienna. Taking the night train, I arrived early on the morning of Saturday, 12 March, as the German armies were invading Austria. Under intolerable pressure from Berlin, Schuschnigg had resigned the previous day. I did not see the German troops from the train : Goering had issued orders that the soldiers were not to approach within fifteen kilometres of the Czechoslovak frontier. Czechoslovakia's time had not yet come.

Nazis were in evidence everywhere. In Vienna itself, the entire population seemed to be out on the streets, intoxicated with excitement, rushing about, shouting, waving banners : those dreadful swastika spiders were everywhere. Lorries careered up and down carrying boys with rifles and shotguns slung over their shoulders, the streets were filled with police cars, black police vans, ambulances, their sirens blaring.

And then came the German troops rolling steadily forward like a grey wave.

I had never seen an army on the march. I had been at military church parades in places like Dover Castle, where I had stayed as a child. I remember even then being moved by the hymn-singing of those bare-headed soldiers. I had seen them at the Cenotaph on Armistice Day. Was it only because they were my own soldiers that the sight of them inspired pity and compassion? These grim, helmeted men excited anger and dread. I thought of *All Quiet on the Western Front* and the days when young soldiers on every battlefield had been the object of our pity and compassion. What sin against the Holy Ghost had Hitler committed to change all this?

In real anguish I wote to Adam. I feared deeply that he would not understand.

'It is difficult to write to you after these days in Europe, especially since I am sure that from China they appear just and inevitable and long overdue. I do not know how I can explain to you that now war has become a certainty and that there is no turning back on either side. It will seem so just to you that that which the social democrats desired [in 1931] should now be achieved, that it was so right of them to desire it, so justified now to achieve it. How can I explain to you in these circumstances that to desire it was a betrayal of the European idea, that the means by which it has been achieved has plunged Europe into the gloom of knowing at last that war is inevitable, that we fight on the same old dreary plane of imperial interests on the one hand, of a war to end war, and a war to make democracy safe on the other.'

Disgusted by everything I saw and heard in Vienna and fearing for what might be happening in Czechoslovakia, I returned almost immediately to Prague. I found the Czechs incredibly calm. They had been officially reassured three times by the German Government, twice personally 'on his word of honour' by Goering, that Germany had no malign intentions whatever towards Czechoslovakia. Neurath, still German Foreign Minister, but later the head of the German Protectorate of Bohemia and Moravia when Hitler annexed the remnant of Czechoslovakia in 1939, personally reassured the Czechoslovak Minister in Berlin 'on behalf of the Führer', not only in the same terms as Goering, but adding that Germany still considered herself bound by the Arbitration Treaty of 1925. Whether or not the Czechs believed these assurances, it was obvious that in the absence of any move by the Western Powers they had no alternative but to try to keep calm in public and in the press, and to avoid involvement in any way. The Czech army did not mobilize.

The people who were not calm, of course, were the Sudeten Germans. Every nationalist heart was filled with immense excitement and overweening pride and confidence that their own 'liberation' could not be far off. The situation I had seen in the Saar now really did reproduce itself and the Sudeten German anti-Nazis were terrified. They heard what was being done to people like themselves in Austria (76,000 were arrested in Vienna alone), and saw their desperate but thwarted attempts to escape. 'Central Europe has become the scene of a man hunt,' I told Adam. 'In fear all countries are shutting their frontiers so that the hunted are like rabbits in a warren, nets on all the holes and ferrets sent in.'

All those Germans who had collaborated with the Czechs or spoken against National Socialism were marked men and openly threatened and jeered at. The 'Activist' parties – those who had served in the Government of Czechoslovakia – all now deserted the Czechs and two of them ran for cover. The German Catholics and Agrarians quickly dissolved their parties and rushed for shelter inside the Henlein Party, which boasted that 212,000 new members had joined in March alone, an increase of 37 per cent on their existing membership. The Social Democrats could not stoop to such measures but Jaksch immediately took his party out of the Czechoslovak Government and adopted a strong nationalist tone.

From now on it was Henlein who was in the saddle, and even had the Czechs not realized that it was with him alone that they must now deal, the British Legation in Prague and the Foreign office in London were bringing heavy pressure to bear on them to this end.

Before I left Prague for London, I paid a last visit to the German Embassy. I had a contact there called Herr von Chamier, a diplomat of the old school, a Junker. Always before, I had been received with a suave politeness. This time it was different.

'I . . . was talked to', I told Adam, 'in a tone of incredible brutality, a tone new to your countrymen, which shows not an added bitterness but a growing contempt for every restraint. "We cannot of course, expect England and France to be pleased to discover that they did not, after all, win the war," he said, and when I said how horrible were the arrests and suicides in Vienna, he answered, "Wir lachen nur darüber." Oh Adam, one feels horribly, horribly betrayed. Why was one brought up to believe the war a horrible crime if all that was important about it was who won it?'

Adam never answered this letter in any detail. Before he received it, but after he had heard of the *Anschluss*, he wrote that I would have to 'revise a good number of [my] premises'. After this there was an unusually long gap in his correspondence with me and a letter in June admitted that there had been 'a certain amount of hostility in [his] silence'. This, he said, was because of my 'aggressiveness', which he could understand and forgive from 'Bohemia' but which was intolerable 'as the pathos of an excitedly successful modern English

167

publicist'. 'We should think still a little more about avoiding the catastrophe by constructive means and attitudes than building strategic positions for the event of its happening,' he wrote. 'If it does, all is up anyway.'

This was precisely the argument of the appeasers whose 'constructive means' meant not only the sacrifice of our 'strategic positions' but also the sacrifice of whole nations like the Austrians and Czechs, and of any hope of an international order based on the assumption that statesmen spoke the truth and abided by their given word. The terrible debasement which National Socialism had brought into international life was that not one of their leaders – or even those non-Nazis like Neurath, Weizsäcker, Schacht and Papen who served them – spoke the truth.

Nor, of course, were the British people being told the truth by their own leaders. Back in England, I was appalled not only by the ignorance of ordinary people about what was going on in Europe, but by their attitude that this could all be left in the hands of the Government and the Foreign Office who were perfectly entitled to keep their activities secret. In so far as I met anyone remotely in touch with official life, I was amazed at how misinformed they were. It was Czechoslovakia and not Germany who was regarded as a threat to peace, not only because she was an artificial State who should never have been allowed to exist in the first place, but because now, it was being said, she was deliberately provoking Hitler by her abominable treatment of the Germans who should never have been subjected to her. People simply did not know that Czechoslovakia was a democratic country with no concentration camps, where Germans actually were freer than they were in Nazi Germany and better treated than any other national minority in Europe. The Czech alliance with France, they said, proved how anti-German she was; her alliance with Russia, that she was part of the 'Bolshevik menace'. It never occurred to anyone that, with her first-class army and huge economic war potential in Skoda and other large armament firms, she might actually be of some value as our ally and certainly of some danger to us if this war potential fell into German hands.

At this time, Penguin Books were bringing out a series of sixpenny 'Specials' on the problems of the day. They were sold on the bookstalls of every railway station in England. Mowrer had just published one on China and a leading French correspondent, Geneviève Tabouis, had written a book about the European crisis entitled

Blackmail or War. They now asked me to do one on Czechoslovakia. I was very glad to do so. There was little time, I feared, for people to hear what was really at stake before irrevocable decisions were taken.

I had just started writing when another crisis blew up in Central Europe. It was the weekend of 21 May, 1938, and I had invited the Third Secretary of the British Legation in Prague, who was home on leave, to stay at High Elms. On the Saturday morning he was suddenly ordered to return immediately to Czechoslovakia. I decided to go with him.

Municipal elections were being held that Sunday in Czechoslovakia. This meant that Germans outside Hitler's control were voting, and some of the candidates were Social Democrats. A scenario not unlike that which preceded the invasion of Austria existed once again. There was the same aggressive and excited local Nazi party rearing for battle, and a Government desperately trying at once to keep order and to prevent anything which might incite intervention from Germany. There was the same tense international situation and finally even the same rumour of German troop movements, reported all over the British and European press.

The British Ambassador in Berlin was assured in the Wilhelmstrasse that these rumours – initiated actually, though in error, by his own military attaché, Colonel Mason MacFarlane – were without foundation, but quite rightly he pointed out that a similar assurance had been given him at the time of the *Anschluss.* Weizsäcker, the German State Secretary, did not wince.

Czechoslovak Intelligence had received similar reports of German troop concentrations, and there were widespread incidents and violence all over Sudetenland. Since their most important military task was to avoid being taken by surprise before they had time to mobilize, the Czechs now mobilized one class of reservists as well as specialized troops. The response was overwhelming. The notices went out at 9 pm on the evening of May 20 and by 3 am next morning, 70 per cent of the reservists were in their places and all the frontier posts were fully manned. Only sixteen men out of 174,000, I was told, had failed to report, whereas 20 per cent of the German reservists, the Czechs insisted, had failed to turn up for the Austrian invasion, during which there had also been widespread chaos in their motorized transports. The efficiency of the Czech mobilization did not escape the notice of the British military attaché in Prague, now a Colonel Stronge, whom unfortunately I never met, and whose reports were not listened to in

London.

The effect in the country was miraculous. All incidents ceased immediately, the calculated German war of nerves was called off and the elections were held in complete calm. More than 20 per cent of the Sudeten Germans still dared to vote against the Nazis.

The whole morale of the Czech people seemed to have undergone a change from the days immediately following the *Anschluss*; the preternatural calm which had made me wonder then whether the Czechs really knew what was happening, had been replaced by jubilation. People in the streets were smiling and laughing as they stopped to talk to each other, and my own friends among the Czech journalists and in the Czech Foreign Office were delighted.

I was staying with the Ripkas, having handed over my own flat to a young Englishman in business in Prague. Ripka was much reassured by the situation. Not only had the Czechs managed their own internal affairs with extreme vigour and efficiency, but above all the Western Powers had at last intervened; the effect had been as he, Mowrer, Churchill and anti-appeasers everywhere had always predicted : Hitler had climbed down.

I called at the British Legation, expecting to find the same confidence there. Instead, I found fury and dismay at the widespread 'misjudgement' of their actions. Hitler and Ribbentrop, they said, had been needlessly angry at our Ambassador's intervention which had, after all, been only 'enquiries' but was now being represented as protests, 'ultimata' even, after which the British would 'take action'. The special railway carriage ordered by the British naval attaché in Berlin, to take him and his family together with some of the children of his colleagues back to England on holiday, had been reported as an evacuation of non-essential personnel from the British Embassy. Rumours of impending war had spread throughout Germany with the most dire results. It was quite untrue that there had been any German troop movements, and as for the Czech mobilization, even the French had protested to Prague about that. It was a deliberate act of provocation by Benes, and I would see shortly how dearly he would have to pay for it. Hitler would never put up with the slap in the face that the Czechs were now boasting they had delivered. British efforts would have to be redoubled to save the situation and make the Czechs see sense.

Much alarmed, I returned to Ripka. I had told him already about opinion in England and how few people realized what was going on;

how Henlein had spoken at the Institute of International Affairs at Chatham House and was the pet of the Foreign Office. Henlein had been in England just before the elections and had even been invited to lunch by Churchill and to tea by Harold Nicolson. This meant that the Nazis were now making a set at the Opposition, as well as trying to influence the Government.

Ripka looked very grave and asked me what part Jan Masaryk, the Czechoslovak Minister in London, was playing in all this. I told him I was sure Masaryk was doing his best, but I feared he was not nearly tough enough. He had an immense desire to please and knew that neither his cause nor his country pleased the British at all. 'They can't even pronounce the name of my country,' he told me once. 'They call it Czechoslavia or Yugoslavakia, but then give up and say, "Oh that's the place nice Jan comes from." ' He was popular in many circles in England but feared to risk his popularity. The impression he had given at the Foreign Office after the visit of the French Prime Minister and Foreign Minister, Daladier and Bonnet, in April was that he was not 'surprised or grieved' by 'the very disturbing conclusions' the British and French Governments had reached about the military situation, and recognized that the Czechs would have 'to go a very long way indeed' to appease the Sudeten Germans. Masaryk seems to have told the Foreign Office that if pressure was to be put on his Government it would not be resented, provided it was the British and French who were applying it and not the Germans.

Ripka was very disturbed, and we decided that he should go to England himself. I was leaving shortly and promised to arrange for him to lunch with Churchill and, if possible, for him to address a meeting at Chatham House.

Once in London I saw Arnold Toynbee, the Director of Studies there, and he made several objections : time was too short; a Sudeten German would have to speak at the same meeting; the fact that Ripka would speak in French meant that few people would come. I was very insistent and eventually a small meeting was arranged for late June when Ripka would be arriving in London.

The lunch with Churchill was a great success, as I knew it would be. Both Winston and Clementine spoke French and both took to Ripka immediately. He had great charm and good manners and relaxed with warm appreciation in the beautiful setting of Chartwell. The food was exquisite, the wine was good, the Churchill family were amusing and friendly, and political understanding was spontaneous.

171

Churchill was particularly interested in Ripka's assessment of France's reliability as an ally.

On 23 June, Churchill wrote an article in the *Daily Telegraph* warning Germany that, if attacked, Czechoslovakia would not be left to struggle alone. France, Russia and eventually Britain would all be drawn to help her. Ripka had insisted, as he always insisted to me, that the Czechs would fight if attacked, as indeed they would have done.

Ripka and I were delighted by Churchill's response. Masaryk, I am afraid, was not. He had not been invited to the lunch and was both astonished and annoyed that a 'mere Czech journalist' should have had such a welcome. Masaryk, I suspect, treasured Sir Ian Hamilton's view that 'Except the Masaryks there are no distinguished persons amongst the Czechs.' Jan was a very human and rather touching personality, lonely and melancholic though constantly cracking jokes, very musical – a 'private face' who should never have been in a 'public place'. Because of his great father, greatness was thrust upon him. He was forced to be the representative of a country in which he had never actually lived – for he was an Austrian by birth, had fought the war in the Austro-Hungarian Army, and had not joined the Czechoslovak Legions who had come over to the Allies. Through his American mother, he became a businessman in the United States after the war and married an American wife. The marriage ended rapidly and disastrously and Jan went almost straight from this to being Czechoslovak Minister in London – a post he filled admirably until the situation became serious.

He tried as best he could to serve his country : he never showed bitterness to his friends who had betrayed it, and he fought valiantly for its recognition and restoration after the war. When, in 1948, Benes gave in to the Communists and Russians as he had given in to the Nazis and British in 1938, Masaryk alone of his Ministers accepted a post in his new communist-controlled Government. A few days later he was found dead below a high window of his Prague flat. It has never been definitely established whether this was suicide or murder. Deep tragedy it certainly was and the end of a tragic life.

But now it was another tragic end which was being prepared : the end of the Czechoslovak Republic just twenty years after its foundation.

20

After Ripka's return to Prague in June 1938, it was decided that I should stay in England, both to keep communications open between Prague and London, especially between Ripka and Churchill, and to write the book which Penguin had commissioned.

Allen Lane and his brother were then the most dynamic and most successful popular publishers in England. They cared passionately about their books, which they saw as a kind of open university, bringing before the public, at a price which everyone could afford, not only a whole range of literature and culture but up-to-date information on a vast number of subjects.

My book was to be one of a new series of Penguin Specials on current political issues. The latest had been *Mowrer on China*, and they wanted to call mine *Grant Duff on Czechoslovakia*. To my protest that no one had heard of me, Allen answered brightly: 'But that's just the point. They'll think they ought to have done.' I was amused, but my respect for Mowrer prevailed. We debated other titles – *Why Czechoslovakia?* or *Will Czechs Fight for Great Britain?* – but eventually decided on *Europe and the Czechs*, since it was the future of Europe and not only that of the Czechs or even Great Britain that was at stake. In the end the two titles we had rejected were given to the first and last chapters, which tried to explain why Czechoslovakia was the focal point of the crisis and how calamitous for our own interests the shift in the balance of power would be if the Czech armies were to be wiped out and all their vast arsenals and military potential were to fall into Hitler's hands. In the rest of the book I dealt briefly with the historical background, showing why Bismarck, although he believed that 'he who is master of Bohemia is master of Europe', nevertheless left this frontier intact; how the Sudeten Germans came to inhabit its mountainous fringes, and how

173

for better or worse, they were an integral part of the Czechoslovak State. I also described how the pan-German fervour of Hitler's Germany was seeking to destroy this polyglot, democratic country.

I was under fierce pressure both to get the book out as quickly as possible, but also to keep it up to date with a rapidly changing situation. The last development I was able to cover was the departure of Lord Runciman for Prague at the beginning of August as an 'unofficial investigator and mediator'. Even then, Penguin could only guarantee publication before the end of September if I contributed my royalties on the first 50,000 copies towards the cost of the speed-up. I agreed, but stipulated in return that Penguin should present a free copy to every Member of Parliament.

The dispatch of the Runciman Mission to Prague was widely acclaimed as a generous gesture of genuine British concern and commitment. It was undertaken, Mr Chamberlain assured Parliament, 'in response to a request from the Government of Czechoslovakia. . . . With regard to the rumour that we were hustling the Czech Government, there is no truth in it. Indeed the very opposite is the case. Our anxiety has rather been lest the Czechoslovak Government should be too hasty in dealing with a situation of such delicacy.'

Ripka telephoned me from Prague with a very different account of what had actually taken place. When Basil Newton told President Benes of this new British move, Benes had been so upset that he threatened to resign. The Czech Generals felt that their Government had already gone as far as it was militarily safe to do towards meeting the Henleinist demands, and they feared that the Mission would now press for more concessions. Benes had finally given in only under pressure from his own 'appeasers', who included the Slovak Agrarian Prime Minister Milan Hodza.

When I passed this information to Churchill, he replied : 'We cannot help them if they do not hold together. Let them look to their own defences.'

I handed this on to Ripka. He was fighting a desperate battle, not only against the potential capitulators within the Czech Government, but equally against those who would gladly have crushed the Sudeten Germans and driven them out of Czechoslovakia, as eventually all were to be driven out after the war, innocent and guilty alike. The tensions inside the country were reaching breaking point. Wenzel Jaksch, who visited London that summer on behalf of the

Sudeten German Social Democrats, praised Ripka highly as one of the most courageous leaders in the country.

The deepening fear and anguish of all those directly threatened by Hitler and his followers were in stark contradiction to the complacent words with which Chamberlain had dismissed Parliament for the summer recess : 'I believe we all feel that the atmosphere is lighter (*hear, hear*) and that throughout the continent there is a relaxation of that sense of tension which six months ago was present (*hear hear*).'

Churchill took no holiday that year, but kept in the closest possible touch with a situation in which he had no influence other than the power of his patriotism and his personality. Always he used it loyally, arguing directly with members of the Cabinet, tackling Halifax and Chamberlain in person and handing on to them any information he received – from a German officer, for instance, about the opposition to Hitler within the Wehrmacht – which might elucidate the situation or stiffen their courage.

The Runciman Mission was doomed to failure from the outset. Armed only with the good intentions of peace-makers, its members soon realized that their one chance of success was to come to an agreement with the Henlein Nazis. The latter now took their orders quite openly from Hitler, and these orders were that no agreement was to be reached. Henlein's instructions were 'always to negotiate and not to let the link be broken', but, 'on the other hand, always to demand more than could be granted by the other side.'

While the Henlein Party prevaricated, Runciman was under great pressure from London to obtain some results before the Nuremberg Party Rally at the beginning of September. Hitler, who was due to make the closing speech on September 12, was expected to use this occasion to bring the crisis to a head. Similar pressure was brought to bear on the Czech Government, and eventually, against strong opposition and with great reluctance, Benes finally accepted all Henlein's demands on September 6. On a flimsy pretext, Henlein broke off negotiations. Runciman and his aides were left waiting at Schloss Rothenhaus, the castle of Prince Max Egon von Hohenloe Langenburg, for Hitler's emissary to come and tell them what the next move was to be.

Ripka telephoned me from Prague to say that negotiations had finally broken down, and that he was sending me details which he wanted me to communicate to Churchill. I replied the next day :

'Your letter did not arrive. I could only tell C[hurchill] what you had told me on the telephone. He thinks our policy of putting pressure on you is at an end, and that they, like Runciman, accept that you have gone far enough. He told me to tell you that in any case you must pay attention to no one so far as your military defences are concerned and that you should take all possible precautions against the [German] military manoeuvres in Silesia.

'He is seeing Chamberlain one of these days. They are trying to push the Government into the only thing that can save peace – a strong joint declaration with France and Russia. But this is *very* confidential and I beg you not even to tell B[enes] where it comes from. He saw Masaryk last night and I do not believe he talked to him about this, but since I believe we will be at war if those gangsters start anything, it is only patriotic to keep one's allies informed.

'Do not give in. We have need of you. C[hurchill] has a good opinion now of the Russians and people think America will support us morally and perhaps militarily within a few weeks. . . .

'We will support you. Opinion here is now very anti-Nazi and the whole country will be united if anything starts. C[hurchill] hopes there might even be a change of Government in Germany. . . .'

Very few people in England, and apparently none at all in Czechoslovakia, knew of the opposition to Hitler's war plans within the German High Command, or of the plot associated with Dr Carl Goerdeler, General Beck and others to seize Hitler by force as soon as he gave the order to invade Czechoslovakia. They then intended to put him on trial before the People's Court. Among those who did know were Chamberlain and Halifax, but they dismissed the plotters as being reminiscent 'of the Jacobites at the Court of France in King William's time'.

It was barely a month since Chamberlain had welcomed the relaxation of tension and blandly denied any desire to 'hustle the Czech Government'. The greatest hustle of all was now produced. On 7 September, in a leading article, *The Times* gave its support to the most extreme of the Nazi demands, the complete cession of the Sudetenland to Germany. Whether Chamberlain or Halifax were privy to the publication of this leader has never been established; it caused such outrage that neither would ever have dared to admit it. The future Foreign Editor of *The Times*, Iverach McDonald, then the paper's correspondent in Prague, hinted at the truth (except for his first five words) when he wrote : 'From the highest of motives both men wished *The Times* to give its own push to events and on September 7 it gave that push.' Despite the *dementi* by the Foreign Office and Runciman's attempt to reassure the Czechs and to coax the Sudeten Germans back to the conference table, the harm had been done. Runciman instructed McDonald to complain to his Editor that the article could not have come at a worse moment.

The Nuremberg Rally was now in full swing, the daily incantations against Benes and the Czechs being received with fierce and sinister baying by the huge crowds massed in the stadium. The war of nerves had reached its height and the moment of crisis, Hitler's speech, was approaching.

Though the violence of his language exceeded all bounds, Hitler actually crossed no Rubicon; he merely kept alive the fiction that it was the interests of the Sudeten Germans that were at stake and that the initiative must come from Prague :

'My demand is that the oppression of three-and-a-half million Germans in Czechoslovakia shall cease and that its place be taken by the free right of self-determination. We should be sorry if through this our relation to other European States should be troubled. But in fact the fault does not lie with us. Besides, it is the business of the Czechoslovak Government to discuss matters with the representatives of the Sudeten Germans and in one way or another to bring about an understanding.'

Chamberlain never took up this cue, and Runciman was no longer in a position to do so.

The speech was the signal for an uprising in the Sudetenland. But despite the long summer of preparation in which a Sudeten German *Freikorps* had been trained in Germany for precisely this moment; despite the German armies massed on the frontiers; despite the seizure of Czechs living in the Reich as hostages to be executed in reprisal for any Sudeten German court-martialled in Czechoslovakia, the 'revolt' was a total flop. It was effectively suppressed within twenty-four hours. Martial law had to be put into operation in only sixteen of the forty-nine German districts, and the Czech Army was not mobilized.

On 14 September the German Minister in Prague sent a Top Secret Urgent Despatch (No. 481) to the German Foreign Ministry :
'Reliable information yields following picture :

177

Leader's staff of Sudeten German Party is in session in Asch as a sort of revolutionary committee without any revolution, and without any contact with Henlein who is said to be staying in the neighbourhood of Asch. General helplessness and nervousness. The majority of the Sudeten German population demonstrated Monday night after the Führer's speech and then went home. Calm prevails everywhere today with the exception of two places near Eger. . . . Information just received puts figure of dead at four Czech gendarmes and two Sudeten German officials. All rumours require checking.'

Once again, as in May, the Czechs had proved themselves perfectly capable of dealing with their own situation. However, Chamberlain was still determined not to let them be the arbiters of their own fate. It was at the very moment when the revolt had collapsed, without one single German soldier being moved across the frontier to give it assistance, that Chamberlain decided to put into operation a plan which, he later explained, he had had in his mind 'for a considerable period as a last resort'. He sent a message to Hitler proposing that he should fly to Germany for a meeting.

To the British public, ignorant of all that had gone before and even of what was happening in Czechoslovakia at this moment, it seemed a daring and imaginative initiative. In reality, it was the last move in a ruthless campaign to deprive the Czechoslovak nation of all participation in decisions affecting its own survival : the final fruits of Halifax's visit to Berlin in 1937 and the appointment of Nevile Henderson to Berlin and Basil Newton to Prague.

Chamberlain flew to Berchtesgaden on 15 September. There was no consultation whatever with the Czechs, who believed that France was still their ally and committed to their defence, and that their territorial integrity was in no way open to question, even by the British, who had, after all, officially repudiated the *Times* leader advocating the cession of the Sudetenland.

In fact, it was only after Chamberlain had actually landed in Germany that this demand was even put forward publicly by Henlein. In his letter to Hitler enclosing the draft of a proclamation to that effect, Henlein wrote : 'It is probable that Chamberlain will propose such a union.'

This was not the version given at the time, nor later by Sir Nevile Henderson, the British Ambassador in Berlin. According to him, after three hours' talk alone with Hitler, Chamberlain 'finally accepted that principle for himself and undertook to consult his Cabinet and to endeavour to secure its consent to it and likewise that of the French and Czech Governments'.

Nothing of this was told to the Czechs. Chamberlain flew back to London to hold a Cabinet meeting on Saturday, 17 September, and to see the French Prime Minister and Foreign Minister the next day. He also received a delegation from the Labour Party.

Now, of all times, it was essential to try to let the Czechs know what was being planned. I tried hard to find out, seeking out everyone who might tell me.

On the Sunday evening I wrote to Ripka, confident, as one could be in those days, that the airmail letter would be on his table the next morning.

'I have the impression that things are going very badly,' I said. 'The Labour people who saw Chamberlain yesterday (this is very confidential but quite exact) got a very bad impression. They are not allowed to talk but I have the distinct impression that Chamberlain has a plan, acceptable to Hitler, which he will impose on you, on the French and on public opinion here.

'I informed Churchill at once and asked for reassurance. He said he had not been informed, has no idea what is going on but that he too has the impression that there is some "miserable plan" which Chamberlain and the Government will try and get accepted. He is confident that if Chamberlain tries now to get you to capitulate to the Nazis, that it will let loose a tremendous campaign here and that the country will split. Churchill himself is going to make a very strong declaration on Wednesday. . . . Churchill says everything depends on the willingness of the Czechs to fight at all costs. In that case, if Germany attacks you, the situation here will change immediately.

'He thinks Germany may attack any time, and the more you establish order in the Sudeten Germany districts, the more necessary this aggression becomes. In the case of a German attack, it is absolutely certain that we will march.

'As a member of a big nation, I am ashamed to say that it is up to you to give us an example. God knows you've given us enough proof already but you must do it again. If Hodza tries to tell the British press that the Czechs are willing to negotiate, shoot him. It won't do any more. It's no longer a question of the Czechs being pacific but of them being brave. If they are ready to fight, people

179

here will be ashamed. I tell everybody everywhere that it is absolutely certain that you will fight. They are sceptical.

'I dare not think of Prague and of you.'

This letter arrived in Prague on the same day that the Czechoslovak Government was informed that Great Britain and France were both backing the German demand to annex a very large and vital part of Czechoslovak territory.

A few days earlier, Ripka, together with a group of fellow journalists and politicians of all parties, had formed a secret council to prepare a plan of action. In Czechoslovakia, just as in England, France and Germany, there were those who wanted to give in and those who wanted to resist Hitler. Few people realized that the struggle was not between countries but inside each country, that the issues at stake transcended national boundaries and day-to-day problems. Even more was at stake for Czechoslovakia than the secession of territory.

Everyone knew that cession of the Sudetenland would mean the end of the Czechoslovak State, but States can rise again. What Benes feared was even worse.

He feared that if the Western Powers stood by while Czechoslovakia was set upon by Germany, Poland and Hungary, the massacre could be so great that the nation itself could be wiped out. What the forces of resistance – and Ripka was one of the leaders – dreaded was something more terrible still : that a nation which does not fight when its very existence is at stake, suffers wounds from which it may never recover.

On behalf of himself and his friends, he sent Benes a strongly worded letter, begging him to stand firm and assuring him of widespread support :

'It depends solely on you whether we shall capitulate or fight. I am aware of the risk of resistance : We may be defeated. But a defeat would not destroy the nation's moral force . . . while capitulation means moral and political disintegration now and for generations to come, from which we could not recover. I implore you not to be influenced by the reluctance and cowardice of some of our politicians.

'Do not hesitate to apply exceptional procedures and measures : You will see that an overwhelming majority of the people will stand behind you. So far people stand firm but the nation's morale will not stand for long. Otherwise disintegration will follow. I am telling

180

you frankly and this is the opinion of many of my
prefer the most terrible risk of war to humiliating cap
will destroy everything that is clean, strong and decisi

'It would indeed be the first time in our history that w
without a fight. We cannot permit such a devastating s

On 20 September President Benes called a meeting of
slovak Government, attended by the Chiefs of Staff. The London
proposals were rejected unanimously.

At this crucial moment, confident that the Czechs were standing
fast, Churchill left for France to visit his friends in the French
Cabinet. The tenuous link between Churchill and Benes was
broken. That night, at 2 am, dismayed that the Czech Government
was still refusing to accept the terms laid before them, the British
and French Ministers in Prague called on President Benes. After a
long day of dreadful shock and anxiety, he had been in bed for one
hour.

Basil Newton, the British Minister, produced a Note from the
British Government threatening the Czechs that if they did not
'take account of realities', the British Government would 'not take
responsibility' for the situation. 'The French Government,' wrote
Churchill, 'at least were sufficiently ashamed of this communication
to instruct their Minister only to make it verbally.' Verbally, however, the French Minister went still further than the British. If the
Czechoslovak Government did not accept unconditionally the
Anglo-French plan, Czechoslovakia would be held entirely responsible for having provoked any war which might ensue, and France
would take no part in it. The Czechs' most important ally had
deserted them.

The two Ministers stayed with Benes till 3.30 am, and at 6.30 am
on 21 September Benes called a Cabinet meeting which lasted till
late in the afternoon. During that day both the Polish and Hungarian Governments entered the lists, demanding Czechoslovak
territory, so that the Czechs knew, should war break out, they
would be invaded not only by Germany but by these Powers as
well. Of all her allies, only the Soviet Union assured Czechoslovakia
of any support. But the right wing in the Czechoslovak Government
were strongly opposed to resistance with Russia as the sole ally,
thus adding the threat of internal dissension to that of invasion.
Truly, decisive, however, had been the behaviour of England and
France. All the rest followed from this.

At five o'clock that afternoon, 'yielding to unheard of pressure', as they said in their Note, the Czechoslovak Government accepted the Anglo-French demands. 'Czechoslovakia,' wrote Sir John Wheeler-Bennett, 'who had faced with courage the threat of her enemies, bowed her head to the desertion of her friends.'

Churchill returned from Paris to find the pass sold. How, he asked me, could Benes have done such a thing? Churchill knew all the political and military circumstances, the months of unrelieved pressure, the disgraceful betrayal, the threatened massacre and destruction by Luftwaffe and blitzgrieg, but perhaps was not fully aware of the stresses of life in Prague. I tried to describe the President's personal and physical suffering, dragged exhausted from his bed and faced with a decision of this terrible nature. Churchill replied : 'A statesman who holds the fortunes of his country in his hands must eat well and he must sleep well. He should never have got up from his bed to receive the British and French Ministers.'

I remembered this when, after the inevitable war had been fought, I read Churchill's account of how, during all these years of crisis, including the war itself, he had always been able to 'flop into bed and go to sleep after the day's work was done'. Only on one occasion, he confesses, did he have a sleepless night. 'I lay in my bed, consumed by emotions of sorrow and fear.' It was the night of 20 February, 1938, when Eden resigned as Foreign Secretary and Chamberlain took control of British foreign policy. 'I watched the daylight slowly creep in through the windows and saw before me in mental gaze the vision of Death.'

One can imagine Benes, seven months later, on that night of 20/21 September, looking out over the beautiful, sleeping city of Prague. The vision of death was conducted to the door by the British and French Ministers.

After the Czech decision to submit had been taken, Ripka went with some friends to see Benes. 'Though he was a man accustomed to stand fatigue without showing signs of it, he was quite unrecognisable . . . ,' he wrote later in *Munich: Before and After.* 'We saw before us a man who was physically worn out and morally crucified. . . . In a voice which could scarcely be heard, he said to us, "We have been disgracefully betrayed." '

On 22 September Chamberlain flew to Godesberg with the Czech surrender in his hand, only to be told, as the Czechs had been told by Henlein every time they yielded to Sudeten German demands, that this was not enough. New demands were made. The areas in question were to be occupied immediately by German troops; nothing should be removed, neither arms from the fortifications, nor state property, nor industrial or commercial equipment – not even cattle from the farms. There would be no vote for those who did not wish to live under Nazi rule; they could vote with their feet before the soldiers poured in, leaving all their possessions behind.

For a few hours even Chamberlain seemed to see the iniquity of Hitler and the futility of appeasement. He retired to his hotel and reported unfavourably to London, where Halifax and the Foreign Office took it upon themselves to warn the Czechs and to remove the previous British injunction against mobilization. General mobilization was ordered in Czechoslovakia on September 23, even before Chamberlain left for England. The Soviet Union issued a statement through her Foreign Minister in Geneva that she was ready to stand by her treaties with France and Czechoslovakia. France ordered partial mobilization on 24 September, and the British Fleet was mobilized on 27 September.

The Czechoslovak mobilization once again went like clockwork. By the evening of 25 September thirty-eight divisions, more than a million men, were in position, ready 'in their strong protective screen of fortifications' to resist the advance of the German Army. Hitler had lost the 'important element of surprise', and the Czechs, 'operating on interior lines, having precise and detailed knowledge of the country and its resources, [and] short lines of communication to their supply depots and arsenals', had almost the entire 'balance of strategic advantage'.

This was the burden of the report sent to London by Colonel Stronge, the British Military Attaché in Prague. And to his opposite number in France, Colonel Moravec, the head of Czech Military Intelligence, witnessing his army's mobilization and calculating that the Germans had only the minimum number of divisions on the Western Front, sent a message ending : 'Your regiments can start marching with their bands in front.'

On 26 September, when Chamberlain and Daladier were meeting in London, the French Commander-in-Chief, General Gamelin, reported in similar terms to a meeting called by Sir Thomas Inskip, the Minister for the Co-ordination of Defence, and attended by the Service Ministers, Lord Gort, the Chief of the Imperial General Staff, and senior staff officers. France, he said, was prepared to attack in the west where the Siegfried Line was far from complete and France's twenty-three divisions were faced by only eight German divisions. The Czechoslovak Army had thirty-four divisions opposing a like number of German units. In his opinion they would fight well, aiming to hold the bottleneck between Silesia and Austria so that the main body of their army could, if forced to retire, retreat and fight on in the east of the country. When questioned in London, Gamelin reiterated that the Czech Army was a good one, had good troops, efficient commanders and an excellent morale considering it was an army of people fighting for their lives.

Even without knowing these military details, we were all greatly heartened until Ripka telephoned me on the evening of 27 September to say that the British were again putting great pressure on the Czechoslovak Government. Not only were further propositions about the transfer of territory being put to them, but these were being accompanied by still worse threats. Chamberlain himself had sent a telegram to Benes warning that if the Czechs did not accept the German conditions by 2 pm the next day 'Bohemia would be overrun by the German Army and nothing which another Power or Powers could do would be able to save your country and your people from such a fate. This remains true whatever the ultimate result of a world war might be.' A quarter of an hour later a further Note was dispatched. In this the threat was even clearer: 'whatever might be the result of a world war, the present Czechoslovak frontiers would never be restored.'

I at once telephoned Churchill. He was very angry with me. Only the previous day he had himself seen Chamberlain and Halifax and they had assured him that all pressure on the Czechs was at an end. Did I, he asked angrily, really need to draw the attention of the Czechoslovak Government to the statement in the press that morning, issued by the Foreign Office, that should a German attack be launched on Czechoslovakia, 'France will be bound to come to her assistance and Great Britain and Russia will certainly stand by France'? The consultations of the last few days had been not only between the heads of the British and French Governments but between the commanders of their armies. What more, he shouted, did the Czechs want? They were having me on and I had better 'take care' – and he all but slammed down the receiver.

None of us then knew that Chamberlain in fact had never

changed course and was still bent not only on coercing the Czechs but persuading the French not to fulfil their treaty obligations to Czechoslovakia. Hitler was to have whatever he wanted, and all Chamberlain wished to know was what that was. To this end, he dispatched Sir Horace Wilson once again to Berlin. Although their meeting was stormy and Hitler made a still more inflammatory speech abusing Benes, his reply to Chamberlain still left the door open. Chamberlain sent an excited reply :

'After reading your letter I feel certain that you can get all the essentials without war and without delay. I am ready to come to Berlin myself at once. . . . However much you doubt the Prague Government's intentions, you cannot doubt the power of the British and French Governments to see that the provisions are carried out fairly and fully and forthwith. . . .'

He also appealed to Mussolini to urge Hitler to agree to a conference to 'settle the Sudeten problem'.

In desperation, Benes now sent Ripka to Paris to try to rally the French. It had been harrowing to stay in England while Czechoslovakia was so dreadfully threatened, and as there was clearly nothing more I could do in London, for a brief moment I joined Ripka in France. But it was already too late. Ripka found his friends, even those in the Government like Reynaud and Mandel, as powerless as Churchill and the anti-appeasers were in London. The Czechs themselves were powerless in Prague. The decisions were being made not in London or in Paris or in Prague, but in Munich, where with Mussolini's help a four-power conference was convened on 29 September.

When the new pressure had been put on the Czechs, Chamberlain had himself proposed that they should be part of any further consultation. Now neither Chamberlain nor Daladier had the courage to insist that the object of their deliberations should be present, never mind consulted. Two Czech Foreign Office officials, one from Berlin and one from Prague, were ordered to be in attendance so that they could receive the decisions of the Four Powers, against which there would be no appeal. This was the treatment usually accorded to a defeated nation, not, as Masaryk had put it to Halifax after Godesberg, to a 'sovereign state which has shown the greatest readiness to make sacrifices for the appeasement of Europe'.

The two Czechoslovak emissaries, Vojtech Mastny, their Minister in Berlin, and Hubert Masarik from the Foreign Office in Prague, were met at Munich airport by a police car and accompanied by the Gestapo to the hotel where the British delegation was staying. They were kept in a hotel room until the conference was over. What happened then was reported by Hubert Masarik :

'At 1.30 a.m. we were taken into the hall where the Conference had been held. There were present Mr. Neville Chamberlain, M. Daladier, Sir Horace Wilson, M. Léger, Mr. Ashton-Gwatkin, Dr. Mastny and myself. The atmosphere was oppressive. . . . Mr. Chamberlain, in a short introduction, referred to the agreement which had just been concluded and gave the text to Dr. Mastny to read out.'

It amounted to the virtual extinction of the Czechoslovak Republic. Not only were eleven thousand square miles of territory torn away from Bohemia's ancient hinterland, not only were three million Sudeten Germans handed over without consultation, but over 700,000 Czechs were also handed to Hitler by the British and French Prime Ministers. Within almost a matter of hours, the Czechoslovak Army had to place the entire defence system of the country in the hands of the German Army, the British and French guaranteeing that the installations would be surrendered intact, a concession which astonished and delighted Hitler.

Two months later, in his secret address to representatives of the German press in Munich on 10 November, 1938, Hitler boasted : 'I myself became most aware of the grandeur of this success when I stood for the first time in the middle of the Czech fortified line. Then and there I realized what it means to take possession of fortifications representing a front almost 2,000 km long without firing one single shot of live ammunition.' And Albert Speer wrote in *Inside the Third Reich* : 'The Czech border fortifications caused general astonishment. To the surprise of experts, a test bombardment showed that our weapons would not have prevailed against them.'

The British military attaché, Colonel Stronge, was the only foreign representative in Prague who had been trusted to go wherever he liked in the fortified zone; he had been shown key sections of the whole system by the Czech Director of Fortifications. He also visited Skoda in Pilsen and Zbrojovka in Brno, two of the most famous armament works in the world. He reported his findings very positively, both to the Foreign Office through his Minister, Basil Newton, in Prague, and direct to the War Office in London. On

1 June, 1938, he was present at the regular meeting of British attachés with the Chiefs of Staff and was summoned for separate interviews with the Chief of the Imperial General Staff, General Gort, with the Secretary of State for War, Mr Hore-Belisha, and with Lord Halifax, the Foreign Secretary. 'Mr Hore-Belisha', Stronge wrote in his 'Personal Memorandum', now lodged in the Bodleian Library, 'was particularly incisive in his questions, whilst Lord Halifax asked about the will to resist in the ranks of the Czech Army and its ability to repel a full scale invasion'. The question which neither they nor the CIGS seem to have asked was what the effect would be on German military strength if Czechoslovakia's military potential fell intact into Hitler's hands.

Hitler himself answered this question six months later in his speech to the Reichstag on 28 April, 1939, giving detailed figures. The Germans gained 1,090,000 infantry rifles, 43,876 machine-guns, 2,175 field guns, 501 anti-aircraft guns, 1,589 aircraft, over 3 million shells and 469 tanks. 'Almost 350 of these,' wrote Milan Hauner in the *Journal of Strategic Studies*, 'were of the standard model LT34 and LT35, superior in guns and armour to any of the available German types Mark I and Mark II. . . . Three out of ten German panzer divisions incorporated them and every third tank which attacked France was Czech built.' It was these tanks that drove back British troops to Dunkirk and St Valéry in 1940.

Colonel Stronge's opinion in 1938 and to the end of his life was that 'it was inconceivable that, if Hitler had been faced in 1938 with the certainty of French and British, and possibly Russian, intervention on behalf of the Czechs, he would have dared, or been permitted, to make war in defiance of the sound professional advice of his generals.'

But Hitler never was faced with this situation. The representatives of Britain and France he faced at Munich were old, ashamed and tired. 'Mr. Chamberlain yawned without ceasing and with no show of embarrassment,' reported the Czech delegate Hubert Masarik. 'The atmosphere was . . . oppressive for everyone present. It had been explained to us in a sufficiently brutal manner, and that by a Frenchman, that this was a sentence without right of appeal and without possibility of modification. Mr Chamberlain did not conceal his fatigue. . . .'

One wonders if Mr Chamberlain slept well that night; perhaps he did for, as he later explained, he was 'pleasantly tired'. I do not think I did, but then I was travelling back to London from Paris. When the boat train drew up in Victoria Station, W. H. Smith were opening their bookstall. I was confronted by banner headlines in all the morning newspapers announcing the Munich Agreement; beside them lay *Europe and the Czechs*. Against the background of a map of Europe all in black, its cover showed the blood-red outlines of a Czechoslovakia that no longer existed. It was my first sight of this now useless book.

Let the last word be that of Colonel Moravec, the head of Czech Military Intelligence :

'Munich became a symbol, and as such will go down in history. It is a symbol of a wish to reach agreement at any price, of negotiating from weakness, of shameful disregard for principles. All who participated in Munich paid for it dearly. Germany and Italy went down to total military defeat; Britain and France fought an exhausting war and their power was considerably diminished.

'When captured German documents and the interrogations of Nuremberg revealed, for all the world to see, the number and deployment of German divisions in 1938 and Germany's inability to wage a two-front war at that time, the question arose : could the High Commands of the Western Powers have been ignorant of these facts as we know them now?

'The answer is : they could not have been, and *were* not, ignorant of them. The mystery of Munich is why the leaders of France and Britain accepted the sacrifice of so much of their own nations' vital interests, knowing what they did.' *

* Frantisek Moravec, *Master of Spies,* Bodley Head, London, 1975, p. 141.

21

I think I could not have borne the strain of those appalling months of 1938 had not a most wonderful change taken place in my personal life.

One of the two cottages which comprised the old flint dower house of the High Elms home farm had fallen empty and my grandmother had offered it to me, generously helping me to furnish it with bits and pieces of furniture. Penguin's advance on *Europe and the Czechs* provided curtains for the windows and blankets for the beds. Clock House was the first home of my own, and in all the terrible pity and fear of public events, the one place where I could find peace and shelter. I loved it passionately.

Now, though I had to leave it for Prague, I knew it was there to come back to.

Before leaving, I had to answer a letter from Professor Toynbee asking me, in the event of war, to join a research team he was forming to work for the Foreign Office. I wrote :

'A week ago I would have answered your enquiry with an unqualified and unquestioning acceptance. To-day, though I may be unjustified in turning it down, I cannot accept without serious thought. Obviously one cannot refuse to serve one's country because one disagrees with its policy but I think my profound revulsion from the recent action of my Government is due to more than disagreement with them on questions of national policy. I have been profoundly shocked and horrified and at a moment when my dominating emotion is one of shame, I cannot offer my services to the Government which has caused it.

'As you know, my family has a long history of public service behind it and I would be proud to continue it in peace or in war, but there seems to me to be values of honour and justice to which one owes

189

allegiance even before one's duty to one's country. If one's country violates those, one cannot serve it.

'Please forgive this letter. It is not my final answer but my immediate reaction to the history of the last ten days. . . . If you want an immediate answer, then I can only say I would be ashamed to work for the Foreign Office at the present moment. If you will give me time to consider more deeply or for our leaders once more to follow the ideals for which this country has stood and fought for in the past, then perhaps I will accept later. I offered my services to the War Office last week. If they should be accepted, I presume that would be a prior claim.'

Toynbee replied :

'I quite understand your feelings and we have now after all, a little time to wait and see what we feel inclined to do on second thoughts.'

My own first thoughts were for Prague and what might be happening there. Benes had resigned on 5 October and was succeeded by Dr Emil Hacha, an elderly lawyer. I was afraid for my friends, especially Ripka who had stood out so manfully against capitulation and had many enemies among those now taking over the government of the country. My fears were premature. Eventually many of the followers of Masaryk and Benes were to be liquidated, but by the Germans, not by their fellow Czechs.

The people who were really at risk in October 1938 were the wretched Sudeten Germans themselves, the very people on whose behalf the whole shameful proceedings were supposed to have been undertaken. The anti-Nazis were trying desperately to reach the safety of the Czech districts still unoccupied by German armies. Hitler demanded the return of all who escaped and a new, embittered Czech Government were acceding to this demand.

My father's old friend, Sir Neill Malcolm, League of Nations High Commissioner for Refugees, arrived in Prague on 10 October to try to ease this tragic situation. He, Wheeler-Bennett and the noble General Faucher, Head of the French Military Mission to Czechoslovakia since 1926, who in shame at his country's betrayal had resigned his post and put his services at the disposal of the Czechs, pleaded in vain.

The Czech Government, having been sacrificed by the British on behalf of the Sudeten Germans, was not disposed to put itself out at Britain's request to save those same Sudeten Germans from the consequences of British action. The Lord Mayor of London set up a Czech

Trust Fund to help any refugees that were able to escape. In the first few months the beneficiaries were predominantly German and Jewish.

Although the moral consequences – the search for scapegoats, recrimination, denunciation, dismissal – so desperately feared by those who opposed capitulation, soon set in, nothing like the horrors of post-*Anschluss* Vienna took place. I had feared for Benes in the event that he, like Schuschnigg, should ever be exposed to Hitler's fury, but the Czechs – even those who had been political opponents – protected their former leaders, whereas the Austrians handed them over or hounded them themselves. Perhaps, after all, there is more to civilization than not eating in one's kitchen.

Benes was allowed to leave the country in peace, taking with him a few of his closest and most trusted officials from 'the Castle'; he also left behind a clandestine group of friends and associates to prepare for underground resistance in the war they considered inevitable. Clearly Benes saw that he must start again and follow the same road which he and T. G. Masaryk had taken during the First World War. Masaryk's son stood with him now, as well as a whole generation of Czechs and Slovaks reared in the Masaryk tradition, sons of the First Czechoslovak Republic, would-be restorers of the Second.

Back in Prague, I found Ripka totally exhausted and very unhappy, but not in despair. He was too much of a fighter, too much of a European, to give in because this one battle, tremendous defeat though it was, had been lost. The forces of evil were still in being and had to be overcome. He recognized that there was nothing else for the new Government of Czechoslovakia to do but try to rebuild the shattered economy of their mutilated country and endeavour to get along with the new masters of Central Europe – keeping their heads down and their thoughts to themselves. Ripka's role, like that of Benes, lay abroad. I urged him to come to England where he could stay indefinitely in my mother's house and write the history of the Munich crisis. He promised to think about it. His immediate desire was to rejoin his family in France and plan with them what and where their future should be. His wife Naomi, a French national, might be able to return to Czechoslovakia and keep open the lines of communication between her husband and his friends and collaborators.

Many of these people came to his flat, both to say goodbye to him and to find out from me, an English national who must surely know and understand, why my Government had handed over their country to Nazi Germany. Their distraught and anguished questions were terribly distressing. Why had it happened? Where had they gone wrong? They had tried to do everything we asked. What was our intention? What were we getting out of it? I could not say 'peace', for we all knew that war was now inevitable. My attempts to explain British policy sounded like an attempt to justify it, and I was bitterly ashamed. Their anguish too was compounded with shame. 'We should have fought even though we were alone,' they said.

After Ripka had left, I returned sadly to his empty flat and sat down to write an article for my old friend Professor G. P. Gooch, editor of *Political Quarterly*. Recalling the words of the French historian Ernest Denis that it was at once the merit and the happiness of Bohemia that its own cause was always bound up with the cause of humanity in general, I wrote:

'If this be true, it would seem that the cause of humanity has gone down undefended, betrayed on the one hand by Britain and France and accepted as past saving on the other by those whom, in the first place, it most nearly concerned.

'There is no place in the present world for an Englishman or Frenchman who would throw a stone at the Czechoslovak Government for refusing to fight, but in a calmer and more detached atmosphere of history, will no historian demand with perplexity why it was that the Czech nation surrendered without resistance? It was of the Greeks that Byron wrote

> Hereditary Bondsmen! know ye not,
> Who would be free himself must strike the blow?

'If the historian or poet of future days is to level his judgement with a just aim, he must take into account not only the decisions of the Czech leaders but the thoughts and feelings of the masses of the Czech nation. . . .

'There is no doubt that the Czechs would have fought to a man had they not had orders to retire. Witnesses of the mobilisation will never forget that night of September 23rd.'

And I went on to describe from the descriptions given to me, not only by Czechs but by English colleagues who had lived through those tragic days, how resolutely and calmly the Czechs – and many Sudeten Germans – manned their frontier fortifications and how

14 Clock House

15 The author, Hubert and Naomi Ripka at Clock House in 1938

16 The author in 1938

desperately, brokenly and angrily they obeyed the order to withdraw.

'To understand the decisions of the Czech leaders,' the article continued, 'it is only necessary to remember that whereas Nazi threats reached a pitch of violence, brutality and intemperance never before equalled in history, Anglo-French influence was used not to steady that intemperance but rather to secure capitulation before it. Pressure to this end was first used in May 1938 and was the occasion for an Anglo-French *démarche*. From that time onwards this pressure steadily increased. . . . Britain and France, faced by what they considered to be a German threat to make war, retreated from their moral, and in the case of France legal, obligation to defend the rights of a sovereign state against the threat of foreign invasion.'

It would be a mistake, I went on, to see in this Anglo-French retreat 'a loss of heart or lack of courage, though to many, including most of the Czechs, there was no other explanation'; rather it was a complete reversal not only of French post-war policy but of the traditional policy of Great Britain.

'If England and France no longer intended to preserve the democratic heritage they won in four years' battle, the article continued, 'if England were no longer interested in the balance of power, nor France in the system of continental alliances painfully pursued in the years succeeding the War, it was obvious that however the Czechoslovak nation might strive to defend that heritage or maintain that balance, it would be powerless to do so against the combined forces of Central Europe. Czechoslovakia stood, as it were, for a cause in which Europe and humanity at large were no longer interested. President Benes may well have considered that the sacrifice of life, necessarily immense in a Czech-German war, would have been absolutely in vain. It would only have added to the sum of human suffering without stemming the tide of human retrogression.

'It was this deep resignation on the part of the Czech leaders, this apparent conviction that the forces of progress were doomed and the sparks of liberty, courage and honour so low in the West that they could not be kindled, which distressed people so profoundly in other countries and may have done wrong to the Czechs themselves. . . . Leaders they could have found who would have fought not merely in self-defence, nor even for the original frontiers of the Czechoslovak state, but for the ideals of liberty and democracy which are again becoming revolutionary cries in Europe. If such a war had broken out, how long would the dictatorships have survived? Which dictatorship would have issued victoriously from it?

'It was no mere coincidence that in the last weeks of the crisis the Nazi press used the word "Hussite" as a term of abuse to conjure up fear among the Nazis. The Czech Hussite armies of the fifteenth century not only defeated the German yeomanry but were welcomed by the German serfs and joined by the peasants who envied the Czech peasantry its freedom. The same danger of internal dissolution faced the armies of Nazi Germany. . . .

'If it be true that the cause of Bohemia has always been bound up with the cause of humanity, then the struggle is not yet over. If the cause of humanity ultimately triumphs over the dark forces and tyrannies which oppress it today, the Bohemia of the Czechs will not be lost.'

In the third week of October I returned to England to continue the struggle, passing through Strasbourg where Ripka had rejoined his family. Once again I lunched at Chartwell to report on my harrowing visit to Prague. After luncheon, Churchill took me into his study and gave me a copy he had signed for me of his speeches, *Arms and the Covenant*, which had just been published. 'You have fought well,' he said, shaking me rather solemnly by the hand. I asked him what he thought I should do now. 'Join the Liberal Party,' he said, 'and work with them.' And he went on to tell me, as he had told Parliament, 'Many people, no doubt, honestly believe they are only giving away the interests of Czechoslovakia, whereas I fear we shall find that we have compromised, and perhaps fatally endangered, the safety and even the independence of Great Britain and France. Do not suppose this is the end. This is only the beginning of the reckoning.'

Shortly afterwards Churchill invited me to meet Sir Archibald Sinclair, leader of the Liberal Party, a man of great charm and sensibility whom I was often to meet in succeeding months, having taken Churchill's advice and offered my services to the Liberals. It was in answer to a query of Sinclair's whether he would really ally himself with Stalin and the Soviet Union that I heard Churchill make his now famous remark that he would ally himself with the Devil to defeat Hitler.

I took part in two by-elections where Independent candidates stood against the Chamberlain Government largely on the issue of appeasement. At Bridgwater, Vernon Bartlett was returned with a large majority. In Scotland, the Duchess of Atholl – the 'Red Duchess' as she was called for her championship of the Republican Government in the Spanish Civil War – was defeated. Thanks to the wide sales of *Europe and the Czechs* in all parts of the United Kingdom – with bitter irony, it became a best-seller now that the cause it championed was lost – many people who had read the book came up to me after meetings where I had spoken, assuring me that they would gladly have fought on such an issue now they realized what it had been. Disillusionment with the Munich Agreement and disenchantment with Chamberlain and Halifax were growing fast.

Penguin asked me to contribute to another Special they were bringing out, entitled *Germany: What Next?* Fellow contributors to the book included L. S. Amery, a strong anti-appeaser and former Conservative Secretary of State for the Colonies; Sir Sidney Barton, British Minister in Addis Ababa during the Italian-Abyssinian War; and Victor Gordon Lennox, the most famous and respected of all the London diplomatic correspondents. We all warned the British public as to what they could expect from Nazi Germany.

As a result of my contribution to this book and of the large sales of *Europe and the Czechs*, I was often asked to speak and write, but I did so with a heavy heart. What was really important to me in those eleven months between Munich and the outbreak of war was no longer any sort of public activity or political cause, no 'primary purpose' greater than myself. Such things, I somehow felt, were no longer in my hands. An inexorable fate was now bearing down upon us and there was nothing more to be done than gird oneself to meet it when it came. I had no doubt at all that war was coming and that all our lives would be swept up in the struggle. Before this happened, I wanted just a short time of private happiness. This I found at Clock House.

I would lie in my little room at the top of the house near the clock tower, listening to the clock pulling up its great chains to strike the hours. Through a small lattice window near the head of my bed I could see part of the roof and a chimney and then the stars. How could I ever have left such a place? I wondered, though I knew I would leave it again, probably very soon, and perhaps for ever. It was not only the first home I ever had of my own, but also the first in which I had someone to look after, a garden to make, animals to care for.

To this blessed shelter I brought Ripka. At first he was reluctant to come, for all his work had been done in cities, but soon he too grew to value the long undisturbed hours writing by the open wood fire in Clock House while I gardened or visited my grandmother. And to Clock House, as well as to my mother's home in Chelsea, throughout that autumn and the following months, came emissaries and exiles from Czechoslovakia to call on Ripka. Benes and Masaryk were in the United States and Ripka was the leading representative of a potential Czechoslovak Government in exile in the West. The last to come was Colonel Moravec and his band of *'coupes gorges'*, as Ripka affectionately called these highly skilled Czechoslovak Military Intelligence officers.

For a few months this Kentish farmhouse provided a gentle respite between all that had just happened and the terrible war which was to follow. I often wonder whether, after all he had gone through and the still more tragic struggles which lay ahead for the Czechs, this was not the most peaceful period in the whole of Ripka's life. As a forester's son, I think he came to love the woods of High Elms as much as I did.

His wife, who had courageously returned to Prague to maintain contact between the Czechs carrying on the struggle abroad and those determined to organize resistance at home, wrote me a most charming letter. Naomi Ripka, the daughter of a distinguished professor from Alsace, was a woman of great energy, courage and intelligence.

'My thoughts are with you all the time,' she wrote. 'Like you, I make perpetual journeys between Clock House and Mulberry Walk and often I really believe I have been there. . . .

'I do not know how to thank you without falling into clichés. Everything one tries to say sounds so stupid. In the terrible nightmare of our epoch, in the midst of all the ugliness facing one from every corner, the affection of friends shines like a diamond and comforts one more than anything else. From this point of view, Hubert and I have such wonderful experiences that my heart overflows with gratitude. I assure you that separation from Hubert is infinitely less hard because I know that he is with you. I know how necessary it is for him to communicate everything he thinks and everything he feels and I see no one who could be a better friend for him at this moment. If he succeeds in coming out of this disaster unbroken, you will have helped him more than anyone by your companionship. And I do not speak of all the worries which he is spared, thanks to you and your mother. . . .'

Ripka was never broken, not by any of the terrible experiences –
defeat and exile, calumny and rejection – which he, like so many of
his compatriots, suffered. In many ways, of the two of us, I was almost
more shattered at this moment. I felt a terrible shame for what my
Government had done.

The quality of the bonds between us and the alliance we felt in the
great struggle of our times comes out strongly in a letter he wrote
to me just after Munich :

'Thank you for the letters which you sent me. As always, they were
very interesting and amusing. But this time I had the distinct impression that all was not well with you and that makes me anxious. I
know you are a little lost and sad. I will do everything to make you
recover. You are quite right that the political situation is not encour-
aging and that the future is full of fearful uncertainty. But one must
not allow oneself to be discouraged. Certainly we will pass through
terrible crises but if we act with faith and courage, we will win
through.

'The human race is so stupid. It would be so easy to work out a
better life for society without revolution and a better life between
nations without war. But people are incapable of making small
sacrifices in order to avoid great ones. But what really matters is not
to lose heart. I count on you. I am always at your side. Wait and see :
we will save Europe.'

22

It was during the lull after Munich that Adam wrote to tell me his father had died and he was returning immediately from the Far East. It was not good news. I was disturbed for both of us and sad for his sake, not only on account of his bereavement but because I saw no good coming out of his return to Germany.

He had been away for nearly two years, years in which great upheavals and tragedies – the Spanish Civil War, the invasion of Austria, the mutilation of Czechoslovakia – had taken place in Europe. Having had no part in these struggles, he was to some extent immune, even indifferent to them. These were all human tragedies, to which the conscience of Europe was slowly awaking, but to Adam, in the Far East, they seem to have taken on the appearance of irreversible historical events. From this detached standpoint, far from the heartbeat of Europe, Adam's political judgement was faulty and distorted.

He had become not less but more German, and more defensive. As German strength expanded, he seemed to feel more strongly the wrongs, sufferings and grievances of his country, and to be more ready than ever to put the blame on others for the leaders his country had chosen. Germany had been 'driven into these ills'. 'I resent,' he wrote to me, 'as utterly hopeless and damaging the high-handed denunciation of a people which contains just as many hard-working "Europeans" which have been defeated and silenced by economic depression and not least by the leading spirit of Europe wanting to perpetuate Germany's defeat in 1918.

'As long as it is not possible for you to consider all that happened in Germany a *European* phenomenon and responsibility no further step can be made. If on the other hand you try to hedge in Germany morally and materially the explosion is bound to happen and destroy

198

what foundations of a Europe in our sense may still be left.'

At the very height of the desperate tension and anxiety of the summer of 1938, Adam had suddenly decided that he must have it out with me. Tragically ironic, in view of events six years later, his first letter was dated 20 July.

'Although you are not very explicit in the views you hold in your letters,' he wrote, 'I cannot fail to realise in all you say and print in papers a tendency with which I increasingly disagree. It would be make belief to doubt that this must one day seriously affect our friendship. . . . I think we have the duty to know how far we can go together and where our ways part. You see in a way they did when you went to Prague and decided to be a journalist. . . .'

If this were true, his letters now were certainly milestones along the same road. He attacked not only my political opinions and me personally (my 'strong personal ambitions', my 'cynicism and sheer love of high life', my lack of 'judgement and hard work') but also my friends. Those in Prague, and Ripka in particular, he dismissed for their 'partly professed and partly honest beliefs', and Mowrer for his 'hopelessly shallow' report on China and for concentrating on evils in countries other than his own.

I was desperately trying to finish the Penguin Special before the position which it was trying to save was hopelessly lost, and had neither the heart nor the time to enter into argument with him.

Two or three weeks later another letter arrived, still resentful though a little more conciliatory. 'I hope my letters have not seemed like "a stab in the back" when you were just in the thick of fighting to get your book done. . .', he said. 'But you must be generous too and admit some justice to the charge I have made against your spirit of defending Europe . . . one of blind denunciation of Germany's ills which although couched in phrases of liberal rights and progress is fundamentally drawing more and more on socially reactionary motives and those of nationalism which made the last war.'

Finally, on 1 September, 1938, one week before the Nuremberg Rally that brought the German-Czech confrontation to breaking point, I sat down and answered him. I tried to state calmly what I thought should be the basis of all political endeavour – freedom – and to explain what I meant by it. But I soon became caught up in my rage at all that was happening in the world, at Adam's failure to see it, and his attack on those who did.

'You are right that your letters are a "stab in the back",' I wrote.

199

'They are a real betrayal. . . . This side *is* more important than any single human relationship – and more and more my only deep and strong affections are for people who care for these things too, and if you do not – then we part.' And I told him very strongly what my feelings were for those he had attacked :

'I admire Mowrer morally and politically and if you accept me, you accept him – or neither. Your criticism of Ripka too I despise as jealousy. Even if it is more, this is not the moment to utter it. He has worked more for Czech-German co-operation than any other Czech and has failed because of the political crimes and follies of your countrymen. He is the most honest, brave and disinterested man I have ever met. His love of his country and his idea of Europe is far more profound than any other I have met and goes far beyond mere self-defence against your countrymen. But today that alone requires heroism and unfaltering determination which I admire profoundly. I care for him very much, and he has come nearer than anyone else to replacing what I lost through your country 25 years ago. That Germany again threatens that is not a reason for my feeling very calm about it, or my tolerating criticism of my friends from you. So there it is. Now you can judge whether we agree sufficiently to be friends. I retract absolutely nothing – either you accept me like that, or not. Now that you are not in love with me you can judge it better perhaps. You could never have stopped me taking this trend except by proving that your country did not mean these things, and your countrymen would have disowned you. I suppose you will go back and be part of it. I cannot condemn you, but I cannot approve either, and perhaps one day I shall think you did wrong. . . .

'Then you reproach me with nationalism and pre-1914 sentiments. You know I have tried always to make a distinction between Governments and people. Germany is a beautiful country – but what has been done to show there is a distinction between Government and people? Nothing. In moments of anger one thinks, "They are the same and I condemn them both" or "They are different, and the people too cowardly and weak to say so."

'. . . Day to day politics . . . now appear quite brutally : Does Hitler want war or not? You will remember there was a thing called the War Guilt Clause. It has been disputed. If there is another war, there will be no dispute again. I deny we drove Germany to accept a regime which meant war. . . .

'It is not "blind denunciation of Germany" – it is a hatred of what

200

your country stands for, hatred of war, of cruelty, of coercion. You know as well as I do that my country hates war. . . . I hate war but I have watched the fear of it bring it on. . . .

'Many people think there will be a war next week. It all depends on one man. I think your proper attitude would be shame and to ask forgiveness. Even I feel ashamed, and I am less guilty than you – but you only reproach me and declaim. Perhaps after all, we cannot be friends. But we have been, and if there is war, and I survive, I shall try to remember. . . . Bless you.'

There was no war : there was Munich and the destruction of Czechoslovakia by 'peaceful' agreement between Germany, England, Italy and France. Adam was shaken. For the first and only time he considered the possibility of not returning to Germany.

'I am strongly tempted,' he wrote from Tsingtao on 1 October, 'to go via America (this entirely between you and myself) to look for a place to work if our continent is really going to be what we both feel threatening, now a conflict has been spared. It is a damned hard choice, but I'd rather be a beggar than a slave and I am not too old to start all over again and I have good friends in America. . . . America also is a prospect of considerable resignation – one has to sacrifice the things Europe still gives freely for a mere potentiality but a potentiality which one may help to work out as a free and self-respecting individual.'

But the tug of his homeland was still terribly strong. 'I want very much and must come home, some time in not too distant a future. I want to see my old father, mother, my brothers and my fields (though I'm really quite unsentimental about all that now.)'

Then, suddenly, came the news of the death of his father. 'I am taking the next ship to Europe,' he wrote to me on 29 October from Hong Kong. 'So I cannot write very much except that it arrives in Marseilles November 25th and that if you should happen to be in France nothing would make me gladder than to be seeing you there first. We could travel back to Paris together and end this voyage there. I do hope you got my last letter from Tsingtao because what I wrote in it was the honest truth.'

Parts of that letter I have quoted above; at the end the original tone between us was restored when Adam described another touching dream he had had of me :

'The other night – I think in Tsinanfu – I dreamt that you were in Peking and that you were having a child and that we were standing with some other people under a leafy chestnut tree and I was leaving the next day and I longed to take you away to a temple in the country – when you said Let's all go to a film together! Silly dream – but you looked very charming. Sometimes I imagine you with your hair done up in a knot and rather superior and maturer than myself and in with all the fashionables. Or I remember some small gesture of yours that used to pain me – and the eager way in which you used to talk and how exciting it was to go to pubs with you. And the background to you is always green and never grey like Prague or Berlin. Love always. A.'

It was this dreadful greyness which now dominated London.

Obviously we had to meet on his way back to Germany to try and get all this straight, even if we could not entirely bridge the chasm that had opened between us. I did not feel I could go all the way to Marseilles, but my reluctance to go no further than Paris upset him and put him on his guard. He confessed later that he had arrived 'armed with a lot of determined emotional independence and defiance of hostility'. I too went to this meeting with considerable reservations.

The meeting of close friends after a gap of nearly two years is always difficult, and there was every reason why this should be no exception. As we breakfasted at the hotel in the Palais Royal where we stayed, or walked along the banks of the Seine, we were both a little embarrassed and shy; also we did not have long to renew our friendship, for his father's death meant that Adam was needed urgently at home.

I cannot now remember exactly how our conversation developed, but what was in each of our minds had been passionately expressed in our letters of recent weeks, which, like all the rest, have survived. I had sent Adam *Europe and the Czechs* to read in the train. Its epigraph was Herodotus' account of the Greeks at Thermopylae, ending with Demaratus' words to Xerxes: 'If you conquer these men and those that remain in Sparta, there is no other nation in the world that will dare to raise their hands against you.'

Adam's strong patriotism no doubt prevented him from seeing any analogy in the situation. In any case, I was almost alone in seeing the Czechs, like the Greeks before them, as the defenders of the Western world against the hordes of a barbarous imperialism. Nor, had he seen the analogy, would he have regretted that there was now 'no other nation in the world that will dare to raise their hands against you'. Germany, in his view, had always been more sinned against than sinning, her just claims denied her and she herself vulnerably on the defensive rather than a potential aggressor.

This had clearly not been the situation at Munich, however, and Adam admitted that he had never conceived possible 'the unilateral settlement of the [Sudeten German] issue by Germany without the Western Powers carrying out their promises to your friends.' And yet it was just these 'promises' – the Franco-Czech-Soviet Defence Treaties and the necessity for Britain 'to back up that ring' – about which we had always argued so fiercely. This was his 'lid theory', which he always believed 'must result in an explosion which would destroy the very suppositions on which Europe rests'. The whole point of the 'lid', as I had quoted Churchill saying to me in 1937, was to confine this explosion inside the frontiers of Germany. Internal revolution had by now become the only alternative to external aggression.

Adam admitted that 'Any system which threatens to or actually dominates the whole rest of Europe and which cannot be changed from within must be considered as definitely coercive and to accept it as final would be the self-abandonment of Europe.' But he denied that this was the system that now existed in Germany. In his view, it was 'conjured up by the Western press to hide another unfair predominance and coerciveness'. He shared the view of Lord Lothian – Secretary of the Rhodes Trust, and thus an important figure in his life – that 'the central fact today is that Germany does not want war and is prepared to renounce it absolutely as a method of settling her disputes with her neighbours provided she is given real equality'.

This is what Adam passionately wanted to believe, and he could quote powerful support for this belief not only from recent British Government statements to this effect, but also from the opinions of people like Lady Astor whom he knew personally. She had been exceedingly kind to him before his departure from Europe, and her son David was as old a friend of Adam's as I was. Both of them might be thought to have been in a better position to understand the situation. If I repeated to Adam what I had written to him in Shanghai – that 'our rulers are people not only with second-class minds but with second-class hearts. They are just morally bad' – he would certainly have found my attitude both irresponsible and extreme. For Adam the dominating fact of the situation was that at Munich our two countries had at last reached understanding on a burning issue : surely we could proceed from there? I could not get through to him why this 'understanding', between the Britain of Chamberlain and the Germany of Hitler, offended my most deeply-felt principles. He had always rejected my condemnation of Germany; now, added to it, was condemnation of England, which he was not prepared to accept either. There was certainly no marriage of true minds in our meeting.

I was the first to leave for home. Adam went back to the hotel and wrote me a cold little note about our relationship :

'Have you ever observed the attitude of professional dancing partners in cabarets to each other? It is very nice and admirable sometimes – though they make sweet gestures in public, their strenuous job makes them very matter of fact and unsentimental in their solidarity and their attachment to each other is bound up with all the hard facts of life, and all the more real because it is unromantic.

'Will we perhaps be a little like that one day?'

Nevertheless, the letter ended : 'My love to you and try for a common policy from your end.'

I found this letter rather chilling, nor, after our meeting, could I see what common policy we could pursue. I answered :

'It was strange to see you again and I have not quite grasped that you are back in Europe. Europe casts such a shadow on its inhabitants that it has somehow cast them into unimportance except as they are related to it. Sometimes people are not related at all and a sort of garden happiness is the result; mostly they are related and either that is purposeful or it is painful. With you it is painful. I suspect that we are enemies. I do not know what you really care for and admire, but suspect that it is not what I care for. I suspect that even your feelings for me are now less affectionate acceptance than a sort of desire to conquer or at all costs stand up and differ. And I'm afraid it has to be like that. I have never met a German with a different patriotism and patriot one must be. . . .

'This is not the sort of letter I wanted to write to you. I am in my house and it really takes me away from all that and I want only peace and a private life. I feel I am no longer an actor on this stage and I need not be an onlooker. . . .'

'Can you not postpone your suspicions till we meet again?' Adam replied from Imshausen. 'Partly, at any rate, I am certain they are wrong. . . .

'The fog around here, and I'm afraid over the Channel, is pretty grim. One does not see much from here at first. The papers are empty and the fields and woods received one with a deep and peaceful kind of joy. But soon enough one feels sterile despair in most veins of life that one follows up and behind any sense of peace there is a deeper one of guilt and shame. But I do care intensely for my home and its people.

'I spoke with a cousin in Frankfort, a friend from Hamburg and an uncle from Berlin. They all think nothing can be done without bowing to the formula. The field after that is wide open and full of opportunities but the starting point is evil and closes down the real walls of one's strength and possibilities.'

I assumed that 'bowing to the formula' meant joining the Nazi Party and working with the Governments of that day, both German and British, and I wish I had protested there and then. A week later he wrote :

'There are many ways in which it seems to me that we would need and be of real help to each other and yet our world is so constructed that what lies immediately ahead of us we must do alone and that what may be best in each of us may imply a subtle kind of pressure, diffidence and even enmity towards each other which is distinctly harmful unless we consciously size it up and bridge it by a bigger common aim beyond the things that are immediate. For this our brief reunion the other day was too short but it filled me not merely with "affectionate acceptance" which you said I had lost, but with a clear hope and joy in our friendship and with renewed, and I think deepened, care for your own self. You always wanted me to and I think I have hardened to a clearer view of the limited realisation and potentiality of our mutual affection and to the fact that we are probably not meant to be supreme happiness to each other. . . . Be good and understand. . . .'

In my next letter, from the Haldanes' home in Perthshire where I was helping in the Duchess of Atholl's election campaign, I did try to be 'good'.

'I'm sorry you felt angry and defensive in Paris,' I wrote, 'but glad it is not permanent. I'm afraid it made me feel just a little hopeless as if we could not work together for the same things because we just did not want them. Sometimes I am very frightened by the intellectual isolation of your country. Now that you are home, could you not teach me to read and study what you think is best in your country, what people you admire as good Germans?. . . .

'I'm afraid I have a terrible desire for peace and quiet, a shetland collie dog and a quiet home in my farm. I think the rest of our lives will not be so quiet that we need give up what we have. I wonder if you feel that about your home? I hope you do and can. I feel what effort we must make must come later and now we need to grow strong inside ourselves.'

But Adam's position, of course, was very different from mine. Mine had been taken up in 1936 and I could now, without ceasing to care or ceasing to notice, temporarily lay it down. Adam had been absent and outside the whole struggle, but on his return he had to decide where he stood and what role he was to play. His strongest desires were to prevent war and to bring about real Anglo-German co-operation; and he bravely set about finding out how this could be done.

He wrote me a long letter from Berlin at the end of December, the full import of which I was only to understand after the war when German historians interpreted it as a reference to the failed plot of the German generals in September 1938 to forestall the attack on Czechoslovakia and depose Hitler. I had not then heard of this plot, so his letter meant nothing to me. It went on to describe, in cryptic terms, conditions in Berlin :

'Instead of the triumphant capital of the future Empire of Europe, I found a sulky, disgruntled and demoralised mess. Few, if any, see the Czech business as you do and I tend to, as the entry to un-limited economic and political possibilities. . . . Schacht . . . said there was no chance at all for a European war, now no longer, as clever Neville had been forging ahead with the other hand while holding the one, and that the other with all that it could pull with it was ever ready and probably stronger already than both of ours.'

To Adam's patriotic ears this must have sounded alarming, rather than reassuring as it did to me. He had always strongly opposed the 'lid theory' that sought peace through superior military strength against Germany. He still could not believe that it was Hitler and Hitler alone who wanted war.

I do not know whether it was his English or his German friends who first put Adam on the disastrous path he was to follow. Given that, above all else, and almost at any price, he wanted peace, it was perhaps inevitable that in England his hopes were pinned on the appeasers. They were easily accessible through his friendship with David Astor since Balliol days, and through his association with Lord Lothian. He must have heard from Hjalmar Schacht (President of the Reichsbank), when he met him in Berlin, that appeasement was still being actively discussed on the economic front, though politically little progress was being made He must also have heard, if he was in touch with the 'Resistance', of the abortive attempts of Goerdeler and others to gain any real hearing in leading British circles. It was in no way ignoble that he should form the ambition to play this role himself. It was, however, a grave error of judgement *not* to see that Appeasement and Resistance were, by this stage at any rate, totally conflicting aims.

Adam visited England in February 1939, before the great revulsion of feeling that came over the British public when Hitler marched into Prague. This was unfortunate timing, for it never allowed him to correct the erroneous impressions he acquired on this first visit after his two-year absence. He stayed with the Astors in London and may have heard direct from Lady Astor about her triumphant luncheon party in May 1938 at which Chamberlain first told American correspondents of his intention to bring about a four-power pact and dismember Czechoslovakia. What further issues and solutions were discussed I have no idea, but Adam could not be blamed for believing that these were the corridors of power down which he could pursue the aims he had in mind. There was quite enough ribaldry about Ribbentrop and others for him to feel that these circles were pro-German and anti-Nazi, as he was himself.

He visited Oxford where he would have heard of Quintin Hogg's success against Lindsay, his old Master at Balliol, in winning the University Seat for Chamberlain. The anti-Nazi talk he heard from many of his old friends he found 'carelessly excited and thoroughly disobliging'.

I am sure that this was how he found me at a rather oddly assorted weekend party at Clock House. Ripka was there, and Diana and her fiancé David Hopkinson, whom Adam was meeting for the first time. He and Diana had had a happy meeting in London a few days before.

I had always longed for Adam to come to High Elms, our devotion to our family homes having been one of the bonds between us. But this visit, somehow, was very different from all my hopes; it must even have been painful, for I have no recollection of it whatsoever. Memory on the whole is merciful, for there must have been a great undercurrent of tension between people all so entangled and so vulnerable to each other, who were meeting at such a moment in world affairs.

Less than two weeks later, on 15 March, Hitler marched into Prague. Although this further aggression was inevitable once the Czechoslovak defences had been dismantled, it deeply shocked British public opinion. It shattered the hopes of appeasement, and for a brief moment brought Czechoslovakia once again onto the forefront of the stage.

Benes and Masaryk were still in the United States and it was up to Ripka, the leading Czechoslovak representative in England, to do what he could for his countrymen. He and I went at once to the Foreign Office, both for news and to win their support with the Home Office for the granting of visas to Czechs whose lives were in danger and whose services would be required in London if general hostilities broke out. This done, Ripka left immediately for France, securing similar facilities for his compatriots there and ensuring the safe return of his French wife and family from Prague.

I do not know by what angry, anguished steps I determined to break off relations with Adam. My letter is missing but his answer has survived :

'I do not accept your reasons for parting but I see that we must part.

'I do not see a "barricade" separating us but a torrent of mixed passions, fears and hate. If you no longer feel it, I cannot convince you now that there is solid ground even on the other side of that torrent and a similar though necessarily different struggle. Clearly we must first be as good and brave as we possibly can at our end of it and if being friends hinders that, we must part. But don't let us make culprits and enemies of each other when we cannot see through all the turmoil and clamour . . . our essential though separate solidarity. . . .

'I hope, darling, your other friends all remain intact, for you need good friends to prevent you from hurting your own self through violence which is no help in defeating the sordid violence of our present world.

'Bless you and always love,   A.'

Of course he was right as far as our personal relations were concerned. But we were caught up in public matters, where it was not a 'torrent of fears and hate' that divided nations or threatened war, but simply the determination of one highly armed and evil régime to assert its mastery over others. Of course, too, as a German national, he had a 'necessarily different' and indeed much harder struggle. It was certainly not 'similar', and I questioned the need for it to be national and judged it to be nationalist.

Adam never explained his own aims to me beyond the necessity of securing peace (and, so it seemed to me, peace at any price). Who his friends were and what were his objectives within his own country, he never told me. Knowing the 'violence', as he called it, of my views about the British circles with whom he was co-operating, it would no doubt have been unwise to reveal clandestine circles in Germany. Who and what the German 'Resistance' was, I had no idea.

I nevertheless got involved, though in total ignorance of the background to Adam's side of it, in the mission which brought him to England in June 1939. It has since become known that it was a clandestine operation stemming from Weizsäcker, the permanent non-Nazi head of the German Foreign Office, and facilitated by a powerful Nazi friend of Adam's, Walter Hewel, who at this moment apparently put peace with England above loyalty to Hitler.

Once again Adam stayed with the Astors, this time at Cliveden for a weekend party which included Lord Halifax and Lord Lothian. Later he also talked with Chamberlain. His object, it seems, was to bring matters of dispute back into international discussion and to try to involve Hitler in the sort of discredit that would revive the German generals' opposition. I knew nothing whatsoever of this, nor of the report he carried back with the hope of its reaching Hitler.

I did know, however, of his return a week later and of his conversations with mutual friends in Oxford which, I warned him, had aroused infinite suspicion. Our parting seems to have been postponed, for he came once again to a weekend party at Clock House in which, with the object of opening a path for him to Churchill, I had included Duncan and Diana Sandys. He did not avail himself of this opportunity, but he did come to see Ripka who, with his wife Naomi, was staying with my mother in London. Adam called at our house and asked to speak with him privately.

He then made an astonishing proposition. The German occupation of Bohemia and Moravia was not proving too satisfactory, he said, and perhaps Czech independence could be restored in exchange for concessions of Polish territory and the international port of Danzig. Ripka had no idea where this proposition originated, but he suspected a manoeuvre by Goering. He rejected it indignantly.

After Adam had left, Ripka, Naomi and I discussed what action should be taken. It was decided that Ripka should write to Churchill. This letter is not in the Churchill files and I have no idea what steps were taken, except that Adam knew almost immediately that Churchill had been informed. I have the original French draft which Ripka dictated to his wife. It is in Naomi's handwriting and takes some pains to conceal Adam's identity :

'A very reliable friend has made known to me that the Germans are making a new effort to gain their objectives in Poland without risking war. They understand that by direct attack they risk the outbreak of a European war. They have submitted the following proposals' (here Ripka outlined the intended exchange of Polish and Czech territory). 'It has the appearance of an unofficial move, but I know that Lord Halifax has been informed though I do not know his reaction.

'I do not need to insist on the dangerous character of this plan : the evacuation of Bohemia-Moravia would be in appearance only. Our people are completely disarmed and at the mercy of Germany. In exchange for this illusory concession, Hitler would gain a glittering success in the Polish question, and Poland would find herself as enfeebled as Czechoslovakia after Munich.

'In view of the absolute reliability of this information, I feel it is my duty to communicate it to you, begging you to regard it as absolutely confidential. My friend would be in the greatest danger were he discovered to be the source of my information.'

We debated a long time what could be the meaning, the motive and the origin of this extraordinary intervention of Adam's. I could not believe that he was consciously doing Hitler's work. Ripka declared that in fact it was far more dangerous than Hitler's brutal politics. He thought it probably came from Goering, but he was disappointed that Adam should lend himself to such a game. 'I really thought him more honest and more European than that,' he said.

What amazed us all was the extraordinary lack of judgement, both political and personal, which Adam revealed in making such a proposition to Ripka. It was out of the question that Ripka, of all people, would ever have lent himself to such a manoeuvre.

All I could say in Adam's defence was that he had been absent a long time in China, had not begun to understand European politics, saw British politics through the eyes of the appeasers and wanted to prevent war at all costs.

'He makes it more certain by such tricks,' said Ripka angrily.

But that this whole operation was of extreme importance to Adam is revealed in his last angry letter to me, the last I was ever to receive.

In that letter he accused me of having, by my 'complete incapacity to understand a natural ally', wrecked something which I should have furthered and failed to recognize values whose destruction were bound to hasten the defeat of my own cause. This was certainly the only occasion in our lives when I actively frustrated something which Adam was trying to do. In what way I failed to recognize values whose destruction hastened the defeat of my own cause, I have no idea. Was Adam in fact after something else than the exchange of Czech and Polish territory? If so, then he really was making use of my friendship, as Ripka wrote to me afterwards, to involve us both *pour ses obscurs buts politiques*. Since he could take neither Ripka nor myself into his confidence, by what right did he demand a blank cheque of confidence in himself?

War broke out between us even before it broke out between our two countries. For this we were both guilty and both innocent. Innocent because neither of us really had this intention or harboured any ill-will in our hearts : guilty because we both allowed it to happen.

I was guilty for provoking the rage of his second and final letter : he was guilty for expressing such rage when he knew it would be the last word.

Here are the letters. Adam's first, which reached me in Paris, was written on brown Chinese rice paper with a blossoming fruit tree as a watermark.

My darling Duff,
     I have a feeling that my last letter was rather inadequate and somehow don't want to leave it at that just now especially since it is becoming highly doubtful whether my August trip to England and America can still come off. I hate this constant pathetic leave-taking, but when we are finally cut off, I do not want the smallest drop of bitterness to poison our mutual memory. Let's bury the best European friendship deep in the soil so that it will not be harmed by any winter or surface destruction and may blossom out again like these Chinese ones.

Bless you sweet,

A.

Mine was written on a page of squared paper torn out of a school exercise book, and given me in the café where I went to have my breakfast and answer Adam's letter.

Dear Trott,

I'm sorry about this paper. It's what the café thinks is what a girl should write on and perhaps, unable to emulate, it is as well to fall as low as possible from the standard of yours.

Thank you for your last letter. I appreciate the gesture but you always did believe that the winter hadn't yet begun when it raged through Europe and froze all hearts. Or rather it made the world hard and glittering and the snow was white and the ice and the sky were black and there were no half shades and compromises but just a fight for the existence of what one cared for. But luckily the world doesn't seem to know how cold it is outside. Notre Dame shines in the evening sun and people fall in love and walk the streets hand in hand. Paris is full of memories but never one of great happiness but always of something unrealised and an urgent insistence that nothing exists but Paris itself and one is a stranger from another world.

> Qu'as tu fais O toi que voila, pleurant sans cesse
> Qu'as tu fais O toi que voila, de ta jeunesse?

It is a curious arrangement to make young people worry because of the troubles inside them, and when they learn to deal with those, to give them real troubles from without. Still, there they are and perhaps it is the point of life to deal with them.

If we'd always been honest with each other we could bury a friendship deep but it is doubt that poisons not pain. Perhaps we will nevertheless survive and know fuller what things it was the other held dear. For now, I suppose, Goodbye. Be safe in body and mind.

S.

Berlin, August 25 1939

Dear Shiela,

The parting remark of your letter has made me angry so that even at this time of day, I must add a few words.

You are right that distrust not pain poisons friendship. But if you imply that my reticence to you lately has in any way been dishonest, you are viciously mistaken. I have never been consciously dishonest to you. To a great extent I have always believed that we did care for similar things and I loved and admired you for your single heartedness. But I also painfully and frequently experienced your complete incapacity to understand and sympathise with a natural ally when his battle had to be fought in an environment different from yours. You would from that incapacity even proceed to wreck a thing which you should have furthered, and fail to recognise values whose destruction was bound to hasten the defeat of your own cause. For that reason alone I have been reticent. I agree that a winter landscape is no subject for subtle colouring and ultimately levels a grim challenge to death or life of one's spark of right sense, but I cannot let that sneaking suspicion in the honesty of our friendship while it lasted pass without protest. It may not be fair or wise to write like this when there is hardly a chance for you to answer, but neither is it tolerable to let things stand as you did, or rather let them rot away under poisonous suspicion as you intended. And finally, darling S, I think these disputes are an awful silly waste and I'm sure should not have to arise. If it's part of the freezing of hearts you refer to, it is not me who has a right to blame you, but if it's part of your own ambitious coldness about your friends' battles, you should eradicate it.

A.

One week later Hitler invaded Poland and on 3 September Great Britain declared war on Germany.

Postscript

During the war we all fought our corners as best we could, 'each in his station, great and small,' Churchill himself in the greatest station of all.

I worked first in Toynbee's section of the Foreign Office and then as Czechoslovak editor in the European Service of the BBC.

Goronwy Rees, who had enlisted as a private even before the war, seeing it as the only honourable course for one who advocated standing up to Hitler, became an intelligence officer on General Montgomery's staff, liaising with Mountbatten's Combined Operations Headquarters, ending the war as a Lieutenant-Colonel and senior intelligence officer to William Strang, the Political Adviser to the Commander-in-Chief in Germany. He died in 1979.

Jawaharlal Nehru, still regarded as a dangerous opponent in his desire for Indian independence, spent much of the war in prison in India. Freed in 1945, he played the leading role in the negotiations leading up to the liberation of India and became its first Prime Minister, remaining in office till his death in 1964.

Hubert Ripka returned to England after the fall of France and became State Secretary in the Ministry of Foreign Affairs in the Czechoslovak Government in Exile. After the defeat of Germany and the restoration of Czechoslovakia within her pre-Munich frontiers, he was Minister of Foreign Trade in Prague until the Communists seized power in 1948. In exile once again, he continued to write and work for international understanding. He died in 1958.

Edgar Ansel Mowrer returned to the United States after the fall of France and in 1942 became Deputy Director of the Office of War Information. He wrote several books on American foreign policy; his last, written with his wife in 1972, was *Umano and the Price of Lasting Peace.* He died in 1977.

Adam von Trott had the hardest and most tragic role. Working in the German Foreign Office as a loyal patriot who loved his country and hated its leadership, he bravely tried to win sympathy and favourable terms for the German Resistance from those who were fighting for the unconditional surrender of his country. Closely involved in the July 20 plot to kill Hitler, he was executed in August 1944.

Hitler's war, thanks to his appetite for aggression and his alliance with Japan, eventually engulfed the greater part of the world. No man in history had ever before caused such carnage and such destruction. Forty million people are said to have been killed, large numbers of them, like the Jews of the holocaust, defenceless victims.

And all because neither the German people nor the leaders of the Western Powers recognized evil in time.

Index

The following abbreviations are used in the Index:
AVT: Adam von Trott
GR: Goronwy Rees
SGD: Shiela Grant Duff